THE
MASTERS
ON THE
NYMPH

Also edited by J. MICHAEL MIGEL

The Stream Conservation Handbook
The Masters on the Dry Fly

THE MASTERS ON THE NYMPH

Edited by **J. Michael Migel**
and **Leonard M. Wright, Jr.**

Illustrated by **Dave Whitlock**

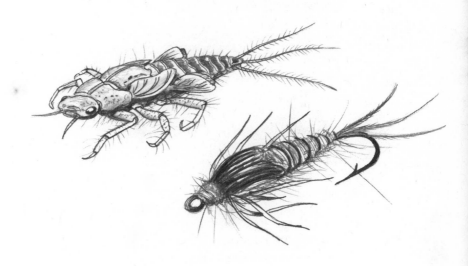

NLB Nick Lyons Books

Doubleday & Company, Inc., Garden City, New York 1979

Copyright © 1979 by J. Michael Migel
ALL RIGHTS RESERVED
First edition
2 4 6 8 9 7 5 3 1

PRINTED IN THE UNITED STATES OF AMERICA

ISBN: 0-385-15151-9
Library of Congress Catalog Card Number: 78-20638
First Edition

NICK LYONS BOOKS
is a division of
ERNEST BENN
New York and London

Contents

Foreword

"EVEN THE MOST SOPHISTICATED TROUT," says Al McClane in his lead chapter to this book, "can be taken on a nymph sooner or later. The versatility of this type of fly is remarkable."

And so it is.

Versatility and sheer effectiveness are clearly what most recommend the nymph to serious fly fishermen, but in recent years another attractive quality has emerged: the challenge. Nymph fishing, once held to be a "lower" form of fly-fishing than fishing the dry fly, has evolved into a complex, demanding, and infinitely subtle art. Dave Whitlock calls it "the most complex of all fly-fishing methods," and whether or not this is so—or whether we should even *rank* the various brands of fly-fishing—the challenge of nymphing is clear. This book invites you to accept that challenge. The wide variety of larval forms available to the trout, the fact that trout feed on nymphs *beneath* the surface (and thus fully in *their* domain, often beyond an angler's vision except perhaps for the "brown wink" Skues found so happy), the vast intricacy of water types and currents and the difficulty of presenting the fly where and how it will best tempt the fish, the multitude of nymph patterns to choose from, more every year—all these factors combine to make this type of fly-fishing richly fascinating.

Masters on the Nymph captures this fascination. Ernest Schwiebert traces the evolution of the nymph, from those "pre-nymphs," the ultra-sparse short-hackled flies, through the first modern master and apologist, G.E.M. Skues, to Edward Hewitt on the Neversink, Doug Swisher and Carl Richards, and other modern innovators and practitioners. Along the way, Schwiebert recounts that wonderful anecdote about the famous encounter between Frederic M. Halford, the fastidious pope of the dry-fly world, and the younger, heretical Skues at the Flyfisher's Club of London. Their feud—and what each said—is delicious.

Then Al Caucci and Bob Nastasi help us distinguish and identify the myriad types of larval forms (a feat that could drive a computer loony), and Poul Jorgensen (who ought to know) explores some of the best ways to dress artificial nymphs, from suggestive to ultra-realistic patterns. Al Troth, a highly innovative tier himself, and Lefty Kreh (that wizard with a fly rod) give invaluable practical tips about nymphing strategies and tactics. Dave Whitlock helps us choose the most suitable tackle from the vast, burgeoning, and often confusing arsenal of rods, lines, and other equipment available to the modern angler; Carl Richards mediates deftly between the many fly patterns and which to use and when; and Pete Hidy discusses the Leisenring lift he helped to popularize and his own soft-hackle nymphs, which he calls "flymphs" but which by any name work marvelously well at times.

I am especially pleased to see that wise and gentle river keeper from England, Frank Sawyer, represented here with a vivid and knowing chapter on "Nymphing in the Classic Style"; his book *Nymphs and the Trout,* on his techniques of nymph fishing, was one of the few to travel across the Atlantic in recent years and find a ready audience here. And his countryman, the young and brilliant Brian Clarke, speaks sanely about "The Nymph in Still Water," the subject of his recent and important book, *The Pursuit of Stillwater Trout.* We have much to learn from the British—whose scores of carefully managed reservoirs have been laboratories for the study of trout fishing in still water since the end of World War II—on this rapidly developing subject. Brian's book, which chronicles the education of a fly-fisherman (away from vague "chuck-and-chance-it" fishing) is an excellent place to begin.

There are a host of contributors of chapters on special and often overlooked aspects of nymphing, too—Chuck Fothergill (on pocket nymphing, the use of lead, and other situational techniques especially applicable to his tumbling Colorado rivers); Sid Neff from Pennsylvania's limestone country (on the delicate and demanding "mini-nymphs"); Charles Brooks (on the huge "maxi-nymphs" he uses for Montana's huge trout); Byron Dalrymple (on nymph fishing for panfish, bass, and even such species as catfish)—and there is an exceptionally interesting and thoughtful piece by Steve Raymond, from the West Coast, on such subsurface creatures as scuds and sow bugs.

As we come to the end, Ed Zern (who is becoming a "master" despite his wonderful self-irony, which *all* masters should have, anyway), speaks about his own introduction to flies fished beneath the surface. He had fished only dry flies, "not out of snobbery" but because his "intelligence was unable to cope with the theory of *wet* flies." But he saw and obviously he has learned. And the editor of the "Master" series, my good friend Mike Migel, charts a day's nymphing and shows how he has come to love "the inner architecture of rivers, not merely the surface. It had been a revelation."

So is this book.

It concerns itself very little with the old and tiresome controversy, "Wet or dry?" That's mostly a purist's problem, anyway. Rather, this book attempts chiefly to *share*.

Most books on the subject—and there are a number of very good ones— cover only one facet of nymph fishing: the entomology, the technique, the practice in England or one specific locale in America. Here we get a happy smörgasbord. In chapters choicely drawn forth from knowledgeable anglers throughout the country and overseas, each writing on his specialty, this book presents perhaps the most thorough portrait of nymph fishing we are likely to get. Its spectrum is broad. The all-too-frequent schism between East and West—where techniques and patterns and water *are* different—has been bridged. There are authors from the Far West, the Rocky Mountain states, the Midwest, the South, and the East. Some chapters introduce a subject in terms basic and clear enough to satisfy the green novice—and to whet his interest; others are sufficiently advanced to make even the experts more expert. Most kinds of rivers (limestone and freestone, east and west), dozens of patterns, locales, and techniques are represented, by those who know them best. (Nor are the rivers and trout neglected in this assault by the masters on the secrets of nymph fishing, on the trout's domain. Len Wright's little coda, on the increasing need to improve our fishing through active participation in conservation groups, shows that all our learned prowess will be worth nothing if we have no wild rivers to fish.)

What we have, finally, is a marvelously coordinated treasury of the best that is currently thought and known about nymph fishing, in the many different forms it takes. Each chapter, like the tiles of a mosaic, contributes its special color to the whole design.

Reading *Masters on the Nymph* slowly, and with much pleasure and fascination, I began to suspect that even *I* might learn to catch a few more trout now and then. Who knows? It might even make *me* an expert some day.

Anyway, I now know what I *should* know to catch trout on nymphs.

NICK LYONS

A. J. McClane *was fishing editor of* Field & Stream *for thirty years and is now editor-at-large at* Sports Afield. *Al has fished virtually every country in the world. He is the author of ten books, and his major work,* McClane's New Standard Fishing Encyclopedia, *is recognized as a classic. Most recently he wrote* The Encyclopedia of Fish Cookery, *published in 1977. He lives in Palm Beach, Florida.*

1
A Fly for All Seasons

A. J. McClane

WHEN YOU LIVE ON A RIVER, as I did for most of my life, you soon come to realize how inconsequential your fishing skills are, compared to the survival skills of a wild trout. There was an undercut bank on the Beaverkill, near our cabin, that I was certain held an eldery brown with jaws like a nutcracker. For weeks I never even saw my fish, though I was on the water at all hours from late spring into autumn. A deeper, greenish pool above was calendar-cover beautiful and full of cooperative trout, but after the stream made its bend, and the current purled back under the hemlock roots and then spun away before dancing merrily over a pebbled riffle—that was the spot. I could smell it as sure as a coming rain in a dry summer. But the undercut was densely canopied by low-hanging boughs almost to water level, and the only way I could get a fly near those roots was by crawling on hands and knees and making a 30-foot cross-stream cast—usually with one elbow in the water.

It was a ridiculous performance, according to wife Patti, daughter Susan, Arnold Gingrich, Bedell Smith, Bert Lahr, and other critics who happened along. At one point I did consider cutting the boughs down, but that would be unfair to my spectral tenant. Four times out of ten I'd throw my backcast into a hemlock behind me and pop my leader. Three times out of ten I'd manage to get my fly caught in the opposite boughs on my forward cast. And when a cast did arrive on the water, only one or two ubiquitous flame-bellied brook trout, so abundant in these upper pools, would appear, making me even more aware of a greater presence.

In my daily elbow exercise I tried every kind of fly in the box. Not even a Muddler caused a stirring in the undercut. Toward the end of that season, when the water was quite low, I reverted to my Catskill boyhood and used a method one step above a wiggly garden worm. I attacked the problem from upstream with a small weighted nymph on a long, fine leader. I made a short cast and paid line out in the current, maneuvering the fly so that it drifted down into the hole to swim near the roots. Then I waited. Long minutes passed before I felt the tug, but instead of immediately boring back into his den, the trout came out, a sooty-black monster, probably momentarily blinded by sunlight. I splashed downstream, hoping to lead my prize away from the undercut. The fish helped by making one strong run, which left him belly-flopping in the riffle below—but also snapped my tippet.

I have caught many trout greater in pounds than this fish measured in inches, and it would have been released in any event. The point of my story is that even the most sophisticated trout—and a brown of about 18 inches on the upper Beaverkill rates summa cum laude—can be taken on a nymph sooner or later. The versatility of this type of fly is remarkable.

There was another place downstream, a short deep run where the river spilled over barren bedrock in a foaming cascade; this was reliable for two or maybe three acrobatic 8-inch rainbows in the side pocket. But in that rushing water I was convinced no greater presence existed at all, unless it was ethereal. For some reason there was always an eerie golden light falling on that pool in the evening as though polarized through a stained-glass window. Nevertheless, it was a pretty spot to cast a fly while watching chipmunks scamper among the ferns and was therefore included in my daily schedule, which was less precise but as dedicated as any Swiss railroad's. (I can get sidetracked by a patch of wild strawberries.)

I must have fished the miniature cascade ninety times that season, from all angles with all kinds of flies. Even my rainbow friends were becoming reluctant, so I tried skimming a little gray caddis pupa over the surface to stir some interest. A darkly spotted brown came barreling out of the depths, and after a long seesawing contest of surging runs against my 6X tippet, he was measured against my rod butt—19½ inches. The nymph had been taken when fished like a dry fly.

Fishing with an artificial nymph is the basic method of trout angling. The nymph will catch fish 365 days of the year—not always the largest and not

Old Beaverkill brown taking McClane's nymph.

always the most, but it will take them consistently. Equally important is the *method* of nymphing, which teaches beginners everything they must know about trout habits and habitat. Nymph fishing can be successful in the coldest or hottest weather, in dead-calm water or a raging torrent, and from the surface to the very bottom of those secret places where great trout hide.

Nymph fishing is old and its development (which will unfold in subsequent chapters) has quite a history, but it did not become popular in America until about 1930. In the half-century since, the totemization of G.E.M. Skues's *Minor Tactics of the Chalk Stream* has certainly inspired but not excelled the works of contemporary masters, most of whom appear in this book. For any angling writer, it is a rare privilege not only to describe his country and time but to give perspective to the sport. Skues succeeded in doing this, but in a strangely delayed way.

It's hard to believe now, but once upon a time "nymph" was a dirty word. In the formal establishment of 1910, Skues was considered a heretic "dabbler in unworthy excesses" by many of his peers. Gentlemen belonged to the Houghton Club, marinated their Stilton in 150-year-old port, and fished with floating patterns. It has never been clear to me why a fly that is sunken, presumably the inferior condition in which artificials originated in the first place, should become the villain in a morality play. Yet within my own lifetime I recall nearly being drummed out of the corps for casting a nymph on the hallowed waters of the Risle. This French chalk stream was still immune to Skues's development by July of 1948, though God knows it's only a verbal stone's throw across the Channel from Hampshire to Normandy. Yet the good word had not been passed.

I had caught and released three lovely trout that were obviously "bulging" in a slick run below the cider mill when our host, Edouard Vernes (who was flailing a dry fly upstream from me and catching nothing), came pounding down the bank and asked to see what manner of "bait" I was throwing into his river. He held my leader tippet between his fingers with a look of complete disdain and gurgled *nam-pff!* I thought he was going to have a stroke. If it hadn't been for an instant character reference from Charlie Ritz, who promised I would mend my ways, Vernes, a millionaire bank chairman who brooked no evil, probably would have snapped my 8½-foot CCF over his knee and sent me by square-wheeled tumbrel to the Bastille. The fact that I was demonstrating for Charlie how to fish a nymph was not mentioned until some years later in Ritz's book *A Fly Fisher's Life*. Even to think of teaching Charlie Ritz anything about trout was almost ludicrous, but my mentor himself had been insulated by the ground rules of chalk-stream society. Eventually Charlie met Frank Sawyer, the doyen of nymph artists, and became a fanatic on nymphing. I have never met Frank Sawyer, but I was flooded with letters from Charlie describing how Sawyer did this or Sawyer did that. It was as though he had translated the Dead Sea Scrolls.

I learned the fundamentals of nymphing back in the 1930s. The only popular American patterns, then purveyed by William Mills & Son, were the flat-bodied, lacquered creations of Edward Ringwood Hewitt—a design also claimed by John Alden Knight, although I can't imagine why. These nymphs came like licorice sticks in three color combinations: black with a gray belly, black with an orange belly, and black with a yellow belly. I seldom caught many trout with these, so, like everybody else who took fishing seriously, I tied my own.

Some idea of where the nymph existed by 1936 can be found in a little fifty-five-page book, *Tying American Trout Lures*, by Rueben R. Cross. Rube, the Sage of Shin Creek, was a master craftsman, yet all he had to say about nymphs covered 4½ pages and concerned four patterns: the Guinea Nymph, the Black-and-White Nymph (grub), the Olive Wood-duck Nymph, and the Carrot-and-Black Nymph. Dan Todd, Ray Neidig, Mike Lorenz, and quite a few other tiers in the Delaware Valley were experimenting with patterns designed to imitate the larval stages of aquatic insects, and some locally effective artificials evolved.

Dan Todd was the Ulster & Delaware stationmaster in Margaretville. He amassed a considerable collection of trout foods preserved in formalin that he kept in his office. One morning a man named Olson (whom Dan detested for his murderous consistency in killing large quantities of trout with spoons and worms) saw a mason jar of pebble-type caddis cases sitting on his desk.

"What's them things?" Olson asked Todd.

Dan looked pained. "I just had an operation. Them's my kidney stones."

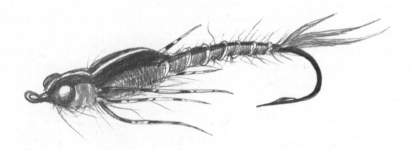

Olson stared closely at the jar. "God Almighty! No wonder you can't fish!"

I was fishing mostly on the East Branch of the Delaware in those days, places like Fuller's Flat and Keener's Flat, which by any standard were classic runs. A Catskill "flat" was often several miles long, containing more riffles and rapids than still water. This was dairy country amid precipitous mountains (it was said that all cows had two short legs), and the name of a flat merely indicated whose meadow provided river access without falling off a cliff.

It was April of 1936 when I caught my first big trout. The weather was cold and snowy and the river was running high. I was fishing a home-tied nymph by casting upstream and letting it sink close to my bank—which was no trick with a waterlogged silk line. I caught quite a number of trout that morning before getting "stuck in the bottom," and when that brown finally came thumping to life it was the biggest thrill a fourteen-year-old boy could ever have. The trout was too big for my landing net, and after getting the head stuck in its meshes I remember wrestling my prize into a snowbank. I walked home, feeling like one big goose pimple, by way of the lumberyard, the butcher shop, the drugstore, and the ill-named Palace Hotel, making sure everybody in town saw my fish. Dan Todd weighed it at the railroad station— 7 pounds 2 ounces, not an adult trophy for the East Branch in those days, since fresh mounts in double figures to 15 pounds or more hung glassy-eyed on every saloon wall.

When I dressed the trout, some of the nymphs that filled its belly were still alive; its digestion rate had almost slowed to a halt in the near-freezing water. What fascinated me was the fact that the fish had continued to feed. Although big trout are often caught on bucktails or streamers, in *very* cold weather a nymph will outfish a minnowlike fly simply because the trout doesn't have to chase it through heavy currents. A nymph can be fished absolutely "dead" and catch fish, while a bucktail cannot; a nymph can also be fished "alive" when the accepted food form is otherwise dead. This is the ultimate conundrum.

I had some fabulous fishing in Montana last year during my annual fall trip. Western rivers are custom-made for the nymph artist, and some lakes produce big trout to no other method, except sporadically. Henrys Lake in Idaho is a classic example; here the trout gorge on green damselfly nymphs and also *Gammarus*, the so-called freshwater shrimp imitated by many nymph patterns. But the lake I have in mind is known for its voluminous mini-mayfly hatches where even the best dry-fly man can spook trout with a size 22 on a 7X tippet. The naturals look like dandruff. There is some action at the beginning of an emergence, and you can hook three, maybe four, nice fish. But the real sport occurs when the "gulpers" (fish of 4, 5, and 6 pounds) appear after rafts of spent mayflies are floating dead on the water. The fish cruise in a leisurely fashion, often porpoising in plain sight as they take ephemeral minutae out of the surface film. With countless thousands of naturals windrowed to a small area, the most perfect imitation is lost in sheer numbers.

After we spent a futile Montana morning casting at repetitive risers and hooking exactly three trout, Tom McNally provided the solution. McNally, who is an expert angler in every sense of the word and chronicles his adventures for the *Chicago Tribune*, learned nymphing fundamentals as a lad on the hard-fished streams of Maryland. He was also a pro boxer in his youth, and now shoots pool with Minnesota Fats, so he reacts to panic situations with sharply honed reflexes—in this case a size 10 fuzzy-bodied brown nymph worked across the surface in a hand-twist retrieve. Absurd? Showing those trout something big and alive swimming through all those tiny inert mayflies commanded a gustatory response that had no equal.

The next morning we began hooking, with modest consistency, rainbows and browns in the 2½-to-4-pound class; these were hammered silver, deep-bodied, arrowheaded trout that leaped and rocketed off like bonefish. Many simply popped our tippets, and we lost several large ones in the lake's numerous weed beds. This method of outfoxing the gulpers was no fluke. Tom and I visited that lake regularly through September and into aspen-yellow October. On any morning when the water was mirror calm his method paid off. Midday winds moaning out of the Spanish Peaks put the fish down under a sea of whitecaps.

In the chapters that follow, you will find a larval feast, a treasure chest of practical information that boggles the mind. My assignment was the joy of nymph fishing, and that brings me back to Rube Cross. When I mentioned his book earlier, I had to go scrambling through my library to check the title. I remembered the volume had a brown cover, but I had forgotton that he wrote an inscription inside, and that told me the year I caught my first big trout. I visited his hayloft shop the following winter to learn more about tying flies. A huge man, half poet, half mountain lion, he was generous to a fault. His dill-pickle-sized fingers spun the most beautiful flies I will ever see. But it's his inscription in my book that deserves to appear in print. The author remains anonymous, yet the words reflect to some degree the transcendental joy of angling:

> *To my young friend*
> *I dreamed,*
> *   that I again my native hills had found,*
> *the mossy rocks, the valley, and the*
> *   stream that used to hold me captive*
> *to its sound.*
> *   And that I was a boy again.*
> *(Anon.)*

Reuben R. Cross
Jan. 3, 1937

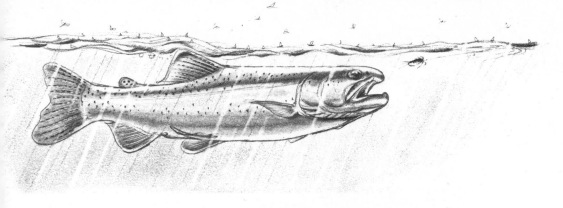

FOUR OF MY FAVORITE NYMPH PATTERNS

These are four old favorites that have taken many fine fish over the years. They suggest subaquatic food forms in general, and, except on those occasions when fish are truly selective, one or another will usually produce if worked at the right depth and retrieve.

Strawman Nymph

Hook:	Regular or 2XL in sizes to suit
Tail:	A few strands of gray mallard or wood-duck flank
Body:	Deer hair spun on hook thinly and clipped in a taper from tail to head, ribbed with pale yellow floss silk. May be tied without hackle, or, if desired, a turn or two of partridge hackle may be added.

Hare's Ear Nymph

Hook:	Regular shank, sizes 6 to 16
Tail:	Brown hackle
Body:	Dubbed very rough with fur from European hare's ear, mixed with fur from the hare's face, ribbed with oval gold tinsel
Thorax:	Tied very full with wing pad from gray goose or duck tied over
Legs:	Dubbing from thorax picked out long and fuzzy; this represents the nymph legs.

Leadwinged Coachman Nymph

Hook:	Sizes 6 to 12 2XL
Tail:	Dark brown hackle fibers
Body:	Bronze peacock herl ribbed with fine black silk
Hackle:	Dark rusty brown
Wing pads:	Small dark black duck upper wing covert feathers (cut to shape)
Head:	Brown lacquer

Iron Blue Nymph

Hook:	Regular shank sizes 14 or 16
Tail:	Cream or gray hackle wisps
Body:	Bluish muskrat fur ribbed with gold wire
Thorax:	Bluish muskrat, no rib
Hackle:	Grayish cream
Head:	Clear lacquer over tying silk

After catching his first trout in a Michigan creek when he was only five, Ernest Schwiebert went on to fish from Labrador to Tierra del Fuego and from Alaska and Lapland to the beautiful Antipodes.

A well known architect and planner with a doctorate from Princeton, he is also involved in the environmental movement, both professionally and philosophically, and serves as an adviser to Trout Unlimited, Game Conservation International, and the Nature Conservancy, and on a special advisory board for fisheries to the National Park Service. His consulting group, Ecosystemics, has participated in socioenvironmental studies in Puerto Rico, South America, Asia, and the United States.

Schwiebert has achieved recognition not only as an angler but as a writer. His articles have appeared in Life, Sports Illustrated, Esquire, Field & Stream, Outdoor Life, Atlantic Monthly, Flyfisher, Sports Afield, *and* Fly Fisherman—*where he currently serves as editor-at-large—and his books include* Matching the Hatch, Salmon of the World, Remembrances of Rivers Past, Nymphs, *and the monumental* Trout.

2

The Evolution Of The Nymph

Ernest Schwiebert

SCHMIDSMÜHLEN IS A TINY GRISTMILL VILLAGE that lies in a sweeping bend of the slow-flowing Vils, which winds through the pastoral Bavarian hills towards Regensburg. Ducks and geese forage in the millrace and waddle through the marketplace in the rain.

The village lies where the Lauterach joins the Vils, and the Lauterach is a classic little river. Its serpentine water meadows and willow-lined channels were my classroom in nymph fishing. More than twenty-five seasons have passed since that April in Germany, but the lessons learned there seem as fresh as yesterday's fishing.

The old river keeper at Schmidsmühlen was patient, and his tutelage solved the nymph-fishing puzzle. His shabby fly book was filled with a partridge-legged pattern that was obviously his favorite dressing. The fly was tied with a pale fox body, ribbed with brown buttonhole twist and with wing cases of brown mottled turkey.

"What's hatching?" I asked.

"We have fine hatches of big drakes coming," the keeper replied, "but the nymph fishes best on most days."

"But with good hatches, why fish the nymph?"

"These nymphs migrate into the shallows and fly off quickly when they hatch," the old man explained. "Because the flies are hard to catch after they emerge, the fish take mostly nymphs."

We walked upstream through the meadows above the village, grateful that the rain had stopped. Beyond a potato field, there was a long reach of river where a few mayflies were hatching. Two fish were already working where the current shelved off under the bank.

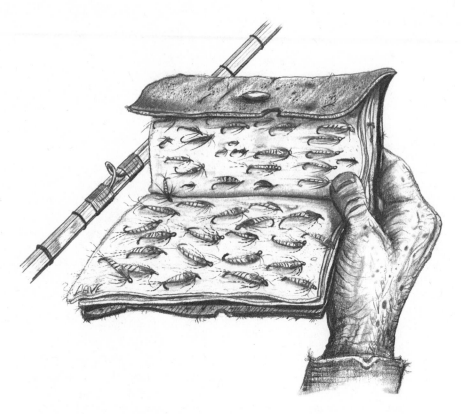

"They're rising over there!" I pointed.

"*Nein!*" The river keeper shook his head. "Those trout are taking the migrating nymphs just under the surface."

"How should we fish them?"

The old man pointed to the riffles upstream. "The nymphs live there, in the running currents," he explained. "When they hatch, they drift downstream, wriggling and working."

"Shall I work the fly too?" I asked.

"*Jawohl!*" the old fisherman replied. "The hatching nymphs can swim, so you should tease them with the rod."

The first cast worked through its swing and went fishless. The second dropped against the grass where the flow deepened into an undercut pocket, and I teased the nymph subtly. Its swing went deeper and there was a strong pull.

"The trout like your nymphs." I laughed.

The old river keeper subsequently taught me what species of nymphs lived in different types of water. His flies were poorly tied, but they were workable imitations of the hatches on his beloved Lauterach. His patterns suggested the color, configuration, and size of each species. The old man understood their varied behavior in the river throughout the year and their singular behavior while hatching. His final trick lay in fishing the artificials to suggest the helplessness or movement of each species in the river.

At that time, nymph patterns in most American fly books were strange creations. Some were British patterns, but few anglers had much faith in them. American dressings were fanciful flies with peacock feelers and guinea-fowl legs tied fore and aft, with no counterparts in aquatic entomology. The Hewitt patterns looked better but were lacquered and lifeless compared to our modern nymph dressings. In those days, my nymph fishing was relatively ineffective, except for the odd fish taken on some dark British pattern tied by Hardy Brothers at Alnwick or on the clumsy copies of the Hewitt nymphs I tied in those boyhood winters.

Although Edward Ringwood Hewitt first published his *Nymph Fly Fishing* in 1934, and John Alden Knight described their joint efforts in *The Modern Angler*, two years later it was Ray Bergman who really introduced an entire generation of Americans to nymphs and nymph fishing.

Hewitt confined his observations to a pamphlet that failed to achieve wide circulation, and Knight's *Modern Angler* did not find the audience it deserved. Both Hewitt and Knight were attempting to adapt British nymph-fishing theory and dressings to our Catskill rivers, much as Theodore Gordon and George La Branche had done for British dry-fly theory on our fast-water streams. John Alden Knight begins his chapter in *The Modern Angler* with these words:

> During the summer of 1931, Mr. Edward R. Hewitt began his real series of experiments in the effort to establish some satisfactory American nymph patterns. He must have tied and tested not less than a hundred different sizes and varieties of nymphs. Some of these took fish better than did others, but none of them was really first grade.

> Not until the summer of 1932 was the problem solved. In talking the thing over one evening, the observation was made that nearly all the natural nymphs in the stream are flat and the patterns we had tried were all round. Accordingly, the flat-bodied nymph came into existence, and with it success in American nymph fishing.

Hewitt and Knight were largely fishing Hewitt's water on the Neversink, with its sweeping riffles and icy flow, and fast-water nymphs there are often

Typical early American nymphs.

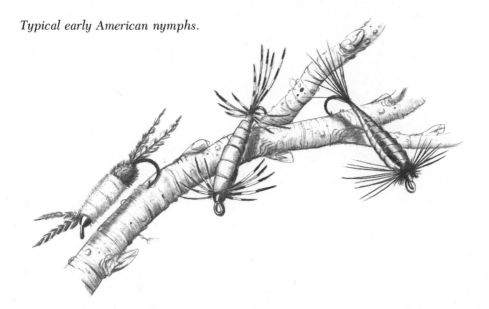

flat-bodied species. Yet our current knowledge of nymph life in American lakes and streams make these flat-nymph theories of Hewitt and Knight seem hopelessly naïve. Modern nymph patterns are tied in both flat- and round-bodied configurations, matching the species found in different types of water, and our aquatic entomology displays a broad spectrum of colors and shapes and sizes. Hewitt and Knight were obviously aware of the varied palette of colors found in our nymphs and larval forms, and a skilled nymph fisherman will find these concluding paragraphs from *The Modern Angler* both perceptive and painfully off-target:

> Most stream insects are brown in colors ranging from almost black to light reddish brown and buff. On the other hand, there are not a few natural insects which have varying colors of green.
>
> Therefore, your kit should include dark, medium and light brown, reddish brown, buff, yellow, olive, dark green, bright green, gray, blue and black. Sizes should vary from one-eighth of an inch to three-quarters of an inch in body length. Of course, you will not be able to find a natural green fur. However, by blending fur and green crewel wool you can obtain a satisfactory olive and dark green. The bright green must of necessity consist of some dyed material.
>
> For early season fishing and other times when the trout are down in the deeper water, weighted nymphs are quite useful. The weighting may be done by winding a spiral foundation of fine fuse wire over the shank of the hook, and then tying the nymph over this foundation. . . .
>
> Many anglers regard nymph fishing as a fad which will run its course and, in due time, be forgotten. This may to some extent prove true. It is more difficult than dry-fly fishing and many anglers, having had no success with nymphs, have gone back to their dry flies, discarding the nymph as just one more gadget. But there are times when the nymphs, although difficult to handle, are invaluable in the taking of trout which would otherwise not be caught.

Bergman soon followed with his book *Trout* and its observations on nymphs and nymph fishing. It was first published in Philadelphia in 1938, and that edition is becoming a rare prize among collectors of fishing books. Like other early American writers, except perhaps Preston Jennings, Bergman failed to base his nymph fishing on a disciplined study of actual nymphs and their behavior.

The tactical lessons found in Bergman are still sound, however, even if his flies did not imitate anything in nature and his knowledge of nymphal behavior was incomplete. It was difficult to master his dead-drift method, particularly when it was fished directly upstream, but I finally learned its secrets on the pocket water of the Ausable in New York. His hand-twist retrieve sometimes took good fish from pools and still-flowing flats, and it took some impressive boyhood baskets of cutthroats and brook trout in Colorado and

Wyoming. But the so-called nymphs found in the color plates in *Trout* were more feathered lures than workable nymph imitations.

There were many times when wet flies seemed to work on nymphing fish, particularly old patterns with shredded wings, discolored bodies, and a few remaining wisps of hackle. Sometimes we took trout easily on a worn hackle pattern or the traditional British dressing of the March Brown with its pheasant wings trimmed short. There was a morning on the Pere Marquette in Michigan when my father took a basket of smutting trout on the peacock-herl body of a small hackle pattern after its hackle had come unwound. Another summer morning on the Upper Manistee during a hatch of tiny olives, I took a boyhood limit of large fish on a badly discolored Greenwell's Glory. Several times I found that porpoising trout could be taken with a roughly dressed Hare's Ear when they refused my dry-fly imitations. During those early years, it never occurred to me that such wet flies worked because they imitated specific hatching nymphs and pupae.

Hewitt and Bergman had caused that myopia, outlining tactics that were merely variations on conventional wet-fly theory. Their methods were limited to the dead-drift presentations, the downstream wet-fly swing with a teasing rhythm of the rod, and a deliberate hand-twist retrieve. Their lack of concern with imitation of the natural nymphs and their behavior often resulted in failure in my boyhood years.

Yet the river keeper on the Lauterach taught me that precise imitation of a hatching nymph, combined with manipulation of the fly that matched its behavior, resulted in taking fish after fish with the clockwork precision that is the best measure of success in matching a hatch.

Later, on the Leizach, high in the mountains beyond Chiemsee in southern Germany, I further perfected my growing skills with a small upstream nymph, fishing the gin-clear millrace flats for trout that I could see clearly. Still more experience followed at Oberammergau, and a richly productive summer was spent on the weedy little Grundbach at Fischen-im-Allgaü, where I fished to much larger trout that were visibly nymphing. The still-flowing flats there were very like the British chalk streams, and their tiny swimming nymphs dictated fresh tactics outside those found in *Trout* and *Nymph Fly Fishing*. The fish soon taught me that casting above their feeding lies during a hatch, and teasing the sinking nymph as it reached them, was far more deadly than a dry fly in those conflicting weed-bed currents.

Our tumbling rivers, and the relatively easy fishing we have enjoyed in the past, have spoiled many American fisherman. Such refinements as matching the hatch and suggesting the precise behavior of particular species were seldom necessary. It is little wonder that many American anglers remain ignorant of nymphs and nymph fishing. Perhaps a better understanding of the nymph and its history will provide a workable foundation for American fishermen in the future.

Although Dame Juliana Berners did not specifically describe nymph fishing in her *Treatyse of Fysshynge wyth an Angle*, written more than five centuries ago, several of its fly patterns are surprisingly like hatching pupae and nymphs.

Leonard Mascall made no mention of nymphs in his *Booke of Fishing* in 1590, published a century after Berners. Although almost another century went by before Charles Cotton contributed his fly-fishing appendix to Walton's *Compleat Angler* in 1676, thereby becoming the father of modern fly-fishing, it was the British writer John Taverner who first described the relationship between nymphs and the aquatic insects anglers had observed on their rivers since Claudius Aelianus. Taverner included his observations in his book *Certaine Experiments Concerning Fish and Fruite*, which he published in 1600:

> I have seene a younge flie swimme in the water too and fro, and in the ende, come to the upper-crust of the river, and assay to flie up: howbeit, not being perfectly ripe or fledged, hath thrice fallen down againe into the bottome: howbeit, in the end receiving perfection by the heate of the sunne, and the pleasant fat water, hath in the end within some halfe houre after taken her flyte, and flied quite away into the ayre, and of such young flies before they are able to flie away, do fish feede exceedingly.

Taverner obviously based these insights on his observations of the stream, since his little book is remarkably free of the biological myths found in Walton.

Charles Cotton may have omitted mention of nymph life in his appendix to *The Compleat Angler,* but several of his dressings sound like hatching-nymph imitations, particularly the hackle types that he recommended in February and March and the whirling dun found emerging in April on the Dove. And it is clear from his narrative poem *"Wonders of the Peake,"* that Cotton was fully aware of the nymph life in his favorite waters:

> But with so swift a torrent in her course,
> As spurs the nymph, flies from her native source,
> To seek what's there deny'd the sun's warm beams,
> And there embrace Trent's swelling streams.

Charles Cotton richly deserves his place in history as the father of fly-fishing, but it was probably the work of Richard and Charles Bowlker that began modern fly tying. Richard Bowlker published the book *Art of Angling* in 1747. Charles Bowlker, his equally talented son, rewrote his father's work in 1780, and it became an enormously popular book that easily dominated discussions of tactics, stream craft, and fly dressing for another fifty years.

Charles Bowlker was simple and direct, not unlike Bergman in our century. Perhaps his prinicpal importance lies in his clearing away of the myth and debris that surrounded earlier fishing theory and in his emphasis on matching the hatch. He displayed no hesitation in disposing of earlier fly-tying techniques, from Berners through Chethan, listing many of their patterns as flies of limited application and then outlining his own thirty-odd patterns. His list included surprisingly modern versions of flies like the Bue Dun, which Chethan had earlier described in a no-hackle dressing, and the classic little Iron Blue. Other standard patterns that apparently began with Bowlker were the Cowdung, Yellow Sally, Grannom, Black Gnat, Whirling Dun, March Brown, and Welshman's Button.

Authorship of so many fly patterns that have survived for more than two centuries is impressive testimony to the importance of the Bowlkers and their *Art of Angling.* Charles Bowlker still advocated the reverse-wing style evolved in earlier centuries. His bodies were slim and graceful in the true north-country tradition, and some were ribbed with buttonhole twist or a few turns of hackle. He believed that his sparse hackles suggested legs, and his delicately palmered fur bodies are imitative of nymphs having well-defined or plumose gill structures. Certainly there are still echoes of Bowlker found in fly-dressing practice throughout Ireland and the United Kingdom: in the traditional Tweed and Clyde dressings and particularly in the slim dressings found on the swift-flowing Usk, not too far from the Shropshire rivers where the Bowlkers learned their skills.

It wasn't until Alfred Ronalds published his *Fly-Fisher's Entomology* in 1836 that the fishing world had its first disciplined book about matching the hatch. This beautiful book married the scientific method to angling. It was completely original in its research and content, and its exquisite copper plates remain equal to most modern lithography. Ronalds was perhaps the prototype of the angling writer, equally schooled in entomology and painting, and his work became a yardstick for future work in fly hatches.

Nymph fishing took another major step when John Younger published his *River Angling for Salmon and Trout* in 1840. His techniques of fishing soft-hackled flies of English partridge and grouse, which are superb imitations of hatching sedges, were simple and effective. Younger believed in casting directly across-stream, depending on the water's speed and allowing his flies to swing with no life other than that imparted by the current. Although Younger did not develop consciously imitative nymphs, his *River Angling* was certainly the first to speculate on their importance since John Taverner.

George Philip Rigney Pulman was writing about the fledgling dry-fly method during these years, and his *Vade Mecum of Fly-Fishing for Trout* (1851) was another seminal book in the evolution of angling. The development of eyed light-wire hooks, oil-finished silk lines, precise knowledge of the British hatches, and the techniques of dressing flies conceived to float all followed quickly in the half century that followed the Pulman *Vade Mecum.*

W. C. Stewart published his *Practical Angler* in 1857 and codified the growing upstream school of presentation. His methods of casting upstream and approaching the fish from below were critical pieces in the dry-fly puzzle. Yet in our excitement over the dry fly, we have tended to forget that the upstream dead-drift method is also the keystone of nymph-fishing tactics. Stewart filled his fly books with dour wet flies like the Woodcock and Brown, Grouse and Green, and Blue-Winged Hare's Ear. Such winged dressings are fine imitations of hatching mayflies, but Stewart also favored even simpler patterns like his golden Plover Spider, Dotterel Spider, Partridge Spider, and Starling Spider. (These soft-hackle wet flies in a subdued palette of body dubbing had considerable influence on Skues in southern England, as well as on Leisenring in the United States.)

Other wet-fly fishermen wrote compellingly of their craft after Stewart and his *Practical Angler*. David Webster published *The Angler and the Loop Rod* that same year, and his methods of dressing the wet fly with rolled wings and delicately dubbed bodies were adapted by Skues fifty years later on the Hampshire chalk streams. Canon Charles Kingsley stubbornly refused to abandon the wet-fly method in his *Chalkstream Studies* and fished often, in spite of his clerical duties at Westminster Abbey, demonstrating both a thorough knowledge of chalk-stream fly life, and the continuing effectiveness of upstream wet flies in the stronghold of dry-fly fishing.

H. C. Cutcliffe wrote *Trout Fishing in Rapid Streams* in 1863, a practical little book grounded in years of experience on the west-country rivers of Devonshire. Cutcliffe also understood the life cycle of the aquatic insects, and in his book he observes, about nymphs, "I find so much spoken about the natural fly and its imitation, but little about the insect before arrived at maturity. How seldom does one imitate the larva or pupa."

T. W. Pritt published a remarkable little book titled *Yorkshire Trout Flies* in 1885. His flies were a collection of simple soft-hackle dressings without wings, using the mottled body and shoulder feathers of plover, pheasant, grouse, woodcock, jackdaw, and snipe. Pritt depended on the flyhatches and the moods of the trout, working his flies dead-drift or letting them swing on the tension of the current, but he also teased their drift at times with his rod. The hand-twist retrieve was also useful in the quiet deeps of Pritt's Yorkshire rivers, and sometimes he skittered his wet flies in the surface film to suggest the egg-laying sedges, much as the three-fly cast was used by old timers during my boyhood summers in the high country of Colorado.

Pritt and the scientific disciplines obvious in the books of Ronalds and F. M. Halford (*Dry Fly Fishing*, 1889) were the prelude to the full-blown philosophy of nymph fishing. The chalk streams of southern England, with their free-rising trout in plain view, were the perfect laboratory for any skilled and creative observer. Their selective fish were a demanding yardstick that could quickly test any fresh theories or fly patterns. George Edward MacKenzie Skues was the genius who would fit the pieces of the puzzle together on the threshold of the century.

Typical Skues nymphs.

The beautiful Itchen was the river that deeply influenced Skues in the evolution of nymph fishing. Skues was a solitary bachelor (like James Leisenring on the Brodheads) and had ample time for his streamside studies. He divided his life between a successful legal practice in London and his fishing. His disciplined intelligence refused to accept the popular wisdom which argued that the skills and knowledge of the wet-fly centuries should be jettisoned in favor of the new dry-fly dogmatics. Although he remained a chalkstream angler throughout his life, except for a few trips to fish the limestone streams of Germany, Skues continued to explore alternatives to the dry-fly method.

Skues first wrote of his experiments in British magazines like the *Field,* and his studies were finally published in his *Minor Tactics of the Chalk Stream* in 1910. The work was based upon its author's penetrating reason combined with a deep-seated suspicion of dogma, a thorough knowledge of existing angling theory and technique, and a cornucopia of original thought. It made a stubborn case for retaining wet-fly tactics on the chalk streams.

Although *Minor Tactics* aroused a chorus of surprising opposition, its arguments were so subtly and convincingly laid that its thesis has never been refuted. The book remains a classic of fly-fishing literature and the genesis of nymph fishing.

Skues continually faced strong opposition to his evolving theories. His writings challenged the *ex cathedra* arguments of Halford and his disciples that dry-fly fishing alone was the method worthy of the British chalk streams. Skues refused to feel guilty for fishing his nymphs in waters that the Halford circle had consecrated to the dry fly method. The feud reached its climax in a famous encounter at the Flyfisher's Club in London, when an aging Halford and his curia of disciples cornered the younger Skues in the foyer.

"Young man," Halford said testily, "you cannot fish the Itchen in the manner you describe."

"But I've done it," Skues replied softly.

Although his first book did not reach print until 1910, only four years before Halford died, Skues had already been fishing the nymph for thirty years. Unlike the earlier writers, Younger and Cutcliffe, who had merely observed that nymphal forms deserved more attention from anglers, Skues searched patiently for precise imitation of nymphs and pupae. The work started in *Minor Tactics* was expanded in 1921 with the publication of *The Way of a Trout With a Fly*, a classic in which Skues displayed a fully polished doctrine of fishing the nymphs, and was codified in his little *Nymph Fishing for Chalk Stream Trout*, which did not appear until 1939. These books are absolutely essential to any working library on fishing.

Skues fully grasped the limitations of his work. Fishing theories confined to chalk streams alone have their problems, since their spectrum of fly life is limited to slow-flowing species. There are many more types of insects found in other aquatic biosystems, such as the tumbling streams of Cornwall and Yorkshire, yet these exceptions to the Skues philosophy in no way weaken its validity. They merely demonstrate that his studies were too limited in scope and lacked a knowledge of biota from both lakes and fast-water habitat. Skues is still the father of nymph fishing.

Other British writers were working in these years, fishing both the chalk streams and the swift-flowing rivers of the north country. Leonard West privately published *The Natural Trout Fly and Its Imitation* in 1912, greatly expanding knowledge of the English hatches. J. C. Mottram, a skilled surgeon who focused his creative intelligence on the problems of trout fishing, wrote *Fly Fishing, Some New Arts and Mysteries*, in 1914, which speculated not only on concepts of dry-fly imitation but also on nymph fishing.

Skues had often written in the *Journal of the Flyfisher's Club of London* in his middle years that a disciplined observer was needed to study the entomology of lakes in Ireland and the United Kingdom. And the greatest reservoirs that have become major trout fisheries since mid-century were still largely in the future when R. C. Bridgett published *Loch Fishing in Theory and Practice* in 1924. Many British anglers still consider it the best general work on the subject. Bridgett was no skilled entomologist, but since he had studied each of the fly hatches on his favorite waters, he did possess a sound working knowledge of insect life. His work treats all conceivable elements of loch fishing, except for a study of specific still-water hatches, and it is clear from his observations that Bridgett himself realized his omission:

> It is somewhat difficult to decide to what extent the angler should be versed in the entomology of the loch, but I think that most will agree

that a little knowledge of the subject is essential. My own opinion is that the slow advance in the art and science of loch-fishing is largely accounted for by the lack of interest displayed in the food of loch trout.

C. F. Walker published his *Lake Flies and Their Imitations* in England in 1960, which expanded our knowledge of still-water entomology and fly dressing. His book covered mayflies, midges, water beetles, dragonflies and damselflies, alders, midges and other two-winged species, stone flies, and tiny crustaceans. Although the specific hatches described are not found in the United States, there are so many parallel species that Walker's observations remain valid for American anglers. Other chapters outline fly-tying theory for imitating these diet forms, and Walker's fly patterns are listed. *Lake Flies and Their Imitations* is firmly based on the philosophy of imitation, and Commander Walker clearly understands the importance of nymphs in lake fishing. Knowledgeable nymph fishermen and flytiers should welcome Walker's book, whether they fish waters in Europe or in the United States.

But perhaps the finest British nymph fisherman since Skues is white-haired Frank Sawyer, the famous river keeper on the beautiful Avon above Salisbury. Sawyer is well known throughout Europe because of the writings of the late Charles Ritz and his own books, *Nymphs and the Trout* and *Keeper of the Stream* (published in 1952).

Although Sawyer is clearly a disciple of Skues, his own experience on the Wiltshire chalk streams has led Sawyer to disagree with his mentor. Skues argued that casting nymphs to rising trout was rather like dry-fly fishing. Sawyer believes that it is utterly different, and he expounded his theories with a gentle passion when I visited his keeper's cottage in Netheravon. Sawyer believes that the nymph method is more difficult than the dry fly, demanding more refinement and skill, and is in no manner inferior to the more fashionable dry-fly fishing.

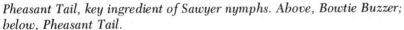

Pheasant Tail, key ingredient of Sawyer nymphs. Above, Bowtie Buzzer; below, Pheasant Tail.

Dermot Wilson observed at his Nether Wallop mill that Sawyer has the singular ability to see deeply into the river and that his skills of observation permit him not only to understand its trout and flyhatches and grayling but perhaps also to see into its soul.

American trout fishermen were slow to experiment with the nymph on our waters. Fishing writers like Hewitt and Knight were familiar with Skues and his books, and in spite of Hewitt's invitation to fish the Houghton Club at Stockbridge with John Waller Hills, where the dry fly and Halford's ghost reigned unchallenged, it seems that nymph fishing had the greater impact on Hewitt.

Ray Bergman published his first book, *Just Fishing*, in 1932. It went through twelve printings. Although it did not treat nymphs as a subject separate from conventional wet-fly practice, its brief discussion of nymphs and its color plates did introduce the new technique to a large audience. Bergman included several British patterns that were imported by William Mills & Son, where the writer worked in his early years, as well as his first nymph-creeper patterns. His caddis and stone-fly patterns were rather primitive, and his nymph creepers were more like streamers than nymphs. Six years later, Bergman published his immensely successful *Trout*, which showed he was now fully aware of nymph fishing by including a full two chapters on the method. Like many other American fishermen, Bergman had little success with the early patterns, although he did fish the Hewitt hard-body types. Bergman experimented with translucent body materials combined with soft hen hackles or guinea-fowl fibers. Although his patterns seem more like lures than imitations of specific nymphs, he was obviously convinced that nymph fishing was important.

James Leisenring completed his *Art of Tying the Wet Fly* in 1941, although the outbreak of World War II caused his little classic to languish in relative obscurity. Leisenring was a simple Pennsylvania toolmaker whose heavy accents echoed his German origins, but his mind had the precision of the finely machined objects that came from his skilled hands.

As Theodore Gordon did with the well-nigh legendary Halford, Leisenring exchanged letters with Skues in England. It was Leisenring who quietly adapted the wet-fly tradition of Cutcliffe, Stewart, and Skues to the fly life of our American rivers.

The decade that followed World War II was richly productive in fishing books. Arthur Flick published his fine little *Streamside Guide to Naturals and Their Imitations* in 1947, which contained several excellent nymph dressings in the Skues style.

John Atherton completed his remarkable *The Fly and the Fish* in 1951, a book filled with a unique mixture of poetry, technical skills, and creative insights. Atherton was an artist who lived in Vermont. His most memorable patterns included exquisite dry and low-water salmon flies and a hopscotching Hewitt skater, but a series of excellent nymph patterns were also included.

Atherton was highly skilled with a nymph, and although his flies are conceived in the flat-bodied Hewitt tradition, they are dressed with greater refinement and skill.

Alvin Grove's *The Lure and Lore of Trout Fishing* was also published in 1951, and it has been acclaimed as one of the finest books in the literature of American trout fishing. It contributed much original knowledge of nymph life, fly-dressing, and nymph-fishing tactics. In the same year the nymph studies of Edward Sens were recorded by Ray Ovington in his book *How to Take Trout on Wet Flies and Nymphs*. Sens was another solitary genius who fished the Catskills, and his work resulted in a superb series of nymphs keyed to our better-known mayfly patterns. His nymphs trace their lineage almost directly to Skues and are perhaps the most popular series available. Sens, however, also added two completely original imitations of hatching caddis flies and started a revolution that still continues in the work of fishermen like Leonard Wright and Larry Solomon. The several hatching-sedge patterns that I worked out for my book *Nymphs* clearly owe a debt to the pioneer work of Edward Sens.

William Blades's *Fishing Flies and Fly Tying* which appeared in 1952, quickly became the standard American book on fly patterns and how to dress them. The book held a special significance for me, since Blades was the acknowledged master who polished my boyhood fly-tying skills at the close of World War II. Blades was the father of the intricate, highly lifelike nymphs, complete with trimmed hackle-stem legs and wing cases, and his theories still live in the work of superb fly makers like Poul Jorgensen, Matthew Vinciguerra, Bill Charles, and Ted Niemeyer.

A. J. McClane, who followed the legendary Ted Trueblood as the fishing editor of *Field & Stream*, published his *Practical Fly Fisherman* in 1953. It remains perhaps the best general book on American fly-fishing since Bergman and is filled with observations on the state of nymphs and nymph-fishing theory at mid-century.

When Sid Gordon published *How to Fish from Top to Bottom* in 1955, he included many original observations on fishing and imitating nymph life. Gordon had several original concepts about egg-laying and hatching sedges, particularly because of their glistening sheath of bubbles. My own book *Matching the Hatch* was printed that same year and included forty-six original imitations of nymphs, larvae, and pupal forms.

Arnold Gingrich served as midwife in assembling *The Gordon Garland* in 1965, which was published in a second edition as *American Trout Fishing* the following year. Among its chapters was a piece on new fly dressings by Theodore Rogowski which included a number of important observations on nymphs. Rogowski pointed again to the importance of Leisenring and his soft-hackled flies as imitations of hatching sedges. Perhaps the most important contribution in his chapter was his silk-stocking nymphs, which used rolled pieces of fine-mesh hosiery to suggest the unformed wings of an emerging nymph. His search for a hatching wing better than the frayed fibers of a Leadwing Coachman or Hare's Ear is still an odyssey that remains incomplete.

Polly Rosborough partially solved the enigma of embryonic wings with marabou fibers, and his little *Fishing and Tying the Fuzzy Nymphs* was published in 1969. It included several mayfly, stone-fly, and caddisworm imitations. There were also a few rough patterns, plus a midge pupa, damselfly, and freshwater shrimp. His damselfly nymph used short marabou fibers to suggest the fluttering rhythms of its caudal filaments. Rosborough is the self-taught sorcerer of the Williamson in southern Oregon and one the finest professional flydressers alive.

The appearance of *Selective Trout* in 1972 quickly established its authors, Doug Swisher and Carl Richards, as major figures in American angling. The book is perhaps best known for its delicate, small, no-hackle subimago imitations, but it is a cornucopia of other flies. *Selective Trout* places considerable emphasis on emerging nymphs and pupae, using hen hackles and soft shoulder-hackle fibers to suggest their partially formed wings. It includes nymphs dressed without wing pads and nymphs tied entirely of fur. Ostrich herl and soft body-hackle fibers are used to imitate wing-case covers. Extended-body nymphs are suggested, along with duck-quill emergers. Their palette of fly patterns also included fur- and quill-bodied midges, as well as soft-hackle flies and Sens-style dressings, but perhaps their most original concept is the wiggle-nymph pattern, a creative adaptation of articulated salmon flies and Blades's stone-fly nymphs.

My own book *Nymphs* was published in 1973, exactly a year after *Selective Trout* reached its surprisingly large audience. Its fly patterns are largely original dressings of mine, and the book was intended to provide American fishermen with a relatively complete guide to our subaquatic insects and crustaceans. Most nymph patterns in recent years have been fancy nonimitative flies without any counterparts in nature. Such dressings are firmly in the Hewitt and Bergman tradition. Yet better fly patterns were unlikely until our fly makers could compare their work with accurate color paintings of as many subaquatic nymphs as possible. Configuration, color, size, habitat, and behavior are equally important in nymph fishing, and my *Nymphs* attempted to make that point.

Swisher and Richards soon followed with their book *Fly Fishing Strategy*, which was published in 1975. There is a fine section on nymph techniques, covering both nymph-fishing casts and manipulation of the fly under the surface film. Some of their subtle techniques deal with working hatching nymphs and pupae in the film itself. Imitations of back swimmers, sow bugs, freshwater shrimps, damselflies, burrowing mayfly nymphs, caddis larvae and pupae, the minute pupal forms of midges, and wiggle nymphs are all explored further. But the most important concept found in *Fly Fishing Strategy* is perhaps the stillborn fly. Many times a combination of weather, temperature, and hu-

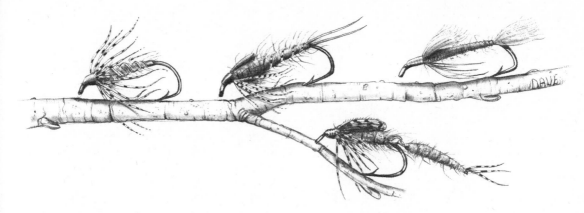

Later American nymphs by (left to right) Leisenring, Atherton, Rosborough, Swisher-Richards.

midity can trap a large percentage of hatching flies in their nymphal and pupal skins. Such conditions can result in many partially hatched insects that fail to escape their shucks rather than the more conventional hatching nymphs. Imitation of such stillborn nymphs is a problem of color mix and of structure, silhouette, and light pattern in the film. The nymphal skin sometimes clings to its emerging fly like a pale halo of color, while in other species the shedding skin is much darker than the thoracic structure and abdomen inside. Although it remains a relatively new development, the stillborn concept is clearly a major step in the evolution of nymph fishing.

Robert Boyle and Dave Whitlock also published their *Fly Tyer's Almanac* in 1975, a book filled with fresh thinking. There are flies tied to imitate leeches and midge larvae and pupae, latex caddisworms and pupal forms, and a wiggle-nymph pattern to suggest a hatching damselfly. Alfred Caucci and Robert Nastasi introduced their book *Hatches* in that same year, and although it is consciously limited to our mayfly species, its color photographs alone make *Hatches* important on any angling shelf.

Charles Brooks completed his *Nymph Fishing for Larger Trout* in 1976, and its comprehensive treatment of nymphing tactics makes it invaluable to American anglers. His earlier work, *The Trout and the Stream*, published two years before, also held considerable information on big-water nymph fishing. Brooks is most interested in heavy water and large fish, but his wisdom has its applications throughout the country. That same year, Gary LaFontaine published his *Challenge of the Trout,* in which the young writer offered a number of fine insights into the nymphing method. Perhaps his most important contribution lies in the attempts to simulate the silvery bubbles that sheath an emerging sedge pupa.

Larry Solomon and Eric Leiser finished *The Caddis and the Angler* in 1977, starting the disciplined study of sedges and their behavior. Although their book avoids the taxonomy of species, it holds much valuable information on the subaquatic stages of the caddis and their imitations.

Our theories of nymph fishing are still less than a century old and display a singular continuity between their British beginnings and evolving practice in the United States. Different problems result in different solutions. Our varied waters have caused American fishermen to work out techniques that go beyond the chalk-stream theories of Skues and Sawyer.

Bold innovation will continue in the future and will have its echoes in tackle and tactics. British fly-fishing entomology has cataloged most of the fly hatches and nymphal forms found in the British Isles. It has taken almost 150 years to complete that work, reaching from *The Fly-Fisher's Entomology* in 1836 to the recent books of writers like Harris and Goddard. Both men are still studying their favorite rivers. Goddard can often be found with Dermot Wilson at Kimbridge along the lower Test, and Harris loves the headwaters of the Liffey and the Rye water outside Dublin, where he is sometimes found behind the gleaming fly counters at Garnett's & Keegan's.

Perhaps the most remarkable aspect of our fishing is the explosive growth of American fly-fishing entomology. Less than a half century has passed since Preston Jennings published his *Book of Trout Flies* in 1935, yet American writers have cataloged a galaxy of fly life in those brief years and their world encompasses an entire continent. The cumulative work of such fishing writers as Jennings, Art Flick, Vincent Marinaro, Charles Wetzel, Alvin Grove, and a phalanx of younger authors is a striking legacy achieved in only forty-odd years.

THREE OF MY FAVORITE NYMPH PATTERNS

For high-altitude lakes in our western mountains:

Diptera (Chironomus pupa)

Hook:	Sizes 14-24 Mustad 94842, fine turned-up eye
Nylon:	6/0 nylon matching body color
Gills:	Short blue dun fibers tied in at midpoint of hook bend
Body:	Black, ruby, purple, reddish brown, brown, dark olive, medium olive green, pale olive, light brown, dirty grayish, amber, dirty yellow, cream, and white rayon floss ribbed with fine silver wire
Thorax:	Polypropylene dyed to match body and dubbed in fat little thorax
Wing cases:	Duck quill sections, or omit in tiny sizes.
Legs:	Soft hackle fibers slightly darker than body colors
Antennae:	Wood-duck, brown mallard or gray mallard fibers
Head:	Nylon matching body color

For western streams like the Firehole River, Yellowstone National Park:

Pale Morning Dun (Ephemerella infrequens)

Hook:	Sizes 12-14 Mustad 3906B sproat 1X long
Nylon:	Dark brown 6/0 nylon

Tails:	Pale barred wood-duck fibers
Body:	Mottled brownish dubbing with an amber quill median, and pale amber lacquer sternites
Gills:	Brownish amber marabou secured with a fine gold wire
Thorax:	Mottled brownish dubbing with an amber lacquer sternum
Wing cases:	Dark mottled brownish feather section tied down over thorax
Legs:	Pale brown partridge
Head:	Dark brown nylon

For Henrys Lake, Idaho:

Freshwater Shrimp (Palaemonetes paludosa)

Hook:	Sizes 8-12 Mustad 3906B sproat 1X long
Nylon:	Olive 6/0 nylon
Uropods:	Olive fibers tied short
Body:	Olive dubbing mixed with hare's mask guard hairs
Overbody:	Matte vinyl overdorsal surfaces, secured with fine monofilament
Springers:	Dark olive-dyed pheasant hackle fibers
Thorax:	Olive dubbing mixed with hare's mask
Legs:	Olive-dyed pheasant hackle fibers
Antennae:	Olive-dyed pheasant fibers
Head:	Olive nylon

Al Caucci and Bob Nastasi have published three major works in the short span of five years: Flytyer's Color Guide *(1978)* Hatches *(1975), and* Comparahatch *(1973). They continue their fishing expeditions from coast to coast, ever-researching stream life and recording the vital data they find and the observations they make. Several major projects are now in the works including a detailed book on caddis flies.*

Al Caucci, a development engineer for over fifteen years, is married and has three children. When not waist-deep in a trout stream, Al can be found skiing a favorite mountain or pickin' his guitar.

Bob Nastasi is a graphics artist, painter, and photographer who lives in Wayne, New Jersey, with his wife and three sons. Bob's talents in illustration, photography, and painting have contributed so strongly to the collaborations with Caucci that his primary work in advertising is being replaced by his work in the field of angling. The illustrations in this chapter are by him. In addition to his insatiable appetite for fly fishing, Bob also enjoys tennis and flying. Both Bob and Al are ice-hockey enthusiasts and music buffs.

3

Nymphs: The Primary Converters

Al Caucci and Bob Nastasi

IT MAY NOT BE APPARENT to the casual observer, or even to the novice fly-fisherman, but beneath the stark beauty of a tumbling trout stream there lives a complex, thriving community of life. This community of microscopic organisms, aquatic insects, and fishes is quite intricate. Each form of life, from the tiniest to the largest, is interlinked and dependent upon the other for survival. Scientists call these communities ecosystems, food chains, or food webs.

Aquatic insects, which include subsurface forms of the mayflies, caddis flies, stone flies, and midges, are the *primary converters* in turning microscopic food into bite-size food for higher forms of life such as the trout. There are many orders of aquatic insects, and many families, genera, and species within each order. In their underwater state all these insects are called nymphs or larvae. The characteristics of these forms are discussed in the following pages.

If a trout stream is healthy, the most significant aquatic insect group will be the prolific mayflies of the insect order Ephemeroptera. Also significant, but presenting fewer feeding opportunities for the dependent trout, are the caddis flies (order Trichoptera). The stone flies (order Plecoptera) and the true two-winged flies or midges (order aquatic Diptera) are usually less important, but on some streams certain species provide heavy periodic feeding; thus they are important to fly-fishermen. There are other insect orders, such as Odonata (dragonflies and damselflies) and Hemiptera and Coleoptera (bugs and beetles), that can also be of major importance on streams with specialized habitats. But for the most part these would be exceptions to the norm on typical mountain streams or rivers, and we will limit our discussion to the first four orders named.

MAYFLIES (EPHEMEROPTERA)

Mayflies and trout have almost identical requirements for nutrients, water temperature, oxygen, and stream-bottom habitat. With few exceptions a stream unfit for mayflies is usually unfit for trout. There are species within the orders of other insects that can tolerate pollution to the extent where oxygen is reduced considerably or is nonexistent. But such waters are not real trout waters, and so they will not be included here.

In thousands of seine tests on hundreds of rivers during the past decade, we have found that the mayfly represents the bulk of the trout's diet. Mayflies exist in every conceivable stream habitat that is not severely polluted or completely smothered by silt. There have been recent claims that mayflies do not tolerate pollution as do insects of other orders, but we have not found this to be the case in our research, at least not on legitimate trout waters. On the contrary, in many cases we've found that where mild domestic pollution was introduced to highly oxygenated, acidic streams in the form of nutrients, the mayfly population has actually increased. Few trout rivers have taken the human abuse that has been given such famous domesticated rivers as the Beaverkill, the main Ausable (below Ausable Forks, New York), and the Au Sable (Michigan) to name a few. Over the last decades these rivers have been altered through logging, road building, and domestic development, yet today they remain some of the best mayfly-producing streams in the country. Our records show many similar examples. The point is that mayfly communities are surprisingly resilient and can withstand most changes in their environment short of lethal industrial pollution or wholesale domestic development.

On the same tack, however, we have found that siltation, as a result of poor farming practice and overgrazing, is the biggest threat to the survival of the mayfly and other oxygen-loving insects such as caddis flies and stone flies. The clearing of land to the banks of a stream results in devastating siltation, which covers up the crevices in the streambed, eliminating the microscopic food farms and apartment complexes where the nymphs and larvae feed and live. The cementing of rocky crevices on the stream bottom changes the entire ecosystem of the stream. The elimination of trees and brush not only causes bank erosion but also makes the stream heat up to intolerable temperatures, which reduces the vital oxygen supply so necessary to both insects and trout.

Mayflies can be classified in six extremely important families so far as the angler is concerned. (This deviation from the current technical mayfly classifications should prove more efficient and easier to use for the fly-fisher, especially at streamside.) The nymphs of these families can be classified into four basic types: crawlers, clingers, swimmers, and burrowers. Each type is equipped with specific body characteristics and appendages, enabling it to survive in its required habitat. The crawlers are variable in size and appearance and generally inhabit stretches of medium current, although they may

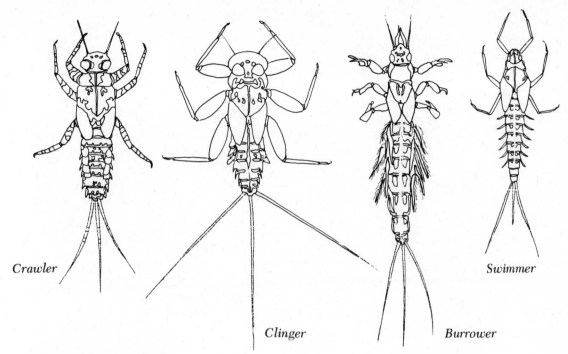

Crawler *Swimmer*

Clinger *Burrower*

Types of Mayfly Nymphs

also be found in fast- and slow-water types; they consist of the prolific Ephe-
merellidae family, the feeble-legged Leptophlebiidae family, and the tiny
mayflies of the Caenidae family. The clingers are of the swift-water Hep-
tageniidae family. The enormous Baetidae family is made up of quick swimmers, while the burrowing types are of the family Ephemeridae. The mayflies
that fall within these basic nymph types, including all related genera and
species, are treated comprehensively in our book *Hatches* (Woodside, N.Y.:
Compara Hatch, 1975), which also includes the evolution, biology, and identification keys of the mayflies. What follows here is a brief summary of the
stages of the mayfly and its vulnerability to the trout in each stage.

When the mayfly eggs hatch on the stream bottom, the tiny nymphs (½
mm in length) feed on algae, diatoms, and detritus in the protective crevices
of rocks. As the nymphs feed, they outgrow each of their nymphal skins and
molt, many times, before they are mature enough to emerge as winged insects.

Contrary to the belief of many fly-fishermen, during the nymphal stage
(which constitutes 99 percent of its life span) the mayfly is practically inaccessible to the trout, except during emergence. Only when they leave their
hideouts during emergence or, a few days or hours prior to emergence, when
they seek out advantageous emergence sites, are the mayflies readily available
to trout. Over the years, our research records and autopsies reveal that most
trout seldom feed selectively on subsurface forms of specific insect species
unless the species is active and ready to emerge, even though the streams
may be teeming with nymphs or larvae.

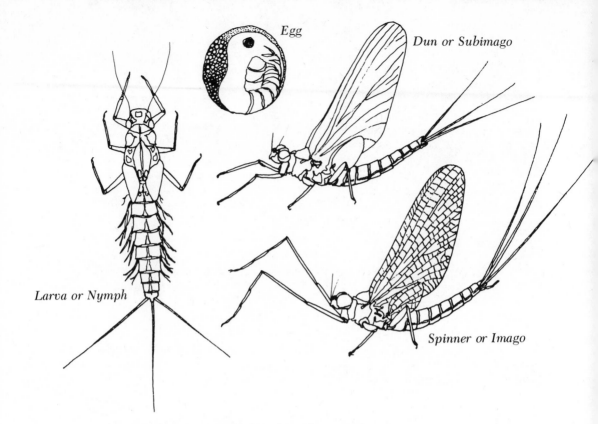

Egg

Dun or Subimago

Larva or Nymph

Spinner or Imago

Life Cycle of the Mayfly

When emergence is near, the mayfly nymph's wing pads become much darker and its body becomes more buoyant as the stomach is filled with air. The winged state of the insect within begins to push, stretch, and enlarge against its outer chitinous skeleton, commonly referred to as the nymphal shuck. The nymphs stop feeding now, and their only interest is in migrating to advantageous emergence positions.

As the nymphs move to these emergence sites, their now-buoyant bodies frequently cause them to lose their footing, and they float dangerously up from the protection of the bottom. Sensing their vulnerability, they swim and wiggle desperately downward to regain their hold on the safe bottom. Many are gobbled up by the trout. The trout's selectivity at this time affords a good opportunity for the angler who chooses the proper nymph pattern and presents it correctly.

When the hatching hour arrives, the thorax begins to split. The nymphs leave the security of the stream's bottom for the last time and ascend toward the surface. This activity results in advantageous feeding opportunities for the trout, which become very selective as to the size, color, shape, and behavior of the naturals.

Some duns successfully pop through the water and into the atmosphere, using the surface tension as an aid in evacuating their nymphal shucks. Some evacuate their shucks underwater. During these periods the trout seldom take the surface duns, preferring the more vulnerable submerged duns or emergers, which have yet to unfold their wings from their thoracic humps. Floating nymph and emerger imitations are best to use at this time.

According to the air temperature or the clumsiness of the individual species, the duns may linger on the surface for long periods of time, setting up even more opportunities for the trout. When they finally become airborne they settle in the foliage, where they hide under leaves or on branches. Here they shed their skins for the last time and transform into the brilliant, glossy-winged insects called imagoes or spinners.

Shortly after the final molt the males mass in swarms over the riffles. The females flit into the undulating swarms intermittently, securing mates. Once paired, they leave the swarm to copulate. Eggs fertilized, the females deposit their eggs to the water in various methods. Some jettison them en masse, dipping their posteriors into the water, while others (such as the large *Ephemera* burrowers) lie prone on the surface, quivering as they extrude their eggs. Others crawl beneath the surface of the water to deposit their eggs on the bottom. Their mission accomplished, both males and females fall to the surface in incredible numbers, spent, completing their cycle. All the trout need do is feed on them effortlessly from a convenient lie.

CADDIS FLIES (TRICHOPTERA)

Like the mayflies, the insects of the order Trichoptera are found in a variety of habitats, but the important species, such as those from the *Hydropsyche*, *Rhyacophila*, *Brachycentrus*, *Glossosoma*, and *Psilotreta* genera, live in the highly oxygenated riffles.

In general, the life cycle of the caddis fly is as follows: The eggs hatch into tiny wormlike larvae that live on the bottom of the stream or river. They

Life Cycle of the Caddis Fly

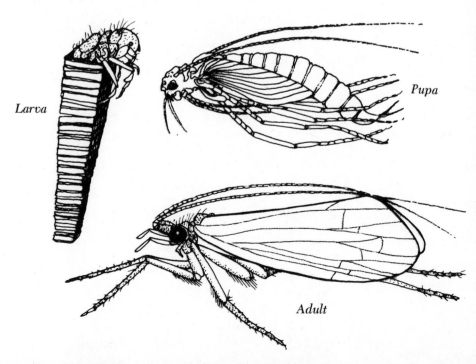

Larva

Pupa

Adult

feed on algae, diatoms, and plant material much as do the mayfly nymphs. Although most are herbivorous (vegetarians), the order is considered omnivorous, as many species are predaceous (both herbivorous and carnivorous).

The larvae may be *free-living, net spinners,* or *case builders.* When the larvae are mature they build various cocoons on underwater objects, where they transform from the larval to the pupal stage, during which stage the adult structure is formed. Case builders generally seal off their cases for pupation. When the metamorphosis is complete, the pupa cuts its way out of the cocoon with its sharp mandibles and rises rapidly to the stream's surface, where it sheds its pupal skin quickly and flies off rapidly as an adult caddis fly. All this may happen in seconds, a sharp contrast to the clumsy and time-consuming emergence of the mayfly.

Many slow-water species crawl out on rocks and sticks or onto the shore. These emergences are generally less concentrated and thus many are inconsequential. Mating flights may follow within hours or days or, in some important species, weeks. Unlike the mayfly, which cannot consume food or liquid after emergence because of its atrophied mouth parts, the adult caddis is equipped with mouth parts to siphon liquids and can sustain itself for exceptionally long periods. Hence, it is a strong, refreshed flier.

The free-living larvae of the abundant Rhyacophilidae and Hydroptilidae families live in crevices and among camouflaging vegetation, where they are rather inaccessible to the trout. For this reason, trout normally do not feed dramatically or selectively on these caddis larvae.

Types of Caddis Larvae

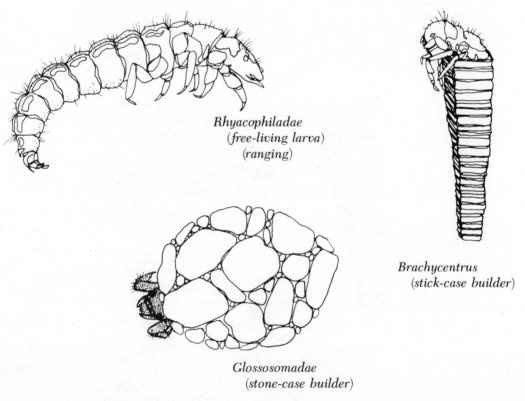

Rhyacophiladae
(free-living larva)
(ranging)

Brachycentrus
(stick-case builder)

Glossosomadae
(stone-case builder)

The net-spinning forms of the Hydropsychidae, Philopotamidae, and Psychomildae families are more or less free-ranging also. They spin silken nets of various configurations that strain small organisms from the current. The caddis flies of the *Chimmara* and especially the *Hydropsyche* genera are important to trout fishermen. They are generally prolific and live in rocky crevices lined with webs that extend to the front of the dwelling, where they spin seine nets. These larval forms, too, are relatively inaccessible to the trout and generally do not constitute much of the trout's diet.

The case builders are the most conspicuous and curious group. Many of the larvae build cases made from pebbles and sand or vegetative matter that are architectural marvels of perfect symmetry and beauty. Some larval cases, such as those from the Limnephilidae family, are made of both pebbles and vegetation. There are two basic types of case construction: saddle cases, where both ends of the larvae protrude, and portable cases, which are sealed at the back ends.

The Glossosomadae larvae are saddle-case builders. Some of the most important caddis species belong to this family. You can see thousands of their cases plastered to rocks while you wade the riffles. The front and back openings are cemented in during pupation. During lull periods, when mayflies aren't emerging, trout may eat these cased larvae, but to get at them they must also eat the case. We've found that trout resort to this only when feeding opportunities are exceedingly lean.

Examples of swift-water portable cases can be seen in the species of larvae that constitute the *Brachycentrus*, *Goeridae*, and *Odontoceridae* families. Limniphilidae larvae cases, such as those of the *Limnephilus* and *Platyphylax* genera, normally inhabit slower water such as that found in pools. Many eastern anglers call them stick caddises. Their ragged cases are made from bark, leaves, sticks, and sand and may reach 2 inches in length. On June days in the Poconos and Catskills we have seen the entire bottoms of pools covered with these moving stick cases. Autopsies on trout during this period showed that trout seldom feed on these cased larvae, although they were unbelievably accessible.

To sum up, trout seldom take cased larvae unless more vulnerable insect stages are not active; thus case imitations are usually ineffective. The pupa, which seals itself in a case or in a cocoon, is normally just as inaccessible or unappealing to the trout as the cased larvae.

The emerging caddis pupae are usually the most vulnerable to trout. Like the emerging mayfly nymph, it is at the mercy of the currents and the trout. Many swift-water species reach the surface and fly off rather quickly, providing the trout with few feeding opportunities. Some species drift freely during their ascent, and trout key in on these insects. Our records show average-size trout of 12 to 14 inches gorged with hundreds of pupae during these conditions. Our studies on caddis flies are still in progress and the final results, we're sure, will prove very interesting.

As you've probably seen, caddis adults are strong fliers and are normally airborne very quickly. This sets up another difficult feeding situation for the trout, especially when compared to the clumsy emergence of the prolific mayfly species that may float for minutes to dry their wings for flight.

Small or freshly stocked trout, or trout in stream sections that are over-populated with fish, such as some of the "Fish for Fun" projects that are normally overstocked, may resort to less-vulnerable insect stages because of the stiff competition for food. This rarely happens on streams with equilibrium, however—those that are seldom stocked or are stocked very discriminatingly and contain wild or holdover fish.

The caddis mating flights can be as thick and awesome as some of the major mayfly spinner flights, but we have been on many of our top trout waters during these flights and seen nary a trout rise. Caddis adults may survive for up to eight weeks, and they form mating flights nightly or daily. These blizzardlike mating flights are really accumulations of insects that may have hatched sporadically every day for weeks and do not necessarily mean that the emergences are concentrated sufficiently to cause heavy or selective feeding. Although the caddis adults may fly close to the surface and occasionally touch, they are normally unavailable to the trout in numbers that would prompt them to feed.

Many ovipositing caddis deposit their eggs on stones and plants near or above the water and are completely unavailable to the trout; others drop egg masses from the air or dip their posteriors into the water rather quickly; still others crawl back into the water to lay their eggs on rocks. The last, when available in great numbers, are the most vulnerable to the trout.

Each season, as our caddis research continues, we find ourselves eagerly anticipating prolific emergences of our favorite caddis species. Discovering species, on new rivers, that cause trout to feed selectively is always a special treat. We're certain that every serious angler will find the activity surrounding caddis unique and challenging, and an experience different from that of the mayfly.

We feel that fly-fishermen should be aware of recent exaggerated claims of the overall importance of caddis in the trout's diet. It has become a fad in current fly-fishing literature for some to overstate the importance of caddis, especially in its adult stage. With all due respect to those who have pioneered efforts on caddis, our findings thus far show that wild or holdover trout seldom feed selectively on caddis larvae, cased pupae, or adults. On the other hand, the emerging pupae of many species are taken very selectively, as are those crippled adults that do not survive the emergence of heavy hatches. On private-club stocked waters and on overly stocked public-river stretches we have witnessed overpopulated trout slashing at skittering or dipping caddis, but we've seldom found this to be the case with wild or holdover trout on most of our top trout rivers. Small trout, 6 to 9 inches, could be the exception.

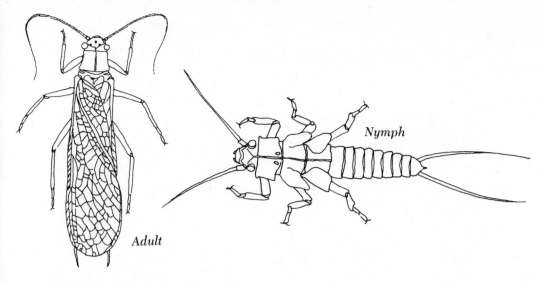

Nymph

Adult

Life Cycle of the Stone Fly

STONE FLIES (PLECOPTERA)

Stone flies are primitive insects; fossils show that they have existed for 220 million years. Stone flies generally represent a much smaller percentage of the trout's diet than do mayflies and caddis flies. This type of generality can be quite misleading, however, for even if stone flies represented less than 10 percent of the trout's diet on a particular stream, it is quite possible to arrive on that stream for several days of fishing only to find that prolific stone-fly emergences or ovipositing flights are in progress, causing trout to feed selectively. It may be the only significant stone-fly activity of the year on that particular stream, yet if the angler were unprepared he would probably have a very unsuccessful fishing trip. Hence, serious fly-fishermen should make every effort to learn about this interesting order of insects and the effect they have on trout.

The size range of stone flies is extreme; some tiny *Capnia* species may be only 4 to 5 millimeters in length, while the legendary *Pteronarcys* flies approach 50 mm (2 inches) in length. Generally, the life cycle of the smaller stone flies is one year, while maturity may take two or three years for the large *Pteronarcys* and *Acroneuria* stone flies.

The combination of seasonal succession, feeding habits, and habitat preferences reduces the competition among the species of the stone fly and species of other orders. For example, the tiny *Capnia* and *Taeniopteryx* stone-fly nymphs spend spring and summer in the substrate as tiny mummylike (depausing) nymphs. They resume feeding on algae and detritus from September to late winter or early spring. Many hatch through the winter and early spring, although April hatches are the best known to fly-fishermen. We have fond memories of early April *Taeniopteryx* activity on the gentle Brodheads in Pennsylvania. The nymph imitations and flush-floating emerger patterns did well when the activity didn't clash with the prolific early-season *Baetis* mayflies, which emerge in similar water-temperature ranges (42 to 52 degrees fahrenheit).

There are six stone-fly families in North America—three are herbivorous (vegetarians) and are of the Filipalpa group; three are carnivorous or omnivorous and belong to the Selipalpia group. The herbivorous group includes Pteronarcidae, Peltoperlidae, and Neoruidae families, most of which feed on blue-green algae, diatoms, and plant matter. The Pteronarcidae family includes the giant stone flies of the *Pteronarcys* genus. *Pteronarcys californica* is called the salmon fly by western anglers and is responsible for legendary hatches on such Rocky Mountain rivers as the Yellowstone, Madison, and Big Hole. *Pteronarcys dorsata* is the eastern and midwestern equivalent of this genus, but the hatches are not nearly as significant.

The Neoruidae family includes the tiny winterish and early-spring hatching stone flies of the *Capnia* (subfamily Capuiidae) and *Taeniopteryx* genera (subfamily Taeniopteryginae). Anglers may recognize their common names: early brown stone fly (*Taeniopteryx*) and early black stone fly (*Capnia*), given to these flies for their early emergence.

The carnivorous or omnivorous stone flies are of the Perlodidae, Chlorperidae, and Perlidae families; the latter are true carnivores. The Perlodidae and Chlorperidae stone flies are omnivorous and many species of the latter are considered herbivorous. The *Acroneuria* nymphs (family Perlidae, sub-

Herbivorites (stone fly)

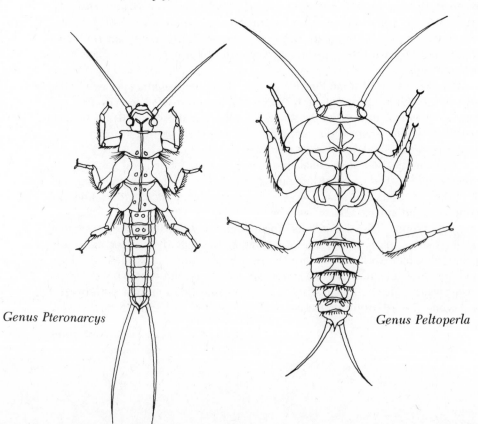

Genus Pteronarcys

Genus Peltoperla

family Acroneurinae) are the most aggressive carnivores. They are prolific on the larger stretches of our best eastern and midwestern trout rivers. They are flattened in cross section and their color patterns are strikingly contrasting and reliable for identification. The plant-eating families are usually round in cross section and concolorous.

Most stone flies crawl out of the water on rocks or other objects before they emerge as adults. Thus the act of emergence generally sets up few feeding opportunities for the trout. A few species may hatch on the surface, especially if the stream lacks boulders or other convenient emergence objects. The best opportunities, as far as the trout are concerned, occur during surface activity or when the nymphs are migrating to their emergence sites. The adults are quick afoot and do very little flying once they reach the shore. Mating takes place not in the air but on the ground or on plants.

As with the caddis, many species of stone flies feed in the winged stage. The Filipalpa stone flies are known vegetation feeders, while the Selipalpia adult stone flies (carnivores) have insufficient mouth parts and do not feed. The large vegetarian *Pteronarcys* stone flies are an exception and do not feed in the adult stage.

Ovipositing is performed in various ways. Many species crawl to the water's edge to deposit their eggs uneventfully. Many species of *Taeniopteryx*, *Capnia*, and *Allocopnia* alight on the water to release their eggs. This presents better opportunities for the trout when the insects are in sufficient numbers. Other spring and summer forms, such as the large Pteronarcidae and Perlidae families, drop eggs en masse from the air.

Over the years, we have found the large stone-fly nymph imitations to be the best producers during periods of inactivity. Imitations of the *Acroneuria* group are especially effective, since these carnivores crawl from their crevices more often than other groups while hunting for food or migrating to other areas. *Pteronarcys* imitations may do better on western rivers or on the headwaters of eastern trout rivers where *Acroneuria* nymphs are scarce. Although these larger nymphs are not available in numbers sufficient to cause selective feeding, they may be to the trout the most appealing subsurface food during periods of inactivity. Thus it is understandable why the large stone-fly nymphs such as the Golden Stone, Catskill Coiler, Montana, Bitch Creek, and Stone-fly Creeper, in sizes 4 through 10, are the top choice of most self-confessed nymphers.

MIDGES AND CRANE FLIES (AQUATIC DIPTERA)

The subject of aquatic Diptera is vast, fascinating, and much too comprehensive to treat here, except in a most general manner. Most Diptera are not associated with trout waters but are slow-water species of the warmer climates. Thus we will limit our discussion to those that seem to be important to the diet of the trout: midges and crane flies. Proper classification of suborders, families, subfamilies, and so on will not be attempted.

The larvae of the Diptera, wormlike and legless, live under or attached to stones, in the muck where they build tubes, and in vegetation (depending on the family or genus). They feed on algae, plankton, and detritus. Generally, the larvae of midges and crane flies are herbivorous, although some of the large crane-fly larvae (which may reach 3 inches in length) are carnivorous and can consume mayfly nymphs and even stone-fly nymphs.

Like caddis flies, Diptera have a complete metamorphosis—a four-stage life cycle: egg, larvae, pupae, and adult. The egg, larval, and pupal stages are generally passed underwater, although some larvae migrate to stream banks to pupate. The larvae may mature in a few weeks or take as long as two years. Most trout-stream species have several broods per season.

The adults are two-winged, as denoted by the name Diptera; the hind pair of wings, reduced to club-shaped balancing organs, are called halteres. Most species are equipped with mouth parts adapted for sucking liquids, and most adults are nonbiting, but those from some families such as Simuliidae (blackflies) and Heleidae (punkies) can inflict painful bites, as most fly-fishermen can attest.

The presence and relative importance of the various species within families will vary greatly from one trout stream to another, according to specialized habitats. We have found, however, that with few exceptions there are only a limited number of families of midges and crane flies that may be important enough to cause selective feeding by trout, especially brown trout, which are the most efficient and selective feeders in the trout family. Even these limited Diptera types are usually important only on sluggish headwaters and on silt-laden meadow or farmland streams, or perhaps on long, flat stretches or quiet pools of mountain rivers.

The larvae of the shallow, swift-water species such as those of the *Simulium* (blackfly), *Blepharocera* (net-winged midge), and *Palpomyia* (punkie or "no-see-um") genera seldom prompt selective feeling by mature fish, but young trout as well as bait fish feed on them often.

The two most important Diptera families, as far as fly-fishermen are concerned, are usually considered to be Chironomidae (midges) and Tipulidae (crane flies). Both are basically slow-water silt dwellers and can be important to the trout's diet on these waters.

Chironomidae species, which number in the thousands, are nonbiting midges. The adults range from 2 mm in size to almost 1 inch, but the most common are the tiny midge forms, approximately 3 to 6 mm (size 28 to 18 hook). The colors of the larvae range from white to red, and to green, brown, and black. The red larvae are called bloodworms and owe their color to a respiratory blood pigment that enables them to exist in streams of low oxygen content. Most of the larvae mix saliva with silt and sand to construct open-ended tubes on the bottom. Like caddis flies, they spin a net across the tube

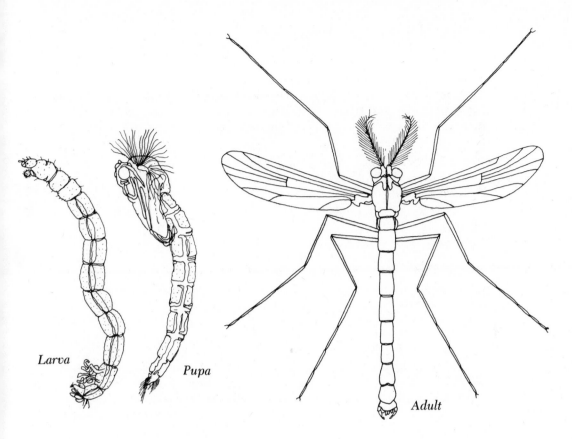

Larva

Pupa

Adult

Diptera
Life Cycle of the Midge

opening that filters plankton and detritus matter. Pupation usually takes place in the tube, and thus they are virtually inaccessible to trout during the larval stage.

The pupae come to the surface to emerge; there they may hatch immediately or hang suspended for a short while. Like the other insect orders, this vulnerable period varies within the species or according to the water and air temperature. A surface ruffled by winds may also cost the emerging pupae precious time. We have witnessed heavy feeding to the pupae and crippled adults on silt-ridden streams and headwater bogs during these emergences.

The same waters can produce selective feeding to the large Diptera forms of the family Tipulidae, commonly called crane flies. These larvae can reach lengths up to 70 mm, but the size range is usually 10 to 50 mm. Most crane flies are semiaquatic and live in wet moss and vegetation along stream margins. Some live in wet meadowlands and pastures, and these forms are obviously not important to the trout's diet. A few genera, however, such as *Antocha* and *Hexatomia,* are wholly aquatic.

Owing to the vast number of species, and size variances within, the midge and crane-fly families are very difficult to anticipate and prepare for, as far as fly tying and the emergences are concerned. Thus anglers should record any activity that may have caused selective feeding by trout, so that they can return to the river better prepared the next time.

Diptera
Life Cycle of the Cranefly

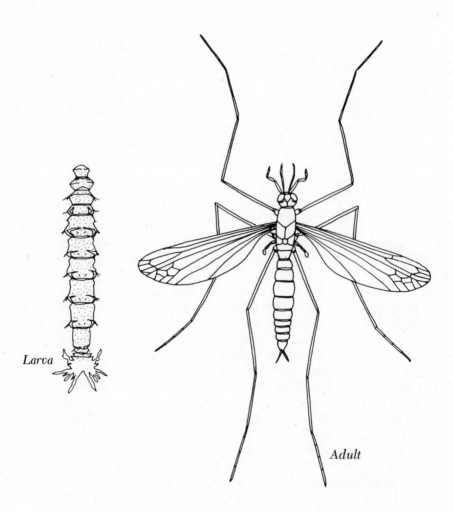

Larva

Adult

Compara-Nymph

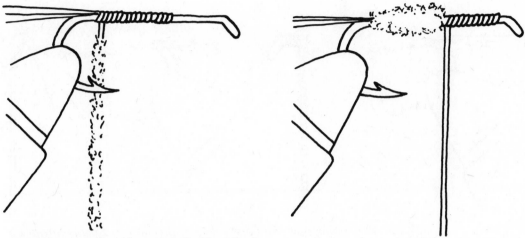

1. Wrap tying thread around shank of hook.
2. Secure wet hackle or flank feather tail fibers to hook shank.
3. Dub rabbit fur to tying thread.
4. Wind the dubbing half the distance from the hook bend to the eye of the hook. Body should be tapered with the thickest diameter at the midsection.

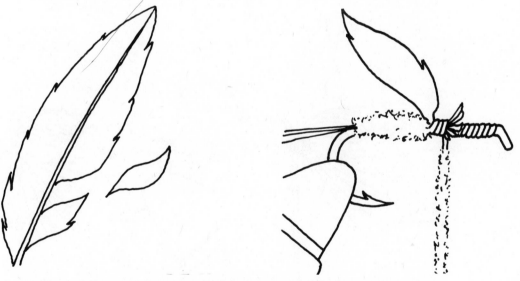

5. Snip a quill segment from a quill feather. The width of the segment will depend on the size of fly you are dressing. Generally, the width should equal the width of the thorax.
6. Wrap quill segment tightly to hook shank.
7. Dub more rabbit fur to tying thread.

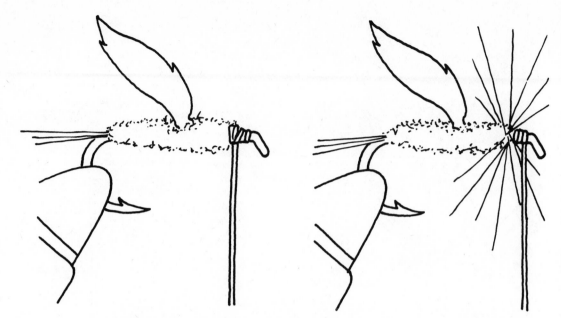

8. *Wrap more dubbing for thorax. Wind tying thread to just behind the hook eye. Most mayfly species have thoraxes that are thicker in cross-section than their abdomens. Discretion should be used in relation to the species you are imitating.*

9. *Select soft-fibered flank or wet hackle feathers for legs.*

10. *Tie in flank or hackle feather.*

11. *Wind several turns of hackle around hook shank.*

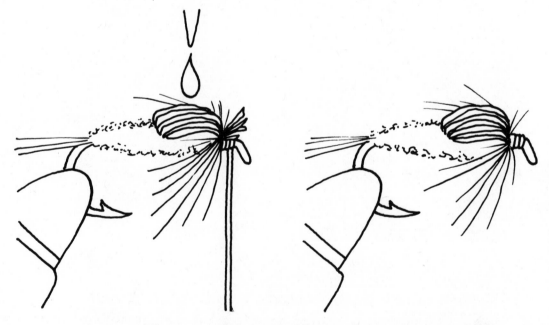

12. *Grip quill segment fibers and pull evenly toward eye of hook. Tie down with four or five wraps of thread.*

13. *Add a drop of clear nail polish, vinyl cement, or head lacquer to wing pad for durability.*

14. *Form head with tying thread and tie off with several jam knots. Add drop of nail polish or lacquer to head of finished fly.*

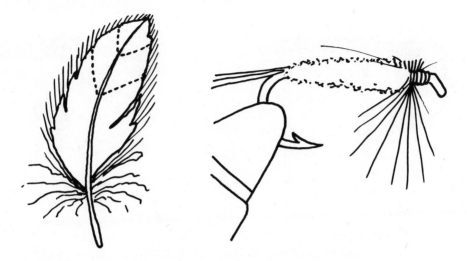

1. *Select properly colored partridge hackle feather, wet hackle, or flank feather. Dotted lines indicate area to be cut.*
2. *Cut feather.*
3. *Repeat steps 1 through 11 for Compara-nymph but do not tie in quill segment. Wind wet hackle several turns behind hook eye.*
4. *Trim hackle on top.*

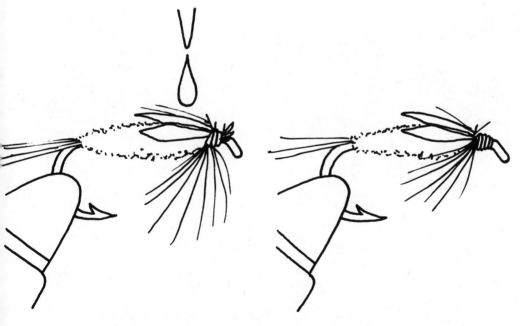

5. *Tie on cut feather (wing pad).*
6. *Add drop of nail polish, vinyl cement, or head lacquer for added durability.*
7. *Form neat head with tying thread and tie off with several jam knots.*

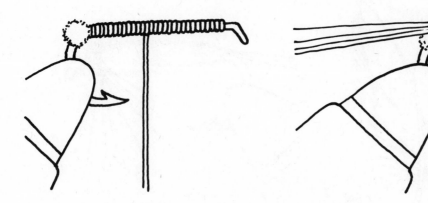

1. Wrap tying thread around shank of hook. Add tiniest bit of dubbing.
2. Form tiny ball of dubbing at bend and bring thread to center of hook shank.
3. Tie in stiff hackle or mink-tail tailing fibers.

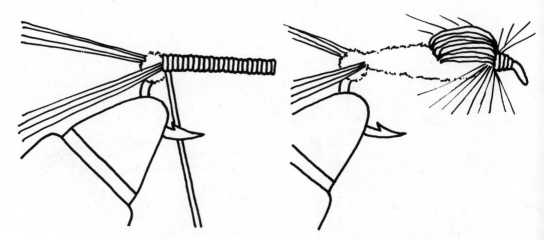

4. Wind tying thread toward ball of dubbing. This operation will force tailing fibers to each side of ball, splaying them in pontoon fashion.

5. Repeat steps 3 through 13 of Compara-nymph, except tie in dry-fly hackle instead of soft hackle. Tie off with several jam knots. Add drop of nail polish or lacquer to head.

6. Trim hackle on bottom so that nymph floats flush in surface film.

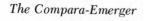

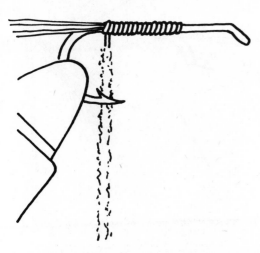

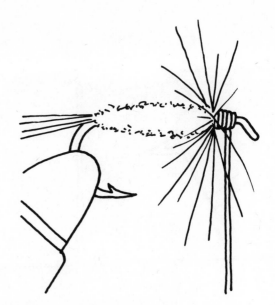

1. Wrap tying thread around hook shank.
2. Secure wet hackle or flank feather tailing fibers to hook shank.
3. Dub rabbit fur to tying thread.
4. Wind dubbing to behind eye (approx. ⁵/₆ hook shank length).
5. Tie in wet hackle or flank feather.
6. Wind several turns of hackle around hook shank (hackle should be tied sparsely).

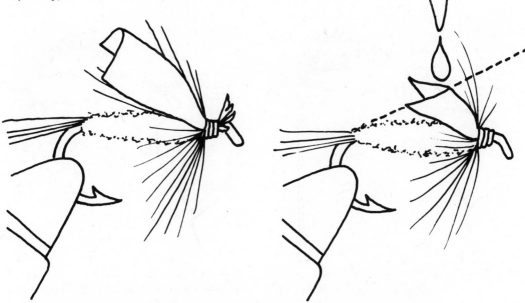

7. Cut segment from a quill feather, twice the width of a normal wing.
8. Fold quill segment and tie down. (We also use flank feather fibers of mallard, woodduck, and teal as well as partridge hackle fibers for this pattern.)
9. Cut quill segment with scissors as indicated by dotted line.
10. Add a drop of vinyl cement to wing for durability and flexibility. Finish with several jam knots and add a drop of nail polish or lacquer to head.

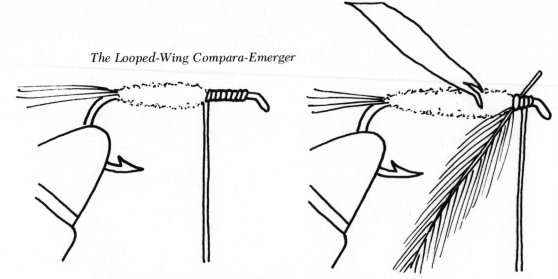

1. Repeat steps 1, 2, and 3 of Compara-emerger and wind dubbing $^3/_5$ length of hook shank.
2. Cut quill segment.
3. Tie in quill segment and add more dubbing to tying thread.
4. Wind dubbing to just behind hook eye and tie in wet hackle or flank feather.

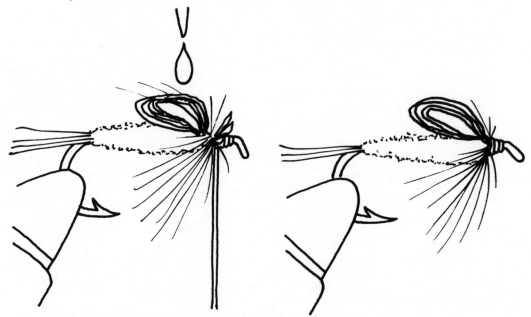

5. Wind several turns of hackle around hook shank.
6. Loop and tie in quill segment. Trim butts of quill fibers and add drop of vinyl cement to looped wing for durability and flexibility.
7. Form neat head with tying thread and tie off with several jam knots and add a drop of nail polish or lacquer.

The Stiff-Hackled Compara-Emerger

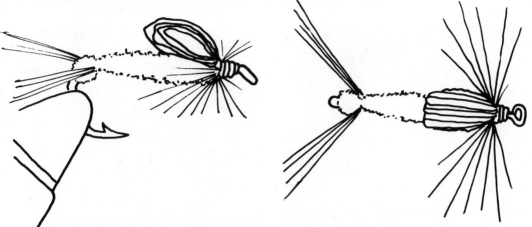

1. Dressing is accomplished by using the same procedure as for the Compara-emerger except: the tails and legs are made of stiff dry fly hackle (mink tail fibers are also used for the tail) using the same procedures as for dressing the Stiff-hackled Compara-nymph.

2. Stiff-hackled Compara-emerger, top view.

The Deer-Hair Compara-Emerger

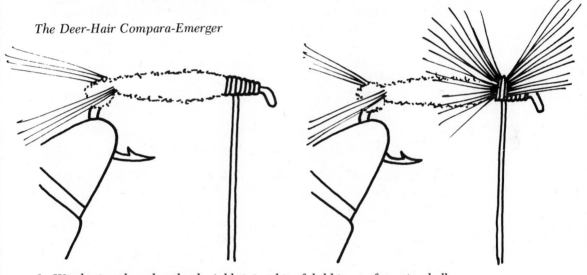

1. Wind tying thread on hook. Add tiniest bit of dubbing to form tiny ball as described in Stiff-hackled Compara-nymph.

2. Return tying thread to center of hook.

3. Tie in stiff hackle or mink tail tailing fibers and complete tail as described in Stiff-hackled Compara-nymph tying instructions.

4. Add more dubbing and wind a neatly tapered body to a position 4/5 distance from the hook bend to the eye. Thorax end of body should also be tapered to act as a base for the desired slant of the emerger wing.

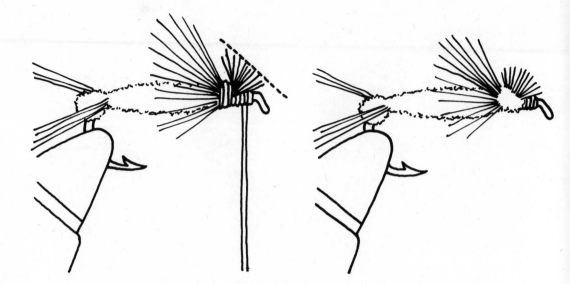

5. *Select a sparse clump of deer-hair fibers. Following the wing proportions of the illustration, secure the deer hair tightly into position. Then wrap approximately 6 to 8 fairly loose turns of thread slightly toward the rear. This will lower the profile of the splayed deer hair.*

6. *With the thumb and forefinger, push back butt ends toward hook bend and wrap tight windings in front of butt ends until they are vertical or leaning toward rear. Trim butt ends as illustrated to form a thoratic hump.*

7. *Add a small amount of dubbing and finish winding thorax. Form neat head and finish by adding a drop of nail polish or lacquer.*

FOUR OF OUR FAVORITE NYMPH PATTERNS

There are no miracle fly patterns that will take selective trout consistently, day in and day out. On the contrary, there is a need for different pattern types to duplicate the size, shape, and color of the current insect activity. As the trout's attention shifts from bottom forms, about to migrate to the surface, to the emergers (slightly below the surface or in the film), and finally to the freshly emerged or ovipositing adults on the surface, the angler must also switch to different pattern types for maximum success and enjoyment of the sport.

For four of our favorite subsurface imitations, we have selected the mayfly nymph and emerger Compara-fly imitations in two different versions. Two are designed to be fished on the bottom or at mid-depth and two should be fished in or under the surface film. They are pictured here.

Except for the hook size and dressings, these prototypes are typical for practically every mayfly species. Our next three choices would be the caddis pupa, stone-fly nymph, and Diptera or midge pupa prototypes.

Four of Caucci and Nastasi's Favorite Nymph Patterns

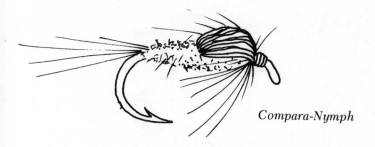

Compara-Nymph

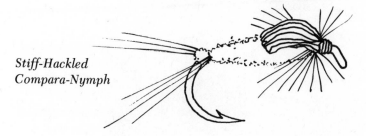

Stiff-Hackled
Compara-Nymph

Compara-Emerger

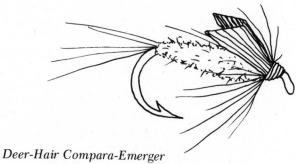

Deer-Hair Compara-Emerger

Poul Jorgensen's name is one of the best known in American fly-fishing, for he is an expert fisherman, a noted conservationist, an innovative fly-tier, and a lecturer, writer, and professional photographer. He is the author of Dressing Flies for Fresh and Salt Water, Trout Fly Charts, and Modern Fly Dressings for the Practical Angler, as well as a book on salmon flies to be published this year.

He is an active officer in such organizations as the American League of Anglers, the Theodore Gordon Flyfishers, and Trout Unlimited, as well as director of the Brotherhood of the Jungle Cock.

Born in Denmark, Jorgensen settled in the United States more than twenty years ago and now makes his home in Columbia, Maryland.

4
Anatomy of the Artificial

Poul Jorgensen

MY FRIEND WAS SHAKING HIS HEAD. He had just been through a one-hour lecture on the subject of entomology as it relates to fly tying and he was now thoroughly confused. "If I have to become an entomologist before I can tie my own flies," he said, "then I'm going back to my old ways of worming."

It's not unusual for a beginner to feel this way, and even after many years of nymph fishing and fly tying I have never found the need for a degree in entomology and do fairly well with just the knowledge gained from reading and from observing the happenings at streamside.

It is important, however, to recognize that the insects we are trying to imitate differ in shape, life-style, and behavior—something the flytier must consider when choosing the hook, material, and method of dressing. If you look through some of the fly-tying books available today, you will notice that all tiers have their own ideas about how a nymph should be dressed and what materials should be used. It is beyond the scope of this chapter to describe all the intricate manipulations required in fly tying, but it is our hope that what is included will encourage the novice to learn more about the fascinating art of fly tying, which for so many has become just as important as fishing itself.

MAYFLY NYMPHS

A few years ago, while giving a slide lecture in Pennsylvania for a group of fly-fishermen, I was asked to sit on a panel to answer questions from the audience. When someone asked what we considered the most important attribute of a mayfly nymph, the moderator passed the question to the gentleman on my right, who without hesitation said, "Color and size."

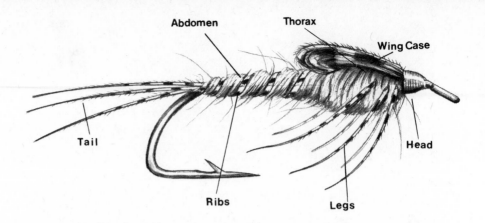

Abdomen Thorax Wing Case Tail Head Ribs Legs

Those are the key words in many cases, and beginners may carry a selection of nymphs in dark, medium, and light shades in different sizes and have a good day's fishing if they know how to use them. But there are times when trout are very selective and will take only a nymph that closely resembles the natural they presently are feeding on, and size and color are just not enough to fool the fish. Unfortunately, most commercial nymphs fall into the conventional category, which means they are dressed by using the same tying method, and were it not for the difference in material it would be hard to distinguish between a March Brown and a Hendrickson. For those who must purchase their nymphs in a sporting-goods store, there is nothing to do but take what's available.

If you take the time to learn to dress your own, however, the possibilities of creating specific nymphs are unlimited. If you use the simple tying method outlined later, try varying the hook length and material application to make your nymph look longer and slimmer, or shorter and fatter, and even pick out the fur on the abdomen to imitate gills in order to conform with the shape and other characteristics of the natural you are trying to copy.

Regardless of the nymph you are using, the presentation has a great deal to do with the outcome of nymph fishing. I therefore strongly recommend that you read the chapters in this book dealing with that subject.

DRESSING A SIMPLE NYMPH

Before you start to tie a nymph it's important to study the materials list carefully and to select the hook that is best suited for the size and type of nymph you are trying to make. There is a whole line of Mustad hooks from which you can choose, and for nymphs they should be made of fairly heavy wire to give them extra weight. Mustad sproat hooks 3906B or 3906, or round-bend 9671 are good for normal-length nymphs, while the Mustad sproat 38941 and round-bend 9672 are best for long burrowingtype nymphs like the Green Drake and the Hexagenia. The hooks, of course, are available in all sizes from 16 to 2 or larger.

The March Brown is one of the better-known nymphs designed to imitate a specific insect, *Stenonema vicarium*, a fly that usually gets active in mid-May through June. While the March Brown is usually dressed on a size 10 hook, there are two other related species of the *Stenonema* genus that are al-

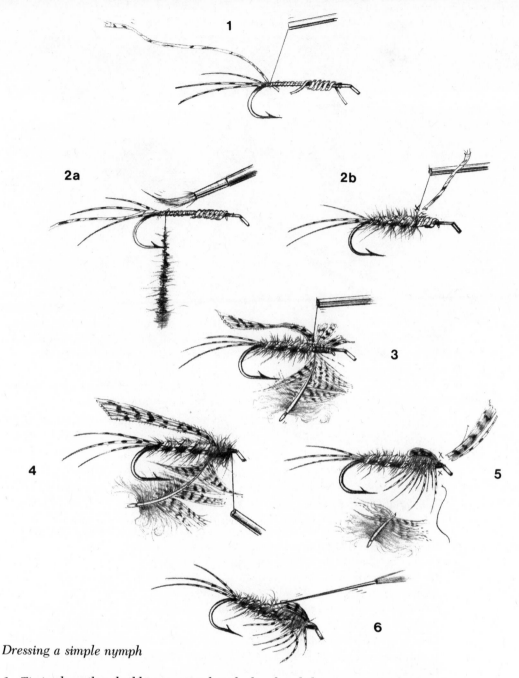

Dressing a simple nymph

1. Tie in the tail and ribbing material at the bend and then wrap some lead wire on the shank for additional weight.
2. Dub some fur on the tying thread, apply a little cement on the hook shank (a), and wind the dubbing to the middle of the shank, followed by the ribbing (b), which is spiraled over it.
3. Tie in the wing-case material, together with the leg hackle.
4. Dub the front of the body.
5. Wind the leg hackle over the front body portion and fold the wing-case material forward over it and tie off.
6. Pick out the fur a little on each side of the rear portion to imitate gills, if needed.

March Brown

most identical. The Gray Fox (*S. fuscum*) is about the same shade but dressed on a size 12 hook. The Light Cahill (*S. canadence*), the smallest of the three, is just a shade lighter than the other two and is dressed on a size 14 hook. All three can be dressed by using the conventional tying method illustrated in the drawings. Because of their behavior when hatching, these nymphs are often fished right in the surface film, so it is best to dress them both weighted and unweighted. To identify which is which, I finish the heads in different colors.

March Brown Nymph

Hook:	Mustad 3906B, size 10
Thread:	Brown
Tails:	Three cock pheasant tail fibers
Ribbing:	Brown embroidery cotton
Body:	Amber seal fur mixed with a small amount of tan fox fur
Legs:	Brown partridge
Wing Case:	Quill strip from short side feather of a cock pheasant
Head:	Brown tying thread

This is one of my favorite impressionistic nymphs and one that has taken fish when everything else has failed. It is best to add some lead wire on the hook shank to get it down deep. For some reason, it seems to work best when fished right on the bottom. Tie in the tail first at the bend, together with three or four strands of peacock herl; then form the yellow floss body, which is rather fat and tapered a little toward the rear. One of the peacock herls is then spiraled forward over the floss as a ribbing, and the other herls are laid forward over the body before the hackle is wound in front.

Telleco Nymph

Telleco Nymph
Hook: Mustad 3906B or 9671
Thread: Black
Tail: Brown hackle fibers
Body: Yellow floss
Ribbing: Peacock herl
Back: Two or three peacock herls
Hackle: Brown
Head: Black

MIDGE-TYPE NYMPHS

There are times when the fish will feed only on the tiniest nymphs in the stream, although it is hard for us fishermen to understand why a trout will take a speck-sized insect and pass up a large juicy nymph. When trout are on a "midge binge" they refuse anything larger than size 20 or 22 and, more often than not, will take a size as small as 28. Artificials for this type of fishing need not be much more than a tail and a little fur wound on the hook. Most of the shades you use for the larger sizes can be used for the midge flies with good results.

CADDIS LARVAE AND PUPAE

Caddis flies are more common on the stream for longer periods of time than any other insect of importance to the nymph fisherman. In their sub-aquatic stage they are rather unusual insects that differ considerably from mayflies and stone flies, both in appearance and development. Some caddis spend their immature life in protective shelters built of sand, small stones, sticks, and other debris found on the stream bottom, while others move freely around among the rocks. When they are ready to hatch they rise to the surface with an erratic swimming motion, and it is at such times they are most likely to be taken by the feeding trout. Anglers can have some good fishing indeed if they have a reasonably good imitation and try to fish it to imitate the natural's behavior as it works its way to the surface. I find it best to cast the artificial upstream and let it sink before applying rhythmic movements with the rod tip to give it a swimming motion as it is being fished.

When choosing the flies for this type of nymphing, I never forget some old standbys: the Breadcrust with its orange body and grizzly hackle collar, and the Green Partridge soft-hackle wet fly. I still carry a good supply in all sizes, together with the more specific contemporary patterns of today. When stocking your fly box you should include both the caddisworm (larva) and the caddis pupa, as they are quite different in appearance. The caddisworm has a slim cylindrical shape with a dark brownish thorax and a dirty-colored abdomen in cream and olive-green, or whatever color of the natural found in the water you are fishing. The caddis pupa is much more interesting. Flytiers have tried for a long time to imitate the glistening sheen of the silvery air bubbles trapped within the translucent pupal skin. The best we have come up with so far are synthetic dubbings like Seal-Ex and others that are very translucent and glistening.

Both versions of the caddis can be dressed on the same type of hook, either Mustad sproat 3906 (or 3906B) or 37160, the one that is now preferred because of its natural curve. Since the naturals rise up from the bottom to hatch, it is important that the artificials be weighted a little with lead wire wound on the hook shank before the body is dressed. If you are one of the many anglers who don't like weighted nymphs, you can wrap some strip lead on the leader with more or less the same result.

Caddis Pupa

The pupa can also be dressed with light brown, green, and gray abdomen and be very effective.

Hook:	Mustad 37160
Thread:	Brown, prewaxed 6/0
Abdomen:	Dark brown Seal-Ex dubbing
Thorax and Legs:	Well-marked guard hairs with fur from the back of a rabbit dyed dark brown
Wing cases:	Gray duck quill sections
Head:	Brown tying thread

This fly is very effective if fished like a caddis pupa, and it is one of the simplest to dress. The ribbing is first tied in at the bend, and then the tying thread is wound to the front where the orange wool is tied in. Make sure

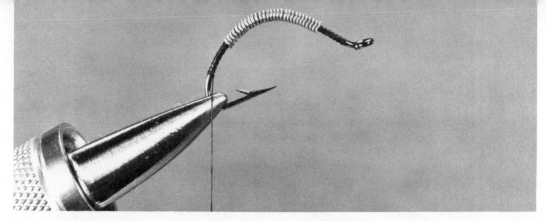

Wind the hook shank with .10-inch lead wire.

Make a tapered fur dubbing in a spinning loop and wind the abdomen. I usually apply a little cement on the hook shank before winding the dubbing.

Spray the duck-quill segments with Krylon or other clear adhesive and tie one section on each side, as seen.

Make the fur leg and thorax section as explained in dressing the Stone Fly, steps 7 through 10; then wind it in front and trim it a little on top.

there is room enough in front for the hackle. Form the body by winding the wool back and forth until it is shaped, as shown; then follow with the ribbing, which is spiraled forward over the wool body. Wind a couple of turns of hackle in front and form a small head with tying thread. After applying a little cement on the head windings, the fly is finished. If you wish, you can wind some lead on the hook shank first for some extra weight.

The Breadcrust

Hook:	Mustad 3906 or 9671
Thread:	Black
Ribbing:	Stripped quill, brown
Body:	Orange wool
Hackle:	Grizzly
Head:	Black tying thread

Breadcrust

Caddisworm

The little Caddisworm varies greatly in size and color, but the most common are the bright green and cream colors. They can be dressed in two ways. The first one is dressed with a latex strip that is wound over a thin wool body, the latex being natural, dyed, or tinted with a waterproof felt-tip marker. The second type is dressed with a fur body only. Both have a small section of the front dressed with blackish-brown fur to represent the thorax and head. If you wish, you can pick out a little of the fur underneath to represent the legs.

Caddisworm

Hook: Mustad 3906B or 37160
Thread: Black
Body: Latex over wool, or fur dubbing only
Thorax: Blackish-brown fur dubbing
Head: Black tying thread

STONE-FLY NYMPHS

The nymph of a stone fly is one of the most impressive insects you can find in the stream, and it is easily distinguished from other nymphs by its two pronounced wing cases (instead of the usual one wing case found on the mayfly species). Since hundreds of varieties of stone flies are found throughout the country, it's important that the angler determine the right size and color for the particular water being fished and learn a little about their general behavior.

The stone-fly nymph's method of hatching should be closely watched, since it provides a clue not only to how to fish the nymph successfully but also to the size and color of the artificial to be used. This nymph migrates early in the morning from the swifter parts of the stream to shallow areas, where it crawls up on rocks and debris to hatch; the empty shucks can be found by the hundreds along the stream, providing you with the basis from which to choose a nymph. During such migrations the nymph is best fished by casting it slightly upstream in the faster water and letting the current carry it down behind rocks in the shallows where the fish are feeding.

While many artificial nymphs have been created to imitate the stone fly, there are some with which I have always had better luck. Art Flick's Stone-fly Creeper, created to imitate the *Perla capitada* (a nymph so common in the Catskill streams), and the Montana Nymph for western fishing are two favorites; their dressings follow this one. These two important nymphs can be dressed by using the conventional tying method explained in the section dealing with mayflies.

There are times, however, when very large nymphs are needed to get the big ones. I designed the semirealistic Stone-fly Nymph for just such occasions. The instructions that follow show it is by no means an easy nymph to dress, but the time is well spent, as many anglers will tell you, if for no other reason than that it results in a trophy fish.

Stone-fly Nymph

Hook:	Mustad 38941 3XL
Thread:	Black, prewaxed 6/0
Underbody:	A piece of plastic, $1/64$ inch thick
Tails and antennae:	Turkey quill fibers dyed dark brown
Abdomen:	Blackish-brown Seal-Ex mix, ribbed with $1/16$-inch-wide strip of latex tinted dark brown
Legs and thorax:	Fur with guard hairs from the back of a rabbit dyed dark bown
Wing cases:	Latex trimmed to shape and tinted
Tinting:	Use Pantone felt-tip markers: Gray no. 404M, Brown no. 464M, and Pale Cream no. 468M

Shape a piece of plastic 1½ inches long and ¼ inch wide in front and tapered down to ⅛ inch in the rear. Make two small notches in front, as shown, and clean the burrs and rough edges all around. Plastic sheets can be purchased in a hobby shop.

Cover the hook shank with thread windings and Duco cement; then tie in the plastic securely on top and wind the middle third with .10-inch lead wire for more weight.

Select the two tails from the leading edge of a turkey primary wing quill, dyed dark brown, and the antennae from the other portions. Then wind a small ball of dubbing directly on the hook shank tight against the end of the plastic. Now tie in the tails on the sides of the plastic, together with the ribbing, which is placed underneath; then tie in the antennae in front, as seen. Wind the tying thread back to the rearmost part of the plastic.

Apply dubbing on the tying thread; then coat the underbody with cement, wind the dubbing to one quarter of the body length from the front, and wind the ribbing over it to the same position. Tie off and cut the surplus.

The wing cases are trimmed to shape from ⅜-inch-square pieces of latex, as shown. The pronotum is shaped from a piece of latex ⅜ inch wide and ½ inch long.

Tie in the first wing case directly in front of the abdomen and tint it completely with brown, followed by gray lengthwise down the middle only. Wipe off the corners with a pale marker for effect. Now form a 3-inch spinning loop at the wing-case tie-in spot.

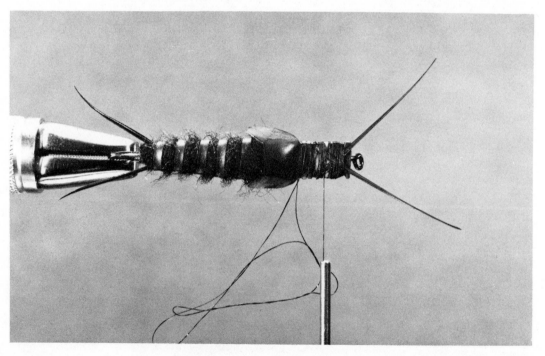

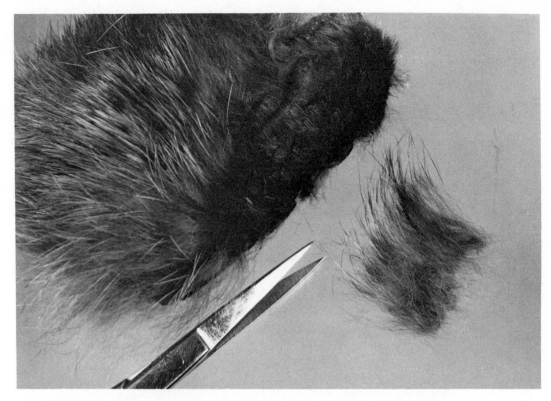

Cut a thin layer of fur and guard hair from the edge of the dyed rabbit skin.

Insert the fur in the loop and proportion it as shown. The tips of the guard hairs should reach to the middle of the abdomen. Use a pair of hackle pliers on the end of the loop for weight and as a spinning tool.

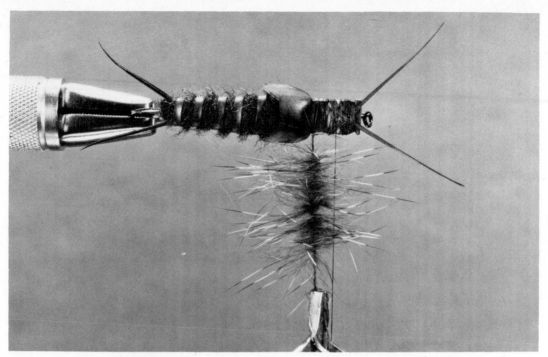

Spin or twist a fur chenille.

Moisten the fur a little and stroke it back so it appears to be coming from one side of the loop only.

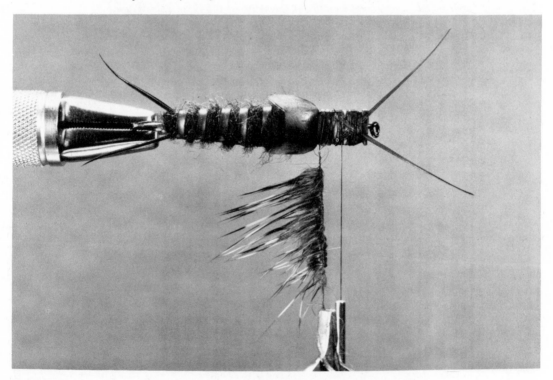

Wind the prepared fur in front of the wing case—with the first turn covering the tie-in windings—to a spot midway between the first turn and the front edge of the plastic underbody. Press down the fur on top or trim it a little if it is too heavy.

Tie in the second wing case and the pronotum piece at the same spot, one at a time, and make the second leg section in the same manner as the first one, tying it off at the notches in front.

Fold the pronotum forward and tie it off at the notches; then trim the surplus to form the head. Tint the latex as described in Step 6 and the nymph is finished. If you wish, the body can be curved a little with a pair of pliers.

FLICK'S STONE-FLY CREEPER

This is one of the best imitations of the famous *Perla capitata*, the amber-colored stone-fly nymph. Start the fly by winding some thin .10-inch lead wire on the front third of the hook shank, leaving enough room for the hackle and a small head. Now tie in the two tail fibers, which should be as long as the hook, together with the hackle stem, which has been soaked in water so it won't break. Wind the hackle stem in close turns up to the lead wire. Wind the seal fur on the front portion; then apply the leg hackle. The wing case is now tied on in front first and then extended over the body all the way to the rear, where it is tied off. It is best to finish the head right after tying in the wing-case material in front and to cut the thread, which now is attached in the rear, right at the beginning of the quill body where the wing case is tied off.

Flicks's Stone-fly Creeper
Hook: Mustad 3906B, size 8
Thread: Primrose
Tail: Two cock pheasant tail fibers
Abdomen: Stripped ginger hackle stem
Thorax: Amber seal's fur
Legs: Grouse body hackle
Wing case: Wood-duck flank feather flat over body, full length
Head: Primrose tying thread

This is a typical western nymph designed for the big rivers of Montana and Wyoming, but it can be fished anywhere black nymphs are needed. It is primarily considered to be a stone-fly imitation, but western anglers will tell you that it may be used as a representative for other nymphs as well. It can be dressed by using the conventional tying method. When using chenille for the body it is necessary to peel some fuzz off the end and expose the center core by which it is attached at the hook bend, after the tail is tied in. This fly should nearly always be weighted to get it down to where the fish are feeding.

Montana Nymph

Hook:	Mustad 38941 3XL
Thread:	Black
Tail:	A few short fibers from a crow feather
Abdomen:	Black chenille
Legs:	Soft black hackle
Thorax:	Yellow chenille (front third)
Wing case:	Two strands of black chenille tied over thorax
Head:	Black tying thread

FOUR OF MY FAVORITE NYMPH PATTERNS

Complete dressings for these four of my favorite nymph patterns are contained in the text of the chapter: Stone-fly Nymph, Caddis Pupa, March Brown Nymph, and Telleco Nymph.

Montana Nymph

Formerly a schoolteacher in his native Pennsylvania, Al Troth now lives in Dillon, Montana, where he works as a professional flytier, outfitter, and fishing guide, teaches fly tying, and presents slide shows and lectures on fly-fishing.

Troth's fishing experiences have spanned over thirty years from east to west, and he relishes variety, being equally at home tossing a 6-inch bucktail or a size 28 midge. United Fly Tyer's Roundtable magazine and Fly Fisherman magazine have carried some of his articles on fly tying.

Some of the more notable flies bearing the Troth name are Troth Bullhead, Terrible Troth Stone, Sow Bug, Scud, and hair dry flies such as the Elk-Hair Caddis, Salmon Fly, and Hair Spider. He credits his hobby of photographing aquatic life with being an aid in developing these fly patterns, many of which have achieved national recognition in angling books and magazines.

5

How to Read the Water

Al Troth

UNLIKE FISHING WITH A DRY FLY, where you can observe your quarry in action, in nymphing you must fish in areas where you may only *suspect* trout activity. The success of a nymph fisherman therefore parallels his ability to read water. Where you "plunk down" the fly is really what it is all about. Regardless of the quality and quantity of equipment or nymph patterns, nymphing lore will come only after considerable time is spent studying, observing, and, most of all, fishing. Many trial-and-error experiences are necessary to develop workable nymphing expertise. Fishing with or observing a good nymph fisherman will save a lot of time, but for the novice angler there are a few shortcuts.

Water flowing through a channel that has a smooth bottom and sides will have a smooth surface; its speed at the surface, except for a slight slowing for friction, would be the same as at the bottom. But a large stone in the channel will deflect the water around itself and form a quiet pocket of holding or feeding water above and below. If the stone is underwater and not visible to the eye, its presence can still be observed, since the stone displaces a similar volume of water and causes a disturbance downstream. Many stones on the bottom slow the bottom currents immensely and cause the surface to appear broken or choppy. In a stream or river this area would be called a riffle (photograph 1).

It is important to be able to visualize how each obstruction in the river affects the bottom currents. Every object that breaks up the smooth outline of the bottom will quicken, retard, or deflect the current. Study carefully all physical details of the stream bottom to ascertain potential hiding and feeding places into which you can drift a fly.

Fish living in moving water are easy to find if you remember that they

79

prefer to lie in currents that require little effort to maintain their position and like to have some nearby cover to which to retreat if a predator threatens. I know of one river that has a large concentration of great blue herons, which are notorious fish eaters. The fish in this water exhibit a great fear of birds, no doubt from harrowing experiences. The shallow, quiet waters make excellent hunting areas for the herons, and the trout seem to wait until the large birds are on their roosts before entering these waters for feeding sessions.

The ability actually to see the bottom of a stream is very helpful. I recall guiding a young fisherman on a smallish spring creek that flowed through a quiet western meadow with heavy growths of aquatic weeds forming channels and pockets, each with one or more feeding trout. A good hatch of small olive mayflies would appear in the next hour, but the fish were concentrating on the small nymphs that were drifting helplessly in the slow currents. Nymphing should be very easy, and the fish appeared eager to take. Fish were moving as much as 2 to 3 feet to intercept a nymph. My client asked if I would

catch a few trout so that he might study my technique. My first five casts were rewarded with four fish. I felt confident he would catch a good number of trout with relative ease.

He waded to an area I selected. Instead of casting above the pocket that held three nymphing trout, he cast his fly over a dense weed bed that contained no feeding fish. His fly was never within 6 feet of a feeding trout. Fish were darting and feeding in the general area, and I tried to direct his casts into the proper places, but with little success. Then I waded out and handed him my Polaroid glasses. He was amazed: my Polaroids cut through the glare and exposed the channels and pockets that had nymphing trout. He excitedly pointed out fish busily feeding all around him. After a few minutes he spotted a nice one and soon had his nymph in a lively 16-inch rainbow.

Since I always wear Polaroids where light conditions permit, I can't imagine anyone who is learning the nymphing art not using them. Aside from making it possible to study the bottom contours and obstructions they aid in spotting the telltale flashes of feeding fish or a trout taking your fly. Polaroid lenses are available in clip-on types for those who wear corrective lenses. (See photographs 2a, without Polaroid, and 2b, with Polaroid.)

Water level is another important factor in selecting lies to fish your trout. In years of normal high spring runoff, the larger flow of water and occasional slight discoloration give the fish a greater feeling of safety and allow them to feed in areas that may be exposed during late-season flows. One river I fish regularly is controlled by a dam that holds water for irrigation and flood control. A meandering river with a moderately heavy current, brushy willow-lined banks, and rubble bottom, it contains excellent insect populations and affords the angler a good opportunity to catch a large trout on a fly.

When the river is high, fish feed in the quiet backwaters and eddies, the supermarkets of the river. These pockets along the bank now have sufficient water depth to give the trout a sense of security, and fish feed there throughout the day. During periods of low water, the same quiet pockets contain trout only during the hours of poor light. Thus you must be ready to cast at the first light of dawn or fish with just enough light to place your cast after the sun has dropped. This is true for almost all streams during periods of low water. Trout are concerned with their safety first and foremost, and suitable cover nearby gives them a feeling of security.

Small freestone streams, particularly those inhabited by brook or cutthroat trout, are excellent for novices to experiment in and increase their nymphing techniques. Bait fishing is akin to nymphing. A good bait fisherman will make a good nymph fisherman because each must locate places where fish do their feeding. In a small stream the feeding areas are not too numerous. You can dabble your fly in every kind of water, but in time you will recognize the lies where you are rewarded by a strike or fish. Usually these brooks or creeks contain small pools, a great deal of pocket water, and short riffles which allow you to work at close range.

Streambed covers and trout.

2A

2B

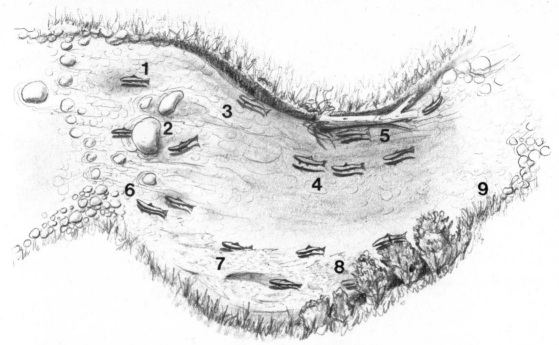

Overhead view of trout-stream nymphing areas: (1) pockets in riffle; (2) in front and behind large rocks; (3) deep runs along cutbanks; (4) deep run and pool water early and late season; (5) fallen tree trunks or roots; (6) shallow flats and pockets just below a riffle; (7) moss and weed beds; (8) beside and under overhanging trees; and (9) grassy undercut banks.

In the spring, many trout are in the deeper wintering holes or pools, but as the water level drops, the fish distribute themselves in the aerated pocket water and riffles. No pockets, however small, should be neglected in your searching casts, for it is surprising how little water is required to hide a fish. Your polaroid glasses will aid in selecting deeper water. Depressions in the stream bottom and heavier riffles will be shown by a darker green color. These areas should be fished carefully. Give special attention to trees and stumps that have fallen into the stream; besides providing shade, hiding places, and breeding grounds for aquatic life, they offer protection from predatory birds and other animals.

Largest trout will hold and feed under roots of fallen trees.

Grassy undercut bands make excellent cover and feeding stations.

Spring creeks usually flow slowly through meadow lowlands. They generally do not experience flooding or low-water problems. Grassy banks, weed beds, and cutbanks offer many hiding and feeding places and harbor good populations of trout. The proximity of cover to the feeding areas provides a high degree of security for the fish. They will feed for longer periods of time when this condition exists, many times throughout an entire day, which is one reason meadow waters are so popular with fly-fishermen.

The size of a spring creek can vary greatly. I have fished some creeks that were only a few feet wide and others that were 50 to 100 yards wide. The Gibbon, Firehole, Madison, and Yellowstone rivers in Yellowstone National Park, and the Henrys Fork of the Snake in Idaho, are representative of large spring creeks or meadowland rivers. The bottom is usually made up of small gravel. The absence of weed growth in the early season can make fishing tough, because lack of cover will have the trout spooky and concentrated in deep holes or along cutbanks. As the season progresses and the weed growth develops, more hiding places are available (photograph 3). The nymph fisherman must concentrate on channels and pockets in the weeds and cutbanks. Riffly water with sufficient depth (2 to 4 feet) will contain trout, and many times the largest, especially if the riffle is too deep to wade. In the late season, larger trout cruise the big open flats after the sun has dropped, and the wakes these fish make betray their presence and location. Although fishing a nymph to these "cruisers" demands accurate casting and promptness of delivery, it can be extremely rewarding.

The vast size of a large river intimidates many fishermen, especially those who have cut their teeth on smaller waters, but large rivers sometimes house enough trophy trout to whet the appetite of any angler, and they deserve special attention. Trout rivers such as the Delaware in the East and Yellowstone, Madison, and Green in the West are considered big waters and are

3

4

often fished successfully by floating in a boat or raft. But the wading fisherman can also do well, although it is difficult to cover a great deal of water afoot on these big rivers (see photograph 4).

The angler must take time to study a section and map strategy. Big rivers are just scaled-up versions or an accumulation of smaller ones, and most big waters follow a similar pattern: pools with riffles between. (An exception is Montana's Madison River. It is very wide with a good current, made up mostly of pocket water and fast, shallow runs, a characteristic that makes it a super fly river.)

The shallower parts of a river produce most of the aquatic life. Riffles are the principal food factories and usually abound with feeding fish. Because it is difficult to describe the variety of stream situations, I have illustrated some of the common waters encountered in nymphing medium- to large-sized rivers.

Photo 5, looking downstream, shows floating logs and debris washed into the bend of the river. This roof of cover hides many trout. The riffle upstream washes food down to the fish. In high water, fish will be up in the riffles and in the eddy on the left; during low flow the best nymphing areas will be closer to the downstream cover. Early morning and late evening will find the trout feeding in the riffle and eddy.

Photo 6 shows a gravel bar running diagonally across the river. The heavy run in the center of the river is a good bet for the middle part of the day, but

5

6

7

during early and late hours trout will move into the aerated shallow riffles below the bar or the eddy below it. This picture was taken in the late season during low water.

Photo 7 is looking upstream, where pockets along the right bank (outside bend) provide quiet water for trout watching for drifting nymphs. The cutbank nearby furnishes excellent cover. Drifting a nymph along the foam or scum line throughout the day can produce good fishing. During hours of waning light the fish can be found in the shallow waters on the inside bend. I caught my first 20-inch-plus fish in such a place.

Photo 8 shows a boulder-studded run that contains many pockets. The fly should be fished carefully below, alongside, above, and between every boulder. Heavy runs such as these contain feeding fish all through the day, even during late-season angling. The nearness of good cover, both from large boulders and heavy broken water, gives a high degree of security. In all seasons, water near the banks will contain trout that are hunting food, although it may be necessary to fish early and late during periods of low water level.

8

9

Photo 9 shows a deeply cut bank on the upstream side of the island. Cover and a quiet cushion of water are available to the trout as they wait for the riffles to wash food down to them. The pocket on the downstream side of an island is another excellent spot to cast your nymph.

Photo 10 shows a pool with a small waterfall where I have taken many fish with a nymph. The best, a 22½-inch hook-jawed brown, was taken from the shallow tail of the pool. The eddies on each side of the head of the pool have also produced many trout. The last area I would fish is the deeper water in the center of the pool. When fish are actively feeding, you will find them more receptive in the shallow waters of the tail or in the eddies at the head.

A young angler allows his nymph to swirl in the eddying currents below a small beaver dam in photograph 11. Pools below small beaver dams on brook-trout waters, or below large earthen or concrete impoundments, can hide large populations of trout. The water below a beaver dam or a wooden splash dam usually has a deep hole directly below the apron. In addition, water falling over the apron or spillway undermines the breast of the dam and provides an excellent hiding and feeding area. I have a special fondness for the tails of these small pools.

Although tail waters below a concrete impoundment hold many fish, fishing in such waters can produce many problems. Wading is dangerous or impossible in water below a power-generating dam because the flow can fluctuate widely at various times of the day. If you can wade during periods of minimum flow, study the bottom and fish much the same as you would fish any river with similar characteristics. In photograph 12, the drift or foam line can be easily followed. Feeding fish will be facing eddying currents, and the spot where currents slow to a standstill is a good place to fish your nymph.

10

11

12

In all waters study the flows that carry the most food. Throw handfuls of dry grass or twigs into the current and watch their routes. This may reveal something a big brown already knows. A pocket thermometer is most useful for late-season fishing. Locating cold-spring seeps or small brooks that offer relief from the warm summer waters can be a great aid in finding trout. One particular stream I fish has been adversely affected by thermal activity, while locating small springs has produced some fishing that otherwise would not be available. The type of trout you are after may influence your quest for suitable water. Keep a fishing diary, noting all the conditions that exist on successful days. On heavily fished waters, trout will not behave normally and may become nocturnal in their feeding habits.

As a fishing guide, I have the opportunity to fish with many outstanding anglers, and every trip to the river provides me with a greater insight into the feeding habits of trout. For instance, the variety of aquatic foods makes feeding areas on some rivers more important than on others. The subtle differences can only be cataloged after a great many experiences. I have been fishing with a fly for over thirty-five years and humbly admit that I am still learning.

How do nymphs appear to the trout? I don't know how many times fishermen have asked me what a particular fly looks like to the trout, especially when they are extracting the outlandish rubber-legged Girdle Bug from the jaw of a good-sized brown. This pattern and another effective western fly, the Bitch Creek, account for many trophy fish in big western waters. Last summer my clients caught over forty trout that weighed more than 4 pounds using these two patterns. Not only did big trout find the Girdle Bug attractive, but fish as small as 6 inches latched on to this oversized "whatever." I cannot think of any counterpart in nature that resembles this bug. It is definitely an attractor-type fly; the white rubber legs wiggling in the current must appear as something genuinely alive. I can still visualize a 3½-pounder I caught one drizzly morning. He swam about 4 feet and slowly inhaled the fly.

Girdle Bug (top) and Bitch Creek attractor nymphs.

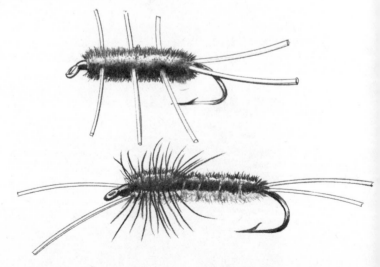

A sparse-dressed nymph (top) appears nearer a real nymph (center) than a heavily dressed one of the same size (bottom).

He was feeding in a dead backwater. Sometimes trout are not too discriminating in their tastes. Examinations of stomach contents have even revealed young blackbirds, no doubt fledglings that fell from their streamside nests in the willows.

Normally I like a nymph that is approximately the size, general color, and form of the natural. Most of my favorite patterns would be classified as impressionistic. I fish too much to spend a lot of time on slavish imitations. I have taken photographs of a live nymph and an artificial in the water, and when the slides were projected and thrown slightly out of focus, just enough to make it difficult to tell the natural from the copy, the fly imitation usually appeared larger than the natural. This is an indication that a smaller, sparsely tied fly would look more lifelike. As a result, the small nymphs I use are simply tied and very sparse.

Trout that are heavily fished over become highly suspicious when a pattern deviates greatly from the natural. This is true on many of the "fly only" waters, where trout obtain their Ph.D.'s in fly dressing. When fish start drifting back to scrutinize your offering, a more exacting imitation is necessary. Spring creeks and other quiet-water situations most of the time require small, sparse patterns. There is a high bank on one of my favorite spring creeks where I can observe the trout without disturbing them. At times they feed actively, moving long distances to pick up a nymph, and at other times they appear to be extremely selective, taking an occasional nymph and letting many naturals go by. When two or more fish are feeding competitively, they are not as fussy about size or pattern. The race to see who captures the fly seems more important.

In high, turbulent, and discolored water, however, flies a size or two larger than the natural have proved effective for me. Trout that are busy feeding usually do not take time to examine your fly as carefully. Some feeding areas are located in such fast water that the trout do not have ample time to inspect your nymphs closely.

If the general appearance of your nymph approximates that of the natural in size, color, form, and action, chances are that you will fool more than your share of fish. If not, you're probably fishing in the wrong places. And that brings us back to where we started. "Reading" the water wisely so that you can place your nymph where the fish should be feeding is the single most important factor in nymphing success.

FOUR OF MY FAVORITE NYMPH PATTERNS

Kemp Bug
Hook: Mustad 3906B or 9672, size 6 to 14
Thread: Danville Flymaster olive
Tail: Peacock herl, clipped short
Body: Peacock herl over padding
Rib: .005-inch-diameter gold wire
Hackle: Furnace
Wing: Grizzly hackle tips tied short

Kemp Bug

Pheasant Tail

Troth's Pheasant Tail

Hook:	Mustad 3906 or 3906B, size 10 to 18
Thread:	Danville Flymaster tan
Tail:	Cock pheasant tail fibers
Abdomen:	Cock pheasant tail fibers
Rib:	.004-inch-diameter copper wire
Thorax:	Two or three layers of copper wire covered with a wrapping of fine peacock herl
Wing case:	Cock pheasant tail fibers
Legs:	Ends of pheasant tail fibers used for wing case
	Note: On it legs on sizes 16 and 18

Girdle Bug (dressing for size 4)

Hook:	Mustad 79580, sizes 2 & 4; 9672, sizes 8 & 6
Thread:	Danville Mono Cord, black
Tails:	.025-inch-square white rubber strands, 1 inch long
Legs:	Three pair white rubber strands, 1¾ inches wide
Body:	Large black chenille, ³/₁₆ inches in diameter

Girdle Bug

Terrible Troth Stone-fly Nymph (dressing for size 1)
I bend the hook shank slightly in the center before tying and normally tie about 6 to 8 turns of 4 amp. lead fuse wire under the thorax section.

Hook: Mustad 9575, sizes 1, 2, and 4
Thread: Danville Mono Cord, dark brown
Tails and
  feelers: Short side of a black-and-white turkey wing quill dyed dark brown; tail ½ inch long; feelers 1 inch long
Body: Dark-brown chenille, 3/16-inch diameter, double-wrapped over thorax section
Overbody: Blend black and brown seal fur and spin in a loop and ribbed thru the chenille; clip on top and bottom
Legs: Clipped neck-hackle stems dyed dark brown or .030-inch-square black rubber; three pairs, 1¾ inches wide

Terrible Troth Stonefly Nymph

Bernard "Lefty" Kreh, *a member of the Fishing Hall of Fame, has been a guide, outdoor writer, and lecturer for more than twenty years, as well as a consultant to tackle companies in designing and testing their equipment. He is also a professional casting coach, and for many years he gave casting exhibitions at boat shows and state fairs, demonstrating the use of fly, spin, and plug tackle. He has held as many as twelve world records on fish caught on a fly rod in salt water.*

Lefty Kreh is Outdoor Editor of the Baltimore Morning Sun *and has written for every major outdoor publication, including* National Rifleman, Outdoor Life, True, Reader's Digest, Sports Afield, *and* Field & Stream. *He is on the editorial staff of* Florida Sportsman *and* Fishing World *magazines and is the author of several books on fishing, some of which have been reprinted in Europe.*

Lefty has fished almost every state including Alaska and in every province in Canada, in Iceland, and over much of Central America and Europe.

6
Nymphing Tactics

Bernard "Lefty" Kreh

NYMPHS ARE IN THE WATER throughout the year in great numbers and varieties. If forced to fish with a single fly all season, most experienced anglers would certainly choose the nymph.

Use a nymph if there is no major insect activity on or above the surface of the water.

Here are several guidelines to follow relating to tackle and using nymphs.

First, use a long rod. In no area of fly fishing is a long rod more important. There are many reasons.

In most cases the nymph should float drag-free in the current. In fact, only when you are trying to imitate the swimming or locomotion of a specific nymph do you *not* try for a drag-free drift.

A good dry-fly man who has mastered the drag-free drift can easily make the transition to nymphing if he transfers his philosophy beneath the surface. The nympher and the dry-fly man should be trying to accomplish the same thing, and I think the single most overlooked factor in successful nymphing is the angler's lack of understanding of the drag-free drift.

Many recognize that as a fly is pulled unnaturally across the surface it will usually result in a refusal by the fish. These fish take most of their food underwater and should be, because of experience, more likely to recognize a fly drifting unnaturally beneath the surface than on it, which means that paying close attention to a drag-free drift will radically increase your catch. There are certain times when a manipulated nymph is deadly, but only for brief periods; the rest of the time the above advice applies.

A limp leader helps reduce drag because it tends to flow with varying currents, but the line is the main culprit in spoiling a good drift. Knowing this, the angler with a long rod is able to keep a larger percentage of his line off the surface than the angler with a shorter stick.

Shown is a nymph with some debris on it. Because nymphs are usually fished near the bottom, the angler should constantly be checking to make sure that no junk is on the fly, spoiling the presentation.

There are other advantages to using long rods. Most expert nymphers try to fish as short a line as possible to be able to detect the moment the fish swallows the nymph. In many cases only 3 to 5 feet of line, plus leader, are outside the guides. The longer rod allows the fisherman to remain in better contact with the line end and to manipulate the fly more easily. In his deadly sinker-bouncing technique, Chuck Fothergill tries to keep all his line off the water, and he prefers a rod of at least 9 feet.

Using a relatively short line to fish a nymph, coupled with a long rod, enables the angler to strike quicker, too. For example, a man casting a 6-foot rod with 4 feet of fly line extended beyond the tip, and with a 9-foot leader, has a fly 13 feet from the rod tip. But the same fisherman with a 10-foot rod is only 9 feet from the fish when it takes. This factor, plus increased leverage, allows the angler to strike much faster.

Remember that in nymphing the fish generally inhales the fly, and a subsequent indication tells you when to strike. In no other area of fly-fishing is the quick strike so important. The long rod gives you an edge on success.

In meadow streams the fisherman frequently must lie prone to make a cast to a visible fish, and here the long rod is a tremendous asset in keeping the backcast high and following the drifting line and fly.

Second, watch your approach. The type of clothing the angler wears makes a great difference. Because a close approach is usually required, and because it's even more of an advantage to be able to see your fish, camouflage helps. Bright, flashy clothes and rods and reels that reflect light, even chrome-plated hemostats that dangle and flash from a wading vest, are all alarm indicators to nearby fish. Clothing that blends with the existing background is my choice.

A low silhouette as you approach a pool is vital too. Standing on a gravel bar or bank, a 6-foot angler must appear as a skyscraper to the wary brown trout, who lives in a constant state of alarm.

Third, study all pools before you make your cast. If you fish a particular stream a great deal, it's wise to remember where you flushed each fish as you wade. Chances are that the fish will return to that spot. What would make a good avenue of approach in early spring may be the totally wrong approach in midsummer. Be aware of these factors and learn from them. And remember that water levels vary at different seasons in creeks and rivers. Fish lie in a pool at different places, depending on such factors as water height, speed, and even where shade exists in summer and doesn't in late fall. The shady side of a pool is often the most desirable spot to drop a prospecting nymph if you don't have a special target in mind. Fish seek such areas to hide and rest.

Waters in shade, especially with an undercut bank, are choice spots to swim your nymph for a big trout.

Swirling eddies (we call them Lazy Susans) or places where foam collects attract insects and are hot spots to test your fly.

Remember that no fish will stay long in very swift water. It must be able

An eddy, or where foam collects, is an indicator that the currents will also gather insects for trout to feast on. Dan Abrams of Jackson, Wyoming, makes a cast to such a place on a local spring creek.

Success!

to gather in more food than it burns up in energy. This means that fish often lie near a swift current that sweeps food to them, so they can dart out, grab the morsel, and retire to more restful waters. When prospecting with a nymph, seek out slow waters that are adjacent to swifter flows. Rocks with an eddy behind them, along with calm water below or alongside, the edge of a riffle, or a bar that breaks the current are all prime places to make a cast.

Rocky shores on streams and rivers, where the current flow is slower and deep, are excellent places to test. Here, Chuck Fothergill swims his nymph along such a spot in the Roaring Fork.

Fishing to visible trout.

Fourth, cast to visible fish. I would rather work a fish I can actually see than blind-cast waters where I think one may be. There are a number of reasons for casting to visible fish. It behooves the angler to make a careful, cautious approach, and to see as many fish as possible. Naturally, Polaroid glasses are a great aid in nymphing, perhaps more so than in any other form of trouting. My personal choice is the lens tinted with a bit of yellow, to build contrast.

If you study their actions, visible fish will tell you if they are chasing emergers, working the bottom for nymphs, or even feeding on dry flies. And if you can see the fish in a pool, you won't make the mistake of casting over those close to you.

Bulging trout are fish that chase their prey toward the surface and grab it just before it emerges into the air. The back of the fish often shows, but not always, and many times the tail is clearly visible as the fish makes its downward turn.

Bulgers can be noisy and splashy, and some anglers confuse them with fish that are sucking flies from the surface. A good thing to remember is that fish taking flies from the surface will generally leave a few tiny air bubbles. Study the surface carefully, and if you see those bubbles you will know that, in general, they are not catching the nymphs.

Fifth, know your nymphs. Once you have determined that fish are definitely nymphing, how do you know what they are feeding on? Presenting an exact imitation of the nymph will certainly put you on the road to success, and there is no question that the more entomology you know, the better your chances are of making a good evaluation. But I have many fine fishermen

Bulging trout.

Here Dan Abrams illustrates a wise approach to a pool before fishing his
nymph. Crawling forward until he can observe all parts of the pool, he studies
it to determine where fish are feeding and resting.

A cast is made to a fish that is bulging.

His reward for a low careful approach, careful study of the pool, and good cast is this nice cutthroat trout.

friends that can't tell you a single Latin insect name, yet they catch fish consistently. Other chapters in this book will help you with the Latin names and in understanding the underwater world, but here I hope to treat the subject so that a novice can at least get into the business of hooking fish on a nymph.

It is wise to learn a little bit about how various nymphs move around underwater. For example, damselfly and dragonfly nymphs, which you would expect in slower stream waters and in ponds and lakes where weeds exist, swim in short bursts of speed. Mayflies and caddis flies crawl around slowly on the bottom. If you are trying to imitate these insects, a drag-free drift close to the rubble will take more fish. There are a few mayflies that do swim rapidly, and if you know which they are, an increased rate of retrieve would be called for when fishing that imitation.

Obviously, if you are trying to fish mayfly imitations that crawl slowly along the bottom, the worst thing you could do is get downstream in swift current and throw your fly directly above you. The current will sweep so fast that the line will be drawn along and the fly pulled upward so quickly that the trout would know it was an imitation.

Stone flies are often ripped loose from rocks and tumble down a riffle, and a fly that is allowed to drift drag-free along the riffle edge will draw strikes.

Sixth, perfect your casts. I believe that the single most-important cast the serious nymph fisherman must learn is the tuck cast, which was shown to me by George Harvey and Joe Humphreys, of State College, Pennsylvania. Watching these two men fish pocket water and along the undercurrent stream banks is like watching an efficient housewife with a vacuum cleaner. Both men are superb anglers, know that getting the drag-free drift is vital, and recognize that most fish will be lying near the bottom where nymphs roll along. So their problem is to cast without alarming the fish, to sink the fly quickly to the streambed, and to let it ride naturally with the currents to the fish. Their tuck cast is the answer, and I've used it to good advantage on western and eastern streams.

To make the tuck cast, direct the fly about eye level over the target but apply extra force at the end of the power stroke (overpower the cast). Tip the rod downward just a fraction as the power stroke is finished.

The nymph, traveling with excessive force, snaps against the bending rod tip, causing the nymph to tuck under the line, forming a horizontal J. This will fall so that the fly enters the water closer to the fisherman than the line end, allowing it to sink deep without pull from the drifting line.

The fly will go close to the bottom and swim along drag-free until the line gets well below the fly and begins to pull on it. This is a simple cast to master, but it can mean the difference between catching a lot of fish and a few.

If you see a fish lying in a clear, shallow spring creek, your best approach is from downstream and slightly to the side. Then you can make a cast with the line away from the fish and the fly can come naturally to it. In fact, this could be considered the basic, or certainly most frequently used, approach to a fish when using a nymph. Aside from the line's falling and alarming the fish,

Stone-fly nymphs tumbling off rocks downstream.

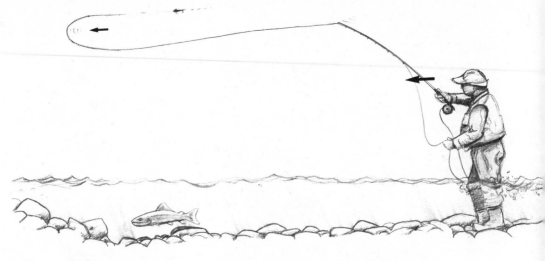

Tuck cast

Cast is made several feet above the fish, at about eye level to the angler, with additional force put into the power stroke.

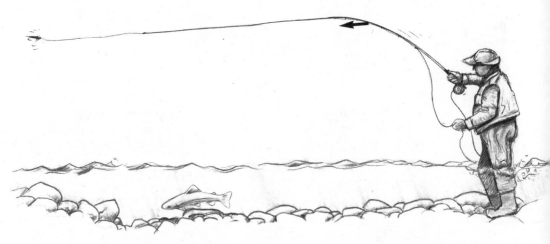

The increase in velocity over a normal cast fully extends the line and places a deeper than normal bend in the rod tip at the end of the cast.

a downstream approach and upstream cast increases the chances of spoiling a good drift. But when fishing nymphs you must make casts upstream, downstream, and across stream, depending on the situation. Obviously, if a fish is lying under a log jam and the only way you can get a fly to it is by drifting it in from upcurrent, then that's what you do.

The rod bends forward under the shock, then recoils backward, snapping the leader and fly under (tucking it under the fly line) so that it heads for the water with the nymph closer to the angler than the nail knot.

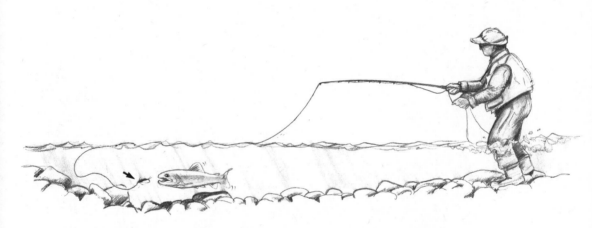

Because the nymph is able to enter the water well ahead of the forward end of the line, it can sink on slack leader and head for the bottom, giving the fly a natural drift until the line on the surface gets downstream from it and begins to lift the fly toward the top.

Seventh, learn to detect the take. Newcomers to nymphing seem to think the fish takes the fly so delicately that you almost have to be a super-fisherman to detect the strike. At times that may be true, but it depends on the kind of water you fish and the type of nymph you use.

I've found that when I fish leeches or dragonfly or damselfly nymphs, the trout generally sock them so hard that I've had the line almost pulled from my fingers. This is also often true when fishing a stone-fly imitation in swift waters. On the other hand, in a stream like the Letort, where drifting a sow-bug or shrimp imitation is deadly, the fish usually accept so lightly that the leader doesn't seem to move or stop. In such situations, if you can see the fish you can often tell when the take occurs. Even if you can't see the tiny nymph, you have a good idea where it is. When the fly is near the fish, if the fish's mouth opens or if it rolls to the side, rises or falls a bit, or makes any movement other than what it was doing for the past few minutes—strike!

Attempting to keep as much line as possible off the water during the drift, and concentrating on watching the leader, the angler should strike any time the leader stops or moves quickly. This is perhaps the most popular method of determining a strike.

If the water is very shallow, or if you want to maintain the nymph at a specific depth, you can grease the rear portion of your leader. While watching the leader knots, which are fairly easy to see, you can often detect a slight pause or erratic movement that signals a strike.

Sometimes greasing a leader right down to the fly can be extremely effective when fishing midge pupae. The problem here is that so many fish are feeding in the surface film that you have difficulty working a specific fish. Greasing the leader right down to within an inch or two of the fly will keep the imitation up there with the pupae for examination by cruising fish.

Since greased leaders do have advantages in various forms of nymphing, I do not nail-knot my butt to the line any more. Instead, I make a tiny loop in the end of the fly line, looping on and off at will any butt sections or entire leader I feel proper for the moment.

In some sticky situations, like Armstrong Spring Creek, Silver Creek, or the Letort and Falling Springs, the trout seem to wear glasses and possess built-in radar. A few anglers are using small closed-cell foam blocks on their leaders to detect a strike. This makes a miniature bobber and does enhance your chances of striking—but it can be a dog to cast.

Another help in knowing when to strike is to attach to the nail knot or one of the leader knots a bright piece of polypropylene yarn that has been well greased with line dressing to make it float.

My personal favorite for a strike indicator is one Dave Whitlock showed me. First, take a razor blade and with several strokes shave your butt section to a tiny hairlike point. Insert this point in the eye of a small needle. Cut a 1-inch section of bright-orange fly line from an old one and insert the needle through the short section. Using a pair of pliers, draw the needle and monofilament through and attach the leader to the line with a nail knot. You end up with a bright-orange short piece of fly line that can be made to ride directly against the nail knot and is very easy to see. It will last the life of the leader and make detecting strikes easier.

Cortland and Orvis, and maybe other manufacturers, sell a special line for nymph fishing that has the end dipped in a bright color to give you an indicator. While it certainly works and the idea has merit, some complain that the tip is too heavy and causes casting and presentation problems.

Mark Sosin, an outdoor-writer friend, came up with a unique and simple method of making a strike indicator on any brightly colored line. Beginning 2 inches from the nail knot, he uses a permanent-ink marking pen and thoroughly darkens the line for a distance of 6 to 8 inches. This solid bar of color separating the main line from the end leaves a bright section right at the knot that is similar to Whitlock's idea.

Lastly, perfect your strikes. When the angler realizes that the trout has accepted the fly, how should he strike? There are several methods.

The slip strike is one of the quickest and safest ways, especially if you are using a delicate tippet. If you are right-handed, when the fish takes the fly, partially open the left hand (releasing the line) and whip the rod tip up sharply. The amount of resistance on the line as it streaks across the palm and through the rod guides is more than enough to drive home the hook, but it's almost impossible to break a fragile leader with this method—and it's fast!

My personal preference on striking when I have only a small amount of line outside the rod tip (not more than 20 feet of line and leader total) is to strike in reverse. Hold an empty rod horizontal and snap downward, observing the tip. You'll see it move upward swiftly, then come down in the direction of the force. This brief upward snap of the rod as you flip it downward will strike a fish more quickly than any other method, and because the tip moves only a short distance it's impossible to break a leader, even an 8X.

The first cast into a pool is always the best one, with each successive cast reducing your chances. When you make a strike by lifting the rod, you remove the line from the pool if it wasn't a fish. But with the downward snap of the tip, you cause the line to jump forward only a few inches underwater, and you can continue your drift.

There is another method of striking worth knowing about. Occasionally the cast will be made upstream, and as the line comes swiftly back toward you, you are unable to gather in the line quickly enough to prevent slack. To combat this you gradually raise the rod as the line comes downstream. Once your rod is in a vertical position, or the tip is held behind you as the line is controlled, and a fish strikes, you should make a forward snap with the rod exactly as you would when roll casting. This will drive the hook instantly foward and hook the fish solid. But because so much slack line exists immediately following the strike, there is no chance of the fish's breaking a delicate leader.

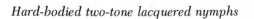

Hard-bodied two-tone lacquered nymphs

FOUR OF MY FAVORITE NYMPHS PATTERNS

Poul Jorgensen's Caddis Pupa
While I dress this in several colors, it is the one I use most.

Hook:	Mustad 3906, sizes 8 to 16
Thread:	Brown
Abdomen:	Medium-brown Seal-Ex
Wing Case:	Medium-gray duck or dove quill
Thorax and legs:	Fur from the back of a brown rabbit

Gray Nymph
This is one of the easiest of all flies to tie. I weight some and leave others unweighted. On unweighted hooks, I use brown thread to separate from those I have added lead to.

Hook:	Mustad 3906, sizes 10 to 20
Thread:	Black
Tail:	Four or five fibers from gray mallard breast
Body:	Muskrat, with the guard hairs left in, spun length of hook.

George Harvey's Stone-fly Nymph

Hook:	Mustad 9672, sizes 8 to 16
Tail:	Pheasant—several fibers from tail of bird
Head:	Brown thread for unweighted, black for heavyweighted
Body:	Underbody is medium yellow, for which I like to use Seal-Ex put on in a spinning loop; tie in at the tail a piece of brown chenille after underbody has been wound forward; bring brown chenille forward and tie off
Hackle:	Gray mallard breast feather, one complete turn

Whitlock's Damsel Nymph
I consider this fly the very best I've used in ponds and spring creeks where damselflies live.

Hook:	Mustad 9672, sizes 6 to 10
Tail:	3 soft ostrich-herl tips or a short small tuft of marabou fibers
Body:	Medium-green fur or Seal-Ex, with fine gold wire ribbing
Wing pads:	Medium-green Swiss Straw
Thorax:	Built up from same fur as body
Legs:	A few sections of grouse feather
Eyes:	Pair of nylon beads made from strand of monofilament

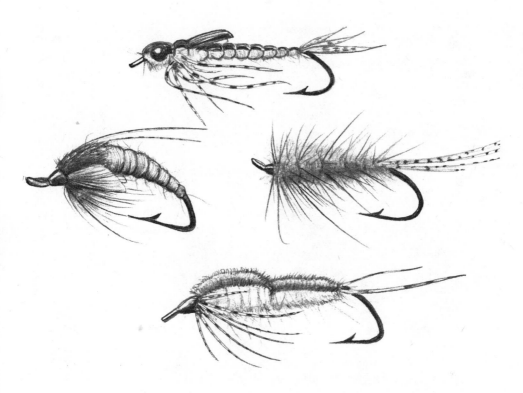

Four of Lefty Kreh's Favorite Nymph Patterns: (1) Whitlock's Damsel Nymph;
(2) Poul's Caddis Pupa; (3) Gray Nymph; (4) Harvey's Stone-fly Nymph.

Dave Whitlock is an illustrator, author, artist, photographer, lecturer, and instructor of fly-fishing and of fly tying, whose skills are totally committed to the sport of fly-fishing and to those conservation programs that support our ecology.

He writes, photographs, and illustrates for all major outdoor and fly-fishing magazines. His most recent books are the Whitlock Vibert Box Handbook *and* Flytyer's Almanac, *the second volume of which will be published in 1978. Dave also illustrated and contributed a chapter to* The Masters on the Dry Fly, *a companion book in this series. He serves as senior adviser of the Federation of Fly Fishermen and as adviser to the American League of Anglers.*

He is recipient of the Buz Buzeck's Flytying Award, the Federation of Fly Fishermen's highest award presented in fly tying, and also recipient of the Max Anders Wild Trout Conservation Award.

He lives with his wife and two sons on the White River in Arkansas, where he created the Whitlock Sculpin, Dave's Hopper, and other special trout, bass, and saltwater patterns.

7
Nymphing Tackle

Dave Whitlock

NYMPHING IS THE MOST COMPLEX of all fly-fishing methods today, because of the great variety of nymph and water types that are important to all trout and other freshwater species. The new fly tackle specifically used for nymphing reflects this complexity, but systematizing your equipment avoids a great deal of misunderstanding and misuse and affords greater success.

Many of today's fly-fishers are studying various aquatic insect life cycles as well as many other subsurface aquatic foods. Students learn that each type has characteristic habitats and specific actions within its environment. The right nymph pattern can still be nearly useless if the tackle does not allow it to be fished properly, while a less perfect, suggestive nymph is deadly if fished correctly.

When I first became interested in nymphing, some twenty-five or thirty years ago, I was told it was almost impossible to catch trout on nymphs unless you possessed ESP. The information, tackle, and patterns then available directly or indirectly verified this. Those were the "good old days," with stiff knotted leaders, large-diameter low-pound-test tippet ratios, poor nylon knots, and a few dozen hard-bodied "nymph" patterns that in color, shape, and size looked like they came from and belonged in outer space.

Thom Green, an old and dear friend of mine, taught me how deadly a soft, suggestive nymph could be if it were weighted and fished just off the bottom on a "dead" or controlled drift. Thom's nymphs looked like accidents, yet he outfished everyone on lakes like Henrys of Idaho and rivers like the White in Arkansas. He caught fish everywhere on these small bunches of tangled fur, and even leaded the hook!

About the same time, Polly Rosborough wrote his book on tying and fishing fuzzy nymphs. Together these two men began converting me from dry

The three most popular type of nymphing rods—graphite, bamboo, and glass

flies, streamers, and woolly worms into a "nympho." As I look back, I can see that each major phase of my nymphing ability came as I adapted or designed better tackle systems—not better nymph patterns.

In today's nymphing for freshwater fish, as I've experienced it, there are three general tackle systems. The size and character of the water, the fish, and the food dictate which one you'll use; tackle for fishing a shallow, fast-flowing freestone stream, for example, will differ in most cases from tackle used for fishing a large, deep river or lake.

At the conclusion of my discussion of tackle components, these three complete tackle systems will be systematized for you.

NYMPHING TACKLE COMPONENTS

Never forget that *you*, the fly-fisher, are the most important ingredient of any tackle system, for you provide the knowledge, skill, and energy to make the rest work. Other components are the rod, the reel, the line and backing, and the leader and tippet.

The Fly Rod

The fly rod is the extension of your hand and arm and controls the nymph fly. Traditionally, nymph rods are supposed to be long, slow or soft-action, and fairly stout. Modern nymphers no longer go along with this. Somehow, in the past, sensitivity was equated with limberness. That is true only if we are speaking of great density or weight as opposed to stiffness, workable perhaps only in the heaviest bamboo or solid-glass rods.

The second purpose of the slow action was to maintain the wetness of the nymph to assure its faster sinking on delivery. A stiff or fast rod, in what used to be referred to as dry-fly action, would tend to snap or pop out the nymph's clinging moisture. Today's nymphs are designed and tied to sink or fish an area regardless of how "wet" they are when they hit the water's surface. Heavy nymph hooks, extra weighting on shank, water-absorbent materials, and well-designed nymph construction determine the nymph's sink rate more than how wet it is when it hits the water.

Today's good nymph rod is reasonably long, rather stiff, sensitive, and very light. It should have the power and stiffness to cast 20 to 80 feet with good loop control without tiring you. Its length, 7½ to 10 feet, together with its light but stiff shaft, should provide positive control for line mending or hook setting. This sensitivity transmits the "feel" of line on water and senses a taking fish. It should also have the power to tire the fish but enough sensitivity to keep the tippet from breaking or the hook from tearing out.

These characteristics are best found in 100-percent graphite fly rods, which make incredible nymph rods that excel in all areas of modern nymphing. On the strike as well as during the pickup of the line, 100-percent graphite rods are much more efficient or positive owing to the response inherent in the carbon fibers. They give a far greater energy transfer from you to the hook point.

A quality medium-to-fast-action glass/graphite composite is my second choice. Third choice would be 100-percent glass or bamboo rods. But remember there are many other factors that determine which rod you use. If you can't afford a graphite, or prefer bamboo or whatever, you can still nymph-fish well if you have your act together.

As in any other type of fly-fishing, line weight is usually determined by what fly sizes, leader-tippet sizes, and types of water are to be fished. Generally, a 6-weight rod of 8 to 8½ feet is a good all-around nymph rod. A fairly wide range of nymph sizes can be cast well with a 6 with good distance and power, yet the rod is sensitive enough to tolerate light tippets and fish well over selective conditions, both in streams and in lakes.

For fishing larger rivers such as the Delaware, White, or Yellowstone, where wind and distance can make further demands on nymph presentation, a 7- or 8-weight rod is an asset. Deep wading and larger, deeper-fished nymphs may even call for 8½- to 10-foot rods. A 9½-foot graphite rod picks up weighted nymphs and sinking lines and throws long casts in gusty winds

*The long fly rod gives the nymph fisherman far greater critical line, leader,
and fly control than short rods.*

without too much difficulty. Just a few years ago, before graphite, after a windy day of fishing on the Missouri, Madison, or Yellowstone with a big bamboo or glass rod, my right arm would be almost useless.

When wind and distance are not factors, on big waters as well as on medium-sized rivers such as Montana's Big Hole, Vermont's Batten Kill, Arkansas's Norfolk, and California's Kings River, and numerous small free-stone and spring creeks, a sub-6-weight rod for nymphing may be just perfect—that is, if you are matching hatching nymphs or smaller crustacea such as scuds or sow bugs. A 5-weight rod of 8 to 8½ feet is an excellent choice for working 20 to 60 feet with nymphs from size 6 to 20. When my special nymph-head fly line is used, a 5-weight nymphing rod is almost ideal.

Fishing the smaller sizes of nymphs crawling on the bottom, swimming, emerging, or in the surface film requires much closer controls than dry-fly fishing. Now smaller rods, 5, 4, and even 3 weights, have their place where conditions cause trout to be selective or spooky. Here the rod must present the smaller line, a long, thin leader, and tiny nymphs without alarming the taking or holding trout. Graphite rods are ideal for this type of nymphing, but composites, glass, and bamboo do almost as well with these smaller lines.

Long nymph rods of 8 to 10 feet, for both floating- and sinking-line nymph-fishing, are generally most efficient. The more line control needed, the longer the rod should be. I use a 10-foot 5-weight graphite rod to fish nymphs up, down, or across pocket-water sections. The 10-foot length almost neutralizes the pocket-water problems of varying current speeds. By holding the rod high and mending line, it is easy to maintain absolute drift control over the water up to 70 feet away!

Roll casting or pickup is twice as easy with a 10-foot rod as it is with a 7-footer. The longer nymph rod also handles more line in the air easier and greatly facilitates difficult angle presentations such as reach casts, slack casts, and positive curve casts.

The main considerations in choosing a good all-around nymph rod are that it be light for its length, relatively stiff for best line control and sensitivity, and reasonably long—at least 8 feet and up to 10 feet.

The Fly Reel

For nymphing, the single-action fly reel is the recognized standard design. Single-action fly reels are those whose spools are mounted and suspended on a straight shaft that is held by a base plate and frame. A handle on the reel spool allows the fly line to be retrieved at 1-to-1 turn ratio. The simplicity of single-action fly reels has withstood the test of time and use. With only a few exceptions, they have undergone very little improvement in design in recent years.

A single-action fly reel for nymphing should have a narrow-width reel spool 3¼ inches or larger in diameter. The spool should hold at least 50 yards of backing, as well as allow good pillar clearance for the fly line. It should

Nymphing reels.

have an audible click-adjustable drag or spool-dampering system. To prevent line tangling, the reel should have clean, simple outlines, and there should be few or no exposed screws. The spool, made of light corrosion-resistant metal or alloy, should be well perforated for good air drying of damp line and should have quick rotation response when the line is pulled out by a fish or by you. After line tension is off, the lightweight spool should also dampen quickly to prevent overrun spin, which causes "backlashing" line or spool tangles.

In addition to the paw-gear flat-spring drag that most good single-action reels use, there are a few reels that have an exposed outer-edge spool flange. This provides a unique second-option manual drag used by "palming" or "fingering" to slow down the revolving spool. This allows an extremely simple and foolproof second method of putting pressure on a fish.

For most nymph fishing, your leader tippets are so light that the paw-click or flange drags are sufficient. Only in a few cases will the fly-fisher need a disk-brake drag system used in single-action heavy-duty fly reels such as the Fin Nor. This would be necessary only if you were nymphing for steelhead, salmon, or saltwater species.

Most single-action fly reels can be used with a right- or left-hand wind. Traditionally, right-handed casters also reel right-handed, but I feel this is the wrong method in most circumstances. The rod hand and arm should be used for that purpose; the other hand and arm are used to manipulate the loose line

Three excellent and popular single-action nymphing fly reels. Note proper spool-line levels!

Two most important features of a good single-action fly reel: a sensitive audible paw-click drag system and an outer exposed flange for palming additional drag.

and operate the reel. Changing hands back and forth is awkward, time-consuming, and inefficient. I use the rod with my right hand and handle the line and reel with my left.

A good "balanced" nymph reel is one that holds the fly line your rod requires, plus an ample supply of backing. Up to a point, the total weight of line, backing, and reel should not be excessively lighter or heavier than needed to "balance" the rod at the point of the rod's grip handle. A heavier reel will usually be less tiring on your wrist in long hours of casting.

Most popular single-action fly reels available today have models with 3¼- to 4-inch spool diameters. This is the best practical size range. Smaller reels can corkscrew your fly line, do not have ample capacity, and take forever to retrieve the line. Before I'd drop below 3¼-inches for even a 3- or 4-weight line, I'd add more backing to fill the larger spool.

Extra spools are important to the nymph fisher who intends to use more than one size or style of line. Two or three lines, such as a full floater, sink tip, and full sinker, are easy and fast to interchange with extra spools.

The multiplying fly reel, which resembles the single-action fly reel, has special spool gearing greater than a 1-to-1 ratio, usually a 2-1 or 3-to-1 ratio. This type of reel is not often used in nymphing. Most fisherman I know who do a lot of nymph fishing feel the multiplier is not usually needed or reliable enough for regular use.

The automatic is seldom if ever recommended. It is generally unreliable and heavy and greatly handicaps the user of small leader tippets. Few have sufficient spool capacity for fly line and adequate backing. The automatics do not have a smooth, sensitive release of fly line or a manual-retrieve method.

The Fly Line

Modern fly lines have greatly expanded the range of water and seasons where nymphs can be effectively fished. The development of sinking fly lines has been one of the most significant factors in the recent rapid growth of nymphing techniques. By varying the shape and density of the plastic coating over the level braided line core, fly lines can present nymphs in any type of flowing or standing water where game fish normally feed on subsurface natural foods.

Basic Line Designs for Nymphing. For all nymphing, there is no one ideal fly line. Several designs and modifications, however, are quite good. Here are four basic kinds.

1. *Level Line.* This fly line has a level core and a level plastic coating. It is available in full-floating and sinking models. The floater is a relatively useless nymph line. In high-density and lead-core models the level line is the best design, as it sinks a nymph very quickly.

2. *Double Taper.* This fly line has a level braided core and a plastic coating that tapers down from a level midsection to a finer point at each end of the

line. The double taper has many nymph-fishing uses. It is best for accurate and delicate presentation and roll casting, and where false casting is necessary. It is not a good distance line. The double taper is made as a full floater, full slow-intermediate sinker, a sink tip, and various-speed full-sinking models.

3. *Weight Forward.* The standard-taper weight forward is shaped like a double taper on its leader tip end but has a longer rear taper into a thin, level shooting or running line section. This line permits longer shooting casts. When over 40 feet of line is out, however, it does not roll-cast, false-cast, or pick up off water as well as a double taper. This is due to a "hinging" effect between the back taper and the shooting section.

The weight forward is made in full-floating, sink-tip, sink-belly, and full-sinking models. Sink-tip and full-sinking models are available in a wide range of densities or sink rates.

Great distances can be achieved with the various high-density weight-forward lines, which are especially useful on lakes and large rivers. Weight-forward sinking models are the most popular design for most deep nymph fishing throughout North and South America.

4. *Shooting Taper or Shooting Head.* This fly line is a further modification of the weight-forward line. It has a level braided core with a tapered coating like that of a double taper and weight forward but is only 25 to 35 feet in length. To the rear portion, which may or may not taper, a nylon line is attached. This provides a "head" of fly line for casting weight and fly control and a much smaller smooth-running or -shooting section that reduces guide friction, allowing greatest distance and minimizing false casting.

The shooting "head" or taper is available ready-made, or it can be cut from other double-taper and weight-forward lines in full-floating, sink-tip, sink-belly, and full-sink models. It is common practice to cut heads from standard fly-line models such as the first 30 feet of either end of a double taper.

Various-level sinking lines make the best and most economical sinking shooting heads as the level line tip sinks faster than tapered sink tips. Depending upon circumstances, these heads are cut at lengths from 25 to 35 feet, the ideal length being 30 feet.

Besides being easier to distance cast, shooting heads are ideal for cold-weather fishing, as the smaller shooting fly line or monofilament does not carry so much water to freeze in rod guides or to wet your exposed hands.

Unless your "head" is just inside the rod's tip-top, roll casting or false casting is quite difficult, and learning how to handle and avoid tangling the shooting line takes some skill and practice. These complications, however, are minor compared to the many other advantages of shooting heads.

Nymphing Line Applications

1. *Floating Fly Lines.* The full-floating fly line is extremely important in nymphing. It is used when fishing nymphs on long leaders in very shallow or intermediate-depth waters. The floating fly line offers the fly-fisher the most

The right nymph tackle system eliminates all hang-ups and allows the fly-fisher to subdue many more large prizes.

positive line and nymph control. When nymphs are emerging or floating, hatching surface-film nymphs must be fished dead-drift or very carefully controlled, the floating line is a must!

A floating line with leader strike indicator and careful mending makes a floating fly line the most practical and deadly of all weapons in the majority of streams and shallow lakes. The leader, nymph, and cast angle determine what depth the nymph sinks to and is fished at. The nymph or leader provides the weight that sinks the nymph to the taking area, while the line is positioned and mended to enhance this fly placement.

The color of floating fly lines has a definite effect on nymph fishing. Line visibility on the water is critical for "reading" the line, leader, nymph position, and mending. The light pastel, white, and fluorescent lines are all easy to see. I greatly prefer white, pale yellow, or green. The fluorescent lines distract me too much and must also be more disturbing to the fish.

There are several floating fly lines now being manufactured especially for nymph fishing, and these attempt to utilize the high-visibility strike-indicator system developed by me a few years ago. These lines, with a 12- to 18-inch section of fluorescent pink or orange color in the finish, make the floating line tip more visible but do not greatly increase the detection of the normally soft, subtle, unseen nymph take because the color section is too long.

When an indicator is much longer than 1 inch, it greatly reduces the early detection of a fish's intake of the nymph, and a permanent line-tip indicator cannot be moved closer to the nymph without shortening the leader.

A short section of indicator, independent of the fly line on the leader, can be moved according to water depth, and so on, for more precise strike detection. In the leader section, there are instructions and illustrations for making this strike indicator.

2. *Sinking Fly Lines.* Fly lines are now available that sink at variable rates, and some are even manufactured in which only specific portions of the line sink. What a revelation these lines have been! They are very complicated, so the reader must use these few words merely as an introduction.

In a sink-tip fly line, the first 10 to 20 feet sink and the remainder floats. These lines are particularly good for fishing nymphs where water is not deep. Shallow lakes and small ponds and streams are some areas where the sink-tip works well. I especially like to use the Hi-D sink-tip to fish to bass, panfish, and trout along lake shorelines, using swimming patterns such as damselfly and dragonfly nymphs. On calm lake waters, the sink-tip also greatly reduces surface disturbance near a retrieved nymph. Next to the full floater, the sink-tip provides the best line and nymph control for presenting nymphs to holding stream fish. The floating portion of the line is watched or mended as with the full floater. Most taking fish must be detected by observing and feeling the strike on the floating portion of the fly line.

When the nymph is taken by an unseen trout, the Whitlock indicator system allows efficient fast detection and hook. Note this trout is lip-hooked as if taken on a seen dry fly.

With a sink- or wet-belly fly line, you have a weight-forward sinking line made with the belly and tip weighted to sink at specific rates—slow to fast. The shooting line floats so that pickup and casting are easier than with a full-sinking line. Most users of wet-belly lines either fish from boats or wade deep. The shooting line is used to accomplish distance and is stripped into the water, the fisherman's mouth, a basket, or boat bottom on the retrieve of the nymph. These lines are better for sinking a nymph in areas where the nymph is to be fished or retrieved over a longer distance or in swifter, deeper water.

A full-sinking fly line is made so that the entire line sinks at a specific rate proportionate to the density of the line's coating. Sink rates vary from quite slow to intermediate to almost as fast as a lead-core trolling line. (In fact, lead-core trolling is often used as a very-fast-sinking shooting-head fly line.) Front tapers on these full-sinking fly lines do not enhance but slightly hinder the tip/leader/nymph sink rate. Therefore, level tip-sinking lines are usually preferred where fast sink rate is critical.

The slowest-sinking nymph lines are ideal for slow, shallow-water nymph *retrieves*. Shallow, mossy lakes are usually best nymph-fished with this type of fly line. The faster full-sinkers are applied where current speed and great depths make fishing nymphs along the bottom difficult. Generally, in still water the full-sinking line is cast out and "counted" down and then retrieved in a style meant to imitate a swimming nymph. In deep or swift streams, the full-sink lines are cast at an angle to the current so as to give the line time to sink to a desired level before current drag sets in.

Basically, with full-sink lines nymphs are drifted, dragged, or retrieved. The line and leader is usually tight so that the unseen strike is telegraphed, seen at the line to water point, or felt at the rod tip or hand. Much of the time fish hook themselves, especially in swift water. However, the fly-fisher also strikes with a line pull and rod lift.

Sinking tight-line masters of deep-lake nymph fishing point the rod striaight at the nymph and hold the tip just at or just below the water's surface to "sense" the fish's take of the nymph.

3. *Shooting-head Fly Lines.* Running or shooting lines are attached to the "head" of floating or sinking fly lines by using either loops or needle knots. Usually 100 feet of shooting line is adequate for most nymphing situations. They can be either a special very-small-diameter floating fly line or a heavy round or flat nylon monofilament. There are many fans of all three types. Each has specific advantages as well as disadvantages.

The shooting fly line is a special small-diameter fly line that retains the feel and properties of true fly line. It is easier to handle and adjust to than the nylons, but it is not as durable in very cold weather and will not shoot for distance as well. Scientific Anglers make this special shooting fly line.

The flat or oval nylon monofilament shooting line is considerably more flexible in cold weather, owing to its ribbon shape, than round monofilament and easier to straighten out and handle. It tends to float better and does not tangle as quickly, but it is easier to damage, kink, or twist, and knot tying is more difficult. This type of mono is manufactured and sold especially for shooting lines by Cortland Line Company under the name of Cobra.

Round nylon monofilament is more durable and has better knot strength, and in good, straight condition it casts or shoots farther, but it wears guides out much faster and tangles more often. Sunset Line Company makes this special shooting mono and calls it Amnesia.

Backing. Nymph fly lines should always be "backed" on the fly reel by an additional portion of braided Dacron or nylon line. Do not use silk or rayon because they rot quickly. Never use nylon monofilament, as it swells and tangles on the reel spool.

Your backing should never test less than 12 pounds, and 17- to 27-pound test is much better! Use at least 50 yards and up to 150 yards, more if the reel will hold it. Use the backing to fly-reel knot for attaching the backing to the reel's spool arbor. Always have backing in one knotless total length. Attach the backing to the fly line with an Albright or needle knot. Backing is joined to the mono shooting line with loops or an epoxy splice.

The Leader

Understanding the nymph leader is a major key to highly effective nymph fishing because in most cases the leader will determine how well the nymph actually fishes. Leaders for floating and sinking lines vary a good deal in design and purpose, so each will be discussed separately.

Nymph leaders are usually tapered, with a butt section somewhere around the strength and flexibility of the fly-line tip tapering down to a small tip section.

There are two designs of tapered nymphing leaders: the compounded knotted leader and the knotless tapered leader. The compound knotted leader is constructed by tying lengths of different diameters together to achieve a taper. Knotless tapers are made by acid-etching level lengths of nylon monofilament or by extruding them through a varying orifice.

Under most nymph-fishing conditions the knotless tapered and level leaders are superior to the compound knotted leaders. Knotless leaders eliminate unnecessary knot failures and knot hang-up on underwater obstacles. They were originally expensive and poorly designed, but today they are practical.

The best nymph leaders are very soft and supple, not stiff as once was popular. Since nymphs do not cause the turnover problem that dry flies do, nearly any length of leader can be used in nymphing. In every circumstance I know of, the limpest, most flexible leaders are best for fishing nymphs in a natural, live manner.

All leaders used for nymphing should be straight and curl-free. They are best straightened by pulling them tight, stretching them, and then slowly releasing the tension. Rubber or leather "straighteners" are not recommended, since they may ruin the nylon leaders' molecular structure and greatly weaken them. The friction and heat generated that straightens the leader will also destroy the nylon's surface structure.

Leader color for nymphing has never seemed too important. Nylon is almost colorless, but it does accept fabric dyes easily. Under certain conditions a leader appears less visible if it is variegated with one or more natural stream color tones, such as olive, gray, or brown, to break up its shine and outline.

Leaders for Floating Fly Lines. Nymph leaders generally used for floating fly lines should, like those used for dry-fly fishing, have a butt that matches the line tip in flexibility and size. Leaders of 7½, 9, and 12 feet are most practical, and these lengths should be matched to the type of nymphs to be fished, with longer, lighter leaders used with smaller nymphs, in clear water, and for selective fish.

The floating-line nymph leader is usually expected to sink, or at least fish just below the surface film. Leader sink material, wetting agents, clay, or toothpaste are used to help the nylon break the surface tension and sink. Sinking nymphs also assist in pulling some part of the leader down. Some of us rub the nymph leader with fresh algae or other aquatic vegetation or stream-bottom silt or clay to "wet" the surface. On the other hand, the leader can be greased with silicone, Mucilin, or Gink to make it *float.* This is done routinely when fishing midge pupae, emerging caddis pupae, or emerging and floating mayfly nymphs.

Lead strips or split shot on the leader, or painting the leader with a compound of thinned pliobond rubber cement and lead powder will enhance sinking of the nymph. Such weighted leaders are usually considered unpleasant to cast, but they enable the more sensitive floating-line nymph method to be used in a far greater range of water areas and depths.

Some tapered-leader manufacturers advertise sinking leaders. Most of these I've tested break the surface-film tension fairly well but have little or no effect on actually sinking the nymph.

The fastest-sinking nymph leader is one that has the limpest smaller diameter. This offers the least attraction to surface film and the least resistance to the downward pull of the line's tip, leader, or weight of the nymph. *This is the most significant property of a good nymph leader regardless of its length, taper, knot, or knotless makeup.*

Leaders for Sinking Lines. Leaders used on sinking lines are generally shorter and less complicated than those used on floating lines. Most should be less than 7½ feet to as short as 2 feet. Only in extreme cases of very clear and/or shallow water does the sinking-line nymph leader need to be longer than 7 or 8 feet.

The main reason for the shorter leader is to make the line's sink rate more effective. As I said earlier, the longer the unweighted leader, the less immediate influence the sinking line has on it and the nymph. The nylon leader actually resists the downward pull of the sinking line or nymph.

The average sinking-line nymph leader is 4 to 6 feet in length, including tippet. Usually a straight piece of nylon, or no more than three sections tied together, make this leader. There is general agreement that the shorter leaders for nymphs fished on sinking fly lines do not handicap or deter most trout or bass from hitting. The prime consideration seems to be getting and fishing the nymph properly. Usually leaders a little heavier (that is, with a larger-diameter tippet) than those in the floating-line method can be used.

Leader Tippets. The last or smallest-diameter portion of the leader is generally termed the tip or tippet. By adjusting the size and length of the tippet, the nymph fisher can alter the performance of the leader to accommodate different nymph sizes and nymph actions. To accomplish this the users of knotted and knotless tapered leaders usually carry several sizes of extra nylon tippet material. Changing tippets is easier, faster, and more economical than changing the entire leader.

In nymphing, the longest tippet possible or practical is usually the best length. The nymph fishes better and has more stretch to resist break-offs.

When using tapered leaders, especially knotless tapers, it is a good idea to add a short wear section between leader and tippet. This reduces knot-tying leader consumption waste. Another method growing in popularity is that of forming a permanent loop at the leader's tip and looping the extra tippet to it in the so-called loop-to-loop junction. The loops are a little larger than a blood or double surgeon's knot and may cause additional hanging up in some very dense, cover-laden waters. But where simplicity and speed are needed, the loop-to-loop method is a good trade-off.

A selection of tippet material should include a pound-test range from 10 to 1 or approximately OX to 8X. Nylon tippet materials come in at least two types, and a good nymph fisher should know and use each under certain conditions.

1. Very soft, very small diameter with high pound-test-to-diameter ratio. Best where nymphing clear and unobstructed water to selective trout. Fair knot strength.

2. Very tough, medium diameter, medium flexible, with a lower-ratio pound-test-to-diameter ratio. Best for nymphing where water is not so clear and/or has lots of water hazards for fish to chafe the leader. Excellent knot strength.

Recommended Knots or Attachments for Various Components. 1. *Backing to fly reel:* backing to reel knot.
2. *Backing to fly line:* needle knot, nail knot, or Albright knot.

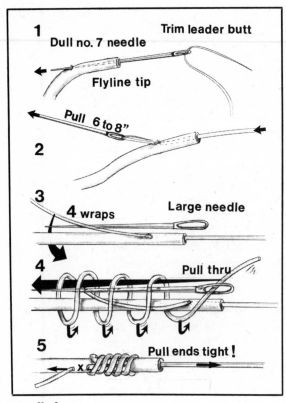

1
Dull no. 7 needle
Trim leader butt
Flyline tip

2
Pull 6 to 8"

3
4 wraps
Large needle

4
Pull thru

5
Pull ends tight !
x

Needle knot.

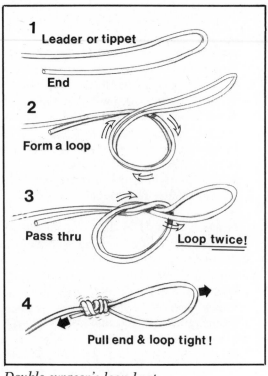

1
Leader or tippet
End

2
Form a loop

3
Pass thru
Loop twice!

4
Pull end & loop tight !

Double surgeon's loop knot—
for loop-to-loop junctions.

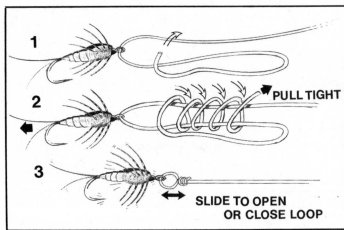

1

2
PULL TIGHT

3
SLIDE TO OPEN
OR CLOSE LOOP

Double surgeon's knot.

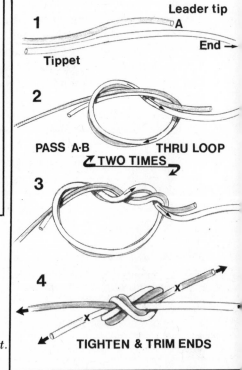

1
Leader tip
A
End →

Tippet

2
PASS A·B   THRU LOOP
TWO TIMES

3

4
TIGHTEN & TRIM ENDS
x   x

Duncan loop knot.

3. *Backing to mono shooting line:* epoxy splice or loop-to-loop.

4. *Shooting monofilament to fly line:* needle knot, epoxy splice, or loop-to-loop.

5. *Shooting fly line to fly line:* loop-to-loop or epoxy splice.

6. *Leader to fly line:* needle knot or epoxy junction.

7. *Leader to leader or tippet:* double surgeon's or improved blood knot.

8. *Leader to nymph:* turned-up or turned-down eye—turle knot or Duncan loop; ringed eye—improved clinch knot or Duncan loop. (*Note:* Open Duncan loop is used when you wish the nymph to swing on a free hinge for more action and less leader influence.)

Whitlock Floating Nymph Head

The Whitlock nymph-head fly line is a nymphing modification of the standard shooting-head-type fly line. It allows a great latitude in fishing floating-line nymphs, in casting ranges, strike detection, and fighting fish. The line roll-casts and picks up easily in practical nymphing ranges of 30 to 60 feet. This type of line greatly reduces the overall casting load on a rod at extreme distances and greatly reduces line water drag when fighting a strong fish. Further, it greatly enhances downstream dead-drift presentation to feeding fish. I prefer it in line sizes 4, 5, and 6, 5-weight being the most versatile.

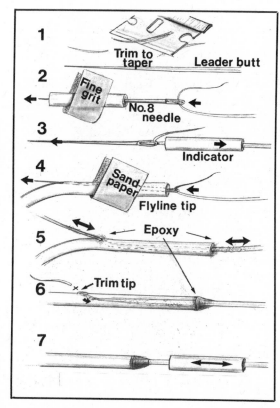

Whitlock epoxy junction and strike indicator— for Whitlock nymph-head fly line.

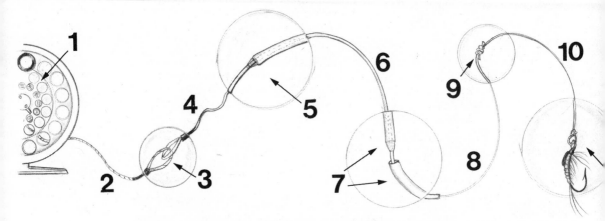

Schematic of Whitlock nymph-head: (1) backing to reel; (2) 100–150 yards 18-pound dacron; (3) loop splice: backing to shooting mono; (4) shooting line: 100 feet; (5) shooting line to fly line: epoxy junction; (6) fly line: 30 feet DT or WF; (7) fly line to leader: epoxy junction and strike indicator; (8) leader: knotless taper; (9) leader to tippet: double surgeon's knot; (10) tippet: 30 to 40 inches; (11) Duncan loop knot to nymph.

Components. 1. *Tippet:* 30- to 40-inch tippet tied to a knotless tapered leader with a 10-inch wear section; tippet 3X to 7X.

2. *Leader:* 7½-, 9-, or 12-foot knotless tapered leader with 3X tip.

3. *Strike indicator:* 1-inch section of orange fluorescent floating fly line on leader's butt section.

4. *Fly line:* the first 30 feet of a double-taper or weight-forward white floating fly line, or a special 30-foot floating shooting-head line; line sizes 4, 5, and 6 are preferred.

5. *Shooting line:* 100 feet of 20- or 30-pound-test Cobra flat monofilament.

6. *Backing:* 100 to 150 yards of 18-pound-test braided Dacron backing.

The nymph head is designed to have a minimum of knot hang-ups. The tippet is attached to the wear section and to the leader's tip with double surgeon's knots. The leader is attached to the fly line's tip with a Whitlock epoxy junction after the indicator is strung on a knotless leader's butt. Shooting mono is attached to the 30-foot line's back end with a Whitlock epoxy junction or needle knot. Backing and shooting monofilament are attached with two small epoxy loops.

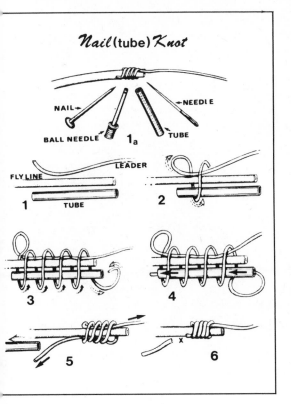

Nail (tube) Knot

NAIL
BALL NEEDLE
NEEDLE
TUBE
1a

FLY LINE
LEADER
TUBE
1

2

3

4

5

6

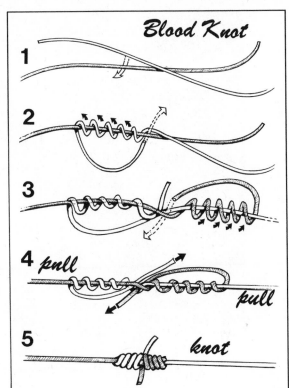

Blood Knot

1

2

3

4 pull
pull

5
knot

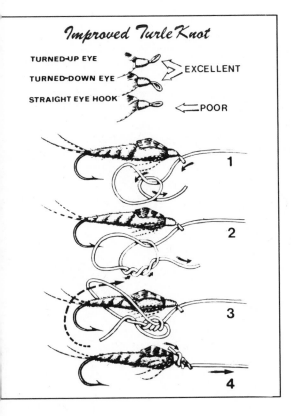

Improved Turle Knot

TURNED-UP EYE
TURNED-DOWN EYE
STRAIGHT EYE HOOK
EXCELLENT
POOR

1

2

3

4

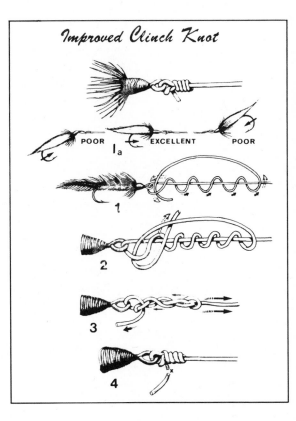

Improved Clinch Knot

POOR
EXCELLENT
POOR
1a

1

2

3

4

A well-balanced nymph tackle system allows the ultimate in casting, line, hooking, and landing control for all types and sizes of trout.

THREE GENERAL NYMPHING TACKLE SYSTEMS

The All-around Nymphing System

Rod: 100-percent graphite, 8½-foot, two-piece, lightweight, stiff-action rod for a 6-weight line; glass-graphite composite for second choice.

Reel: 3½-inch spool to hold 6-weight line and 150 yards of backing. Spool 1, weight-forward 6F white fly line with 9-foot knotless 3X tapered leader and strike indicator; spool 2, weight-forward 6F/s high-density sink tip with a 6-foot 3X leader.

Match the Nymph and Presentation-line Control System

Rod: 9½-foot lightweight, stiff-action rod to cast a 4- or 5-weight line.

Reel: 3¼- to 3½- inch diameter spool with outer palming flange to hold 4- or 5-weight line and 150 yards of 18-pound-test backing. Spool 1, 4- or 5-weight Whitlock nymph-head fly line with 9-foot knotless tapered 3X leader; spool 2, 4- or 5-weight brown weight-forward floating fly line with 12-foot 4X knotless taper and orange strike-indicator section.

Large-River and Lake Nymphing System:

Rod: 9-foot stiff-action, medium-weight fly rod that will cast a 7- or 8-weight fly line.

Reel: 3¾-inch spool diameter that has outer palming flange and sturdy click-drag system; should hold 150 yards of 27-pound-test backing. Spool 1, weight-forward 8F floating fly line with a 9-foot knotless 2X leader, orange fly line strike indicator on leader; spool 2, weight-forward 8F/s high-density sink tip with a 6-foot 2X leader tip; spool 3, high-density shooting head with a 4- to 6-foot 2X leader tippet.

FOUR OF MY FAVORITE NYMPH PATTERNS

Dave's Red-fox Squirrel Nymph

This is my favorite all-purpose nymph, as versatile and effective for a nymph as the Adams is for a dry fly. It works well where mayflies, stone flies, caddis pupae, and scuds of similar colors exist, and where there are no nymphs.

Hook:	Mustad 9671, sizes 4 to 18
Body weight:	6 to 10 wraps of lead wire at thorax
Thread:	Black
Tail:	Sparse tuft of red-fox squirrel back hair, including both guard and underfur ½ length of hook shank
Rib:	Small oval tinsel
Abdomen:	Red-fox squirrel belly fur
Thorax:	Red-fox squirrel back fur (with guard and underfur included)
Wing case:	Dark-brown swiss straw or turkey tail
Legs:	Either guard hairs of red-fox squirrel back or one turn of dark partridge hackle

Stone-fly Nymph

This pattern is my favorite deep-fished stone-fly nymph tied in appropriate color and size to match resident adult stone-fly nymphs. (*The Second Fly Tyer's Almanac* by Robert Boyle and Dave Whitlock, to be published in 1978, will contain full tying instructions.)

Hook:	Mustad 9672 or 36890, sizes 2 to 12
Body weight:	Loop of lead wire laid along hook shank to build shape of body too
Thread:	Herb Howard's prewaxed 6/0 to match underbody color of nymph
Tail:	Two wild-boar bristles or nylon monofilament the color of natural stone-fly nymph
Rib:	Small gold oval tinsel or single strand of nylon floss to match underbody color
Abdomen (top):	Swiss straw or turkey quill section to match nymph's top or dorsal side color
Abdomen (bottom):	Fur dubbing or Seal-Ex
Thorax:	Same dubbing as for bottom of abdomen except tied larger and fuzzier

Wing case:	Swiss straw or turkey quill extended from abdomen back to form bulky wing case
Legs:	One body feather of pheasant or grouse to match color scheme laid over abdomen top before wing case is tied down
Head:	Same dubbing as thorax and abdomen with overlay of wing and back material
Eyes:	Heat-beaded (balled) strand of nylon monofilament
Antennae:	Two boar bristles or nylon monofilament strands

Dave's Swimming Shrimp (backword or forward swimmer)

This is my favorite freshwater shrimp, scud, and saltwater shrimp imitation. Shrimps and scuds swim backward with tails or forward with legs. They do not form a "C" unless they are dead or in tight confinement, so most shrimp patterns do not realistically imitate moving live shrimps. This pattern can be tied as either backward or forward swimmer by reversing body parts on hook shank.

Hook:	Mustad 94842, 9671, or 36890, sizes 18 to 4
Body weight:	6 to 12 lead wraps at rear of hook shank
Thread:	Light gray, tan, or light olive, Herb Howard's prewaxed
Rib:	Small gold wire or single strand nylon floss
Antennae:	2 to 6 strands of tying thread 1 to 1½ times the length of hook shank
Body:	Blend of sparkle orlon wool, Seal-Ex, and beaver belly
Legs:	Picked out longer dubbing fibers (heavier at head area)
Back:	Strip of clear poly bag or single layer of swiss straw the color of shrimp's body
Eyes:	Heat-beaded (balled) strand of nylon monofilament
Tail:	Small section of back material extended down over hook bend or hook eye

Floating Nymph

An emerger imitation of many mayflies, stone flies, or caddis pupae. This is a most deadly hatch matcher for me as nymphs emerge into adults in the surface film. Nine out of ten time it beats the floating adult patterns. Grease *only the wing case* with Mucilin, Gink, or Dilly wax so nymph will hang tail-down in surface film and case is visible to fly-fisher!

Hook:	Orvis Supreme 94831 or 94842, sizes 24 to 10; any light-wire dry-fly hook will work
Thread:	Herb Howard's 6/0 prewaxed, the color of fly's body
Tails:	2 or 3 fibers of soft bird hackle
Rib:	Small gold wire
Abdomen:	To match color of Spectrum or Flyrite synthetic dubbing
Thorax:	Larger amount of same dubbing as abdomen
Wing case:	(Most important!) A large "bubble" or expanding wing of

Flyrite to match adult's wing color, usually light dun, pale
yellow, white, or tan
Hackle: One or two turns of soft cock hackle or grouse hackle; trim
off top and bottom leaving a few fibers on each side of thorax

In addition to these four nymphs, I have the greatest confidence in the new
Whitlock Damsel Nymph, which Lefty Kreh has covered in his chapter. It is a
super big-fish taker in toughest conditions when swimmed off the bottom
to cruisers.

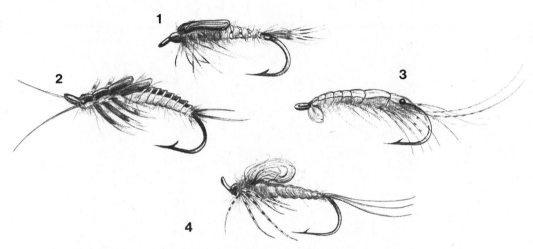

*(1) Dave's Red-Fox Squirrel Nymph; (2) Dave's Stone Nymph; (3) Dave's
Swimming Shrimp; (4) Floating Nymph.*

Carl E. Richards was born in Pittsburgh, Pennsylvania, in 1933 but grew up in Columbus, Ohio. He began fly-fishing when he was eight years old and professional fly tying for a local store at the age of nine. His summers were spent in Michigan, fly-fishing for trout and angling for river smallmouths in Ohio.

Richards graduated from Ohio State University School of Dentistry and promptly moved to Michigan because it had more trout fishing than Ohio. He now lives in Rockford, Michigan, where he practices dentistry and writes books and articles on fly-fishing. He co-authored Selective Trout, Fly Fishing Strategy, and Tying the Swisher-Richards Flies and was a contributing author in Art Flick's Master Fly Tying Guide and The Masters on the Dry Fly. He has also written many articles for national sports magazines.

8
Pattern Selection

Carl E. Richards

THE TALL IDAHO HILLS were springtime green and the surrounding alpine meadows were in full yellow bloom. At Bone Fish Flats large rainbows were sipping naturals tight against grassy banks in the quiet flow of Henrys Fork, probably America's richest hatch-producing trout stream. The great pink-sided fish were rhythmically sipping something, exactly what I couldn't quite figure out. They were fiendishly selective. Three gray-green shadows cruised the shallow shoreline, happily gorging natural flies and consistently refusing my offerings.

I had that age-old problem of trying to match a multiple hatch, a period when more than one insect is hatching and/or egg-laying at the same time. This is a constant battle of wits on the Fork, where the water is so rich in aquatic insects that it often offers as many as ten or twelve choices to the trout. I had been casting over these fish for about thirty minutes with no results. There were some brown drakes emerging but the fish didn't seem to be taking them, certainly not my imitation of this large mayfly.

The fish seemed to be surface feeding, but when the rise forms occurred I could see nothing in the water. This meant the naturals must be flush in the film, very small, or slightly subsurface. There were species of caddis flies, mayflies, and midges, both hatching and egg-laying. I couldn't seem to hit on which stage of which species the fish were working on.

Now usually, if you try hard enough and long enough, one foolish fish can be teased into striking, and after forty-five minutes I finally got a nice 19-inch rainbow to take a small Quad-Wing Caddis. I didn't think that was the main dish and suspected my fish took my fly only as an hors d'oeuvre. But at least I had a fish to study.

I then put into use the most important piece of equipment to come along

in years: the stomach pump. Gently I inserted the plastic tube down the fish's throat, injected a few cc's of water, and pulled back on the syringe. Out came the stomach contents in the precise order they were ingested. Now the whole story of the feeding period was an open book: small dark *Baetis* nymphs, the smallest, least discernible insect of this multiple hatch—and the fish were taking them right on the surface before they hatched into duns.

I tied on a small, dark floating fur nymph, well greased, and other feeders quickly fell for my pattern. As I was no longer guessing, I was successful.

It is usually possible to find out exactly what rising trout are feeding on, and it is foolish not to do so. Yet few anglers take advantage of this opportunity. The whole object of this little story is to emphasize the importance of learning what the trout are feeding on, for the key to pattern selection is giving them what they are already taking. To use as valuable a tool as the stomach pump you must catch at least one fish, but if trout are rising this is usually possible.

On the stream, the nymph fisherman—or any other fisherman, for that matter—is faced with either of two general situations: (1) fish rising, actively feeding, either surface or subsurface, to a hatch of insects; or (2) fish not obviously feeding, no hatch in progress (which of course is most of the time on most rivers). Let's take each problem separately.

FISH OBVIOUSLY FEEDING TO A HATCH OF INSECTS

The stomach pump has made nymph fishermen out of many a thoughtful dry-fly man. The pump has exploded some of the old theories we were taught

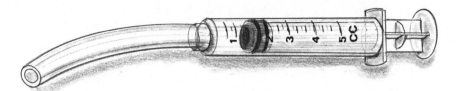

Simple stomach pump.

as unquestionable truths. Consider, for example, this statement: "Trout take nymphs at the beginning of the hatch and duns toward the end." This old truism is so far from correct that it is dead wrong. I have taken fish after fish that appeared to be surface feeding exclusively, only to find after examining the stomach contents that they were actually taking two or three or four nymphs and then a dun, then a few more nymphs and then another dun. This means the dry-fly, match-the-hatch type of angler should be fishing floating nymphs most of the time! And, in fact, quite often a well-designed floating nymph is deadly during the hatch and much more effective than a standard dry-fly imitation.

Naturally, the pattern you select should be a close imitation of the live nymphs that the trout are feeding on—a fur-bodied fly with a high wing pad to simulate the wing in the process of bursting out of the nymph casing, three widespread tails, and a very few leg fibers tied underneath, beard- or DeFeo-style. The general outline of the artificial is very important and should closely simulate the natural. These flies should be tied on 3X fine wire hooks so they can be fished dry and dead-drift. Obviously, the aritifical should be the same size, color, and shape as the real nymph (never the dun), and herein lies the problem. During a multiple hatch everyone—even the most expert fishing entomologist—must obtain a sample of the natural and examine it *in the hand.* This is the only way to be certain of a correct imitation. The best way to obtain a reliable sample is by using a stomach pump. If this is not possible (after all, to use it you must capture one fish), other, less reliable methods are required.

Seine the river and see what life is present. If only one species of mature nymph is found, you are probably safe in assuming that this is the correct nymph to imitate. If many different species are present, as in our previous situation on the Fork, you must do a little more exploring to select the correct pattern. Small, lightweight binoculars are often invaluable in discovering what surface feeders are taking. If everything else fails, wade over into the line of

Typical floating Mayfly Nymph.

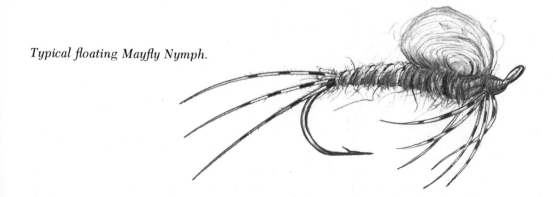

drift where the fish are working, even if it disturbs them, and look closely at the surface. You may notice a small, almost invisible species of insect that actually is emerging in much greater numbers than the larger, more obvious, flies. Many times I have found that an imitation of the smaller species in a floating nymph is much more effective than larger patterns.

It has been established that trout prefer to feed on nymphs just under the film and in the film. During an emergence of natural insects, the ratio is about six nymphs to one winged dun. Why this is so we can only conjecture, but to me it is reasonable to believe the fish have learned by experience that a nymph will take a long time to hatch, dry its wings, and escape. Thus the fish does not have to hurry to capture the nymph, as he would with the dry adult. And since large trout abhor wasting energy they pick the food form they can sip at their leisure. It is easier for them to feed on nymphs, and they do so.

Quite often, trout that are apparently surface feeding are actually feeding on caddis pupae. These insects may be taken on the way up from the bottom or on the surface film. It is often difficult to recognize an emergence of caddises since the adults lie low in the water and lack the high visibility of the sail-like wings of the mayfly. In addition, they don't usually ride the film for any appreciable length of time. If fish are rising to something seemingly invisible and a few caddises are in the air, even if none are seen on the water, that is your clue to a caddis emergence. Caddis pupae are very effective both weighted and twitched up as a natural rising to the surface or tied on a 3X fine-wire hook and fished dry. In general, they should be tied with a fat fur body, a few long legs (which also represent antennae), a wing case hanging down under the body, and a darker thorax.

The rise of fish to a caddis hatch is often quite baffling. Several books have indeed been devoted to the caddis, but the many individual species and their quite diverse habits make it a complicated subject to digest. One cannot, with any degree of certainty, make generalizations. For instance, a great many pupae rise quickly to the surface and then soon emerge from the pupa in the adult stage and fly away. Thus a weighted pupa allowed to sink and drift to the trout-taking position and then quickly twitched to the surface is quite deadly. Many other species of pupa, however, drift in the film for a long time, and in this instance using a floating pupa on a 3X fine-wire hook fished dry is a more effective technique. In some species the emerging pupa runs across the surface to the shore. These species must be fished in a similar manner, which is completely different from the first two types.

Another complexity encountered with the caddis is that the emergence and egg-laying flight often occur simultaneously. At this time many caddis adults dive or crawl underwater to deposit their eggs. The angler in some instances is faced with rising pupae and diving adults (a classic wet-fly situation). Picking the correct imitation in such complex situations is very difficult indeed. The use of the stomach pump can lead to a quick solution, but if its use

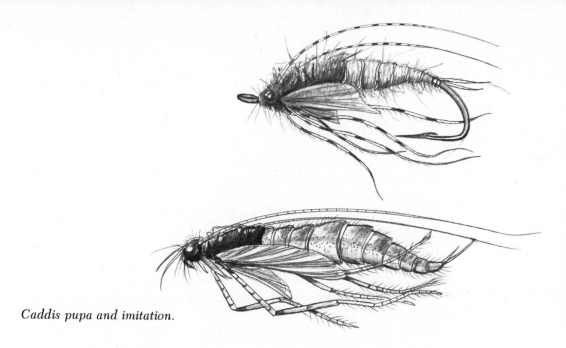

Caddis pupa and imitation.

is not possible, only close observation and a thorough knowledge of the possibilities will give any hope of a correct solution.

All the floating artificial nymphs are, by their nature, difficult for the angler to see, as are the naturals on which the fish are actually feeding. This is as it should be, but it does require attention and you must learn to strike easily during a false rise lest a disturbance be created on the water. You have to keep track of approximately where your fly is floating and gently raise your rod tip when a rise occurs in the vicinity of the artificial's position.

Midge pupae are fished much like caddis pupae, since the hatching habits of the naturals are similar. They are much easier to tie, being only a slim fur body with a darker fur thorax tied underneath, and they are usually much smaller (sizes 20 to 28) than the average caddis (sizes 14 to 20).

Most stone flies crawl out on the bank to emerge, so a weighted imitation fished on the bottom and near shore is effective at the appropriate time. The few smaller species of stone flies that do hatch in the water can be fished like the floating mayfly nymphs. A fur nymph of the appropriate color and size, either weighted or on a 3X fine-wire hook (depending on the method of emergence of the natural) is very effective.

Three Midge Pupa designs.

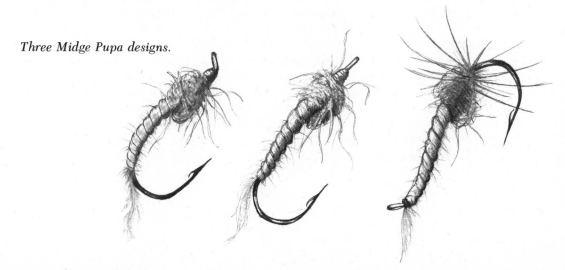

Small stone fly emerging (left) and imitation floating Stone-Fly Nymph.

NYMPH FISHING WITH NO HATCH IN PROGRESS

Periods when no hatch is on and fish are not obviously feeding occur most of the time on most rivers. On all but our most fertile streams the hatch period is but a few hours a day, so it is important to learn to take trout during these so-called dead periods. A well-fished nymph is perhaps the dealiest imitation that can be used. During these dull periods the most effective patterns are usually representations of naturals that are present in the stream or lake you are fishing and that the trout are used to feeding on day in and day out. The only certain way to learn what naturals these are is to seine the river, examine rocks, submerged logs, and aquatic vegetation, and see for yourself what is there. After discovering the most prevalent form, tie on a good translucent fur nymph and fish it on the bottom, dead-drift or crawling, but *as slowly as possible*. Remember that the current at the surface is much faster than the current on the bottom, as much as seven times faster, so what appears to be a dead drift at 7 miles an hour surface current is actually dragging furiously at the bottom. Unless you can slow the fly down to the speed of the bottom current, your nymph will not be very effective. Many techniques exist to accomplish this, and they are covered in other chapters of this book.

These nymphs, which are to be fished deep, are usually tied on regular or heavy wire hooks and would be tied to simulate mainly mayfly nymphs and stone-fly nymphs, although dragonflies, damselflies, caddis larvae and pupae, shrimps, scuds, and a myriad of other possibilities exist. Here again the stomach pump should be used once you land the first fish. What is in the fish is what you should be using.

Another way to select an effective pattern is to go by water type. Pick an imitation of a natural prevalent in a specific type of river. The larger the nymph form (realistically tied) the larger the trout that is likely to take.

Our faster, boulder-strewn, freestone streams almost always have a good population of various stone-fly species. Many of these nymphs are of medium to large size. Eastern and midwestern rivers have good populations, and most larger western rivers have huge populations. In these streams a really well-tied stone-fly nymph of medium to large size is always an excellent choice. Large fish are often hooked on such weighted imitations when fished right on the bottom with fast-sinking lines. Such rivers as the Big Hole, Madison, and Yellowstone are famous for their hatches of *Pteronarcys* species. These giant stone flies are so large they resemble hummingbirds in flight. The larger

Typical deep-fished nymph designs: top row, Mayfly Nymph, Stone-Fly Nymph; middle row, Dragonfly Nymph, Damsel-Fly Nymph; center, Caddis Larva; bottom row, Freshwater Shrimp, Scud.

species undergo a three-year life cycle, so naturals are always present in various sizes and exact imitations are not usually necessary, especially in the faster tumbling currents.

Just as large stone-fly nymphs are fine fish attractors in our many free-stone streams, a large mayfly wiggle nymph, tied to resemble a medium size (size 10 3XL) *Ephemera* nymph (brown drake, green drake) and the much larger (size 4–6 3XL) *Hexagenia* nymphs are great fish finders on our larger, slower moving lime streams and spring creeks. These large mayfly nymphs are burrowers and are from 15 to 36 mm in length, and large fish will savor them. The nymphs must emerge from their tunnels quite often to molt and grow and thus are available to the trout even during winter months. The *Hex-*

Large stone-fly nymph and imitation.

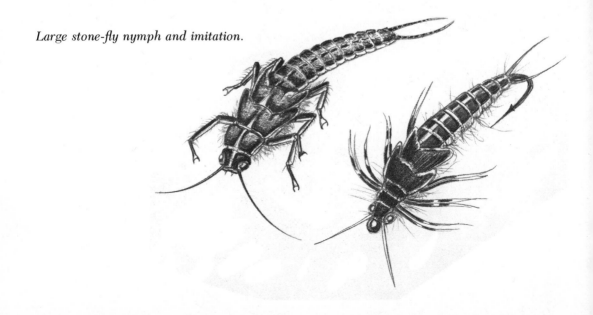

Hexagenia *Wiggle Nymph*.

agenia nymphs are found in silt beds, while the smaller *Ephemera* require a river bottom of well-mixed sand and gravel. These *Ephemera* species are usually considered eastern species, but this is wrong. Though not widely recognized, heavy brown drake hatches occur on some large western rivers with suitable habitat. Imitations of these slow-water dwellers should be fished slowly, creeping along the bottom when the nymph fisherman is searching the water.

The smaller colder spring creeks such as Silver, Armstrong, and other similar streams almost always have large populations of shrimps and scuds living in their lush weed beds and lime-rich waters. The smaller fur plastic-backed imitations fished slowly on the bottom will often turn an otherwise dull period into an exciting day.

It is always advantageous to seine the bottom, be it freestone or spring creek, and look closely to see what type of food is in the river and available to foraging fish.

No matter what order of insects you wish to represent, your pattern should have life and translucence incoporated into its makeup—fur for the body, soft fibers for the legs such as hen hackle or patridge body fibers, and a little gold wire for the rib. Such materials simulate life and movement. The same flexible fibers should be used for the tails, which should usually be three in number and spread wide to imitate the naturals. Body and thorax should be made of soft translucent fur or of a man-made fiber like Poly II for life and translucence. The hard bodied, ultra-realistic flies that look so realistic in the hand and take so long to tie are not usually effective fish-taking imitations. Some of the exact imitations look so good in the fly box that one can imagine them crawling away; in the water, however, they seem dead, stiff, and lifeless.

In slow-water streams, and especially lakes, wiggle nymphs are even more effective. These are tied so that the abdomen can undulate up and down to simulate the swimming motions of a natural mayfly. These wiggle nymphs are usually fished deep, both during a hatch and when none is anticipated.

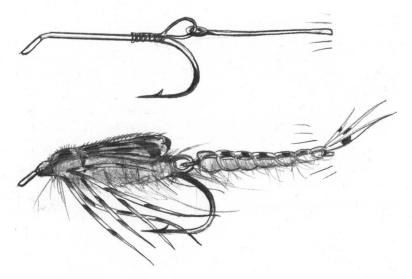

Detail of Wiggle Nymph.

One of the most valuable nymph patterns I use during a rise is a cross between a nymph and a newly emerged dun. These are called stillborn duns or emergers. They simulate an insect that is in the process of crawling out of its nymphal shuck. Often it becomes stuck, never succeeds in hatching, and either drowns or is eaten. Trout prefer them to the fully upright duns, since they seem to know they have more time to capture the stillborn. These patterns are tied with a simulation of the shuck hanging out the tail end of the fly and usually one or both wings stuck in the nymphal case. On midge hatches, these stillborns are often the only effective pattern.

I cannot say too often that the one major thing readers can do to improve their catches tremendously and learn about trout feeding habits and diet is to obtain and use a stomach pump. This simple piece of equipment has completely changed my stream strategy and vastly simplified my pattern selection. It has proved to me that I should usually be using floating nymphs or emergers during a hatch instead of a standard dry fly, and it has changed me from a mostly dry-fly type to a floating-nymph-type fisherman, at least during a rise.

A friend of mine, Dr. Fred Oswalt, has invented a new, safer type of pump that has two tubes instead of one: a very small input tube and a much larger outtake tube. First the syringe is fulled with water, then the plunger is depressed and water forced into the small tube and into the trout's stomach. The water circulates, going out the larger tube and carrying with it the ingested food.

This design creates no extra pressure on the stomach walls, as a carelessly used regular pump does. It's more effective and much safer for the fish than the simple syringe-and-tube arrangement. This is important if you believe as I do that catches should be released unharmed to provide future sport for everyone. To keep a great stream full of fish provides exciting fishing for tomorrow and the day after tomorrow!

FOUR OF MY FAVORITE NYMPH PATTERNS

Hendrickson
A realistic yet simple fur nymph. The size and color can be varied to imitate many mayfly nymphs.

Tails:	3 fibers from a tan-flecked wood duck or merganser flank feather tied in so they are spread wide and slightly shorter than the body
Abdomen and thorax:	Medium-brown spun fur, darkened on dorsal with a Pantone felt-tip marker (leave a small section in the middle of abdomen as is, lighter than the rest)
Rib:	Thin gold wire
Wing case:	Very dark duck-wing primary sections
Legs:	Dark-brown hew hackle tied DeFeo-style
Hook:	Size 14 1XL, regular wire or 3X fine

Floating Mayfly Nymph (protypical pattern)
Color and size to match species to be imitated.

Hook:	Sizes 10 to 24, 3X-fine wire
Tails:	3 fibers top-quality cock hackle slightly shorter than body
Abdomen and thorax:	Fine-grained fur or Poly II
Wing case:	Darker fur or Poly II piled up on top
Legs:	Hen-hackle fibers, DeFeo-style

Caddis Pupa (olive)
Color can be modified to simulate other species.

Hook:	Sizes 16 to 20, 3X-fine wire or regular, depending on whether to be fished floating or rising from the bottom; weighted if to be fished deep
Abdomen:	Fat, short fine-grained bright olive fur
Legs:	6 soft fibers from a Hungarian partridge breast (darker feathers)
Wing case:	Very-dark-gray hen-hackle tips tied under body
Thorax:	Darker gray olive fur
Antennae:	2 long tan-speckled fibers such as wood duck, 1½ to 2 times the length of body, tied back over the dorsal of the body

Floating Midge Pupa

Olive color to be varied depending on naturals to be imitated.

Hook:	Sizes 18 to 28, as light as possible; ringed eye
Tails:	None
Thread:	Olive, as fine as possible
Abdomen:	Very-fine-grained olive fur spun on tying thread, tied very, very thin, almost no more than thickness of bare hook shank
Thorax:	Slightly thicker olive fur
Wing case:	Dark-gray spun fur piled up high *under* hook shank

Frank Sawyer was born beside the river Avon in Wiltshire, England, and became a river keeper when he was eighteen. For the past fifty years, he has been keeper and manager for the Services Dry Fly Fishing Association, whose six-mile stretch of the Avon runs through the heart of Salisbury Plain. He became interested in the natural history of river life and spent many years studying insects in their nymphal forms, after which he evolved a series of artificials now produced for sale by his wife and daughters.

Sawyer started to write articles for various sporting magazines after the last World War and later wrote three books, Keeper of the Stream and two versions of Nymphs and the Trout. He became a regular radio broadcaster for the BBC and then did many programs for television, including several on fishing which were transmitted direct from the riverside. Among other activities he is the inventor of the humane rabbit and small-vermin traps which brought about the law to ban the steel-toothed gin in the British Isles. For this he received public awards from the RSPCA and from the Ministry of Agriculture Fisheries and Food.

Sawyer has fished and demonstrated the art of nymph fishing both in many parts of the British Isles and in Austria, Germany, France, and Sweden, where he built up an international reputation as a nymph fisherman. He teaches casting, and lectures on all things to do with fishing and the general maintenance of trout streams.

In recognition of his services to fishing he was awarded the M.B.E. by the Queen in her Birthday Honours List in June 1978.

9
Nymphing in the Classic Style

Frank Sawyer

THE NAME G. E. M. SKUES will forever be associated with nymph fishing throughout the world as long as there are anglers who wish to catch fish. He had his own ideas about taking trout on nymphal patterns long before I was born, and though I am sure he would never have claimed to be the only one with such views in mind, or indeed in practice at that time, nevertheless it was he who wrote about it and stood his ground against the great number who then considered the dry fly to be the only sporting way to fish the chalk and limestone rivers and streams in southern England. That the views of the late F. M. Halford and many of his compatriots have been disproved time and again since then, and that nymphing has become accepted as an art equal if not actually surpassing that of the dry fly, has only followed the Skues doctrine. So before writing anything more I would like to pay tribute to his memory. Without the help I got from him and his old friend and mine, the late Sir Grimwood Mears, I would never have had the courage, or indeed the ability, to write about nymphs myself. That I have written in the past and do so again is only following in the steps of the old master, whose wish it was that I should do so.

Times have changed considerably since Skues retired as a fisherman, and I sometimes wonder what he would say, or write, if he could come back to his old haunts and fish the Itchen and other waters as we have to fish them today. One thing is quite certain: He would not have the chance to catch the numbers of wild trout that were present in those reaches at the turn of the century, and maybe his opinion on many things would alter. Although I knew Skues during the last few years of his life, I never saw him fishing, and the only real information I had about his riverside activities was given to me by Sir Grimwood Mears, who knew him very well and had fished with him on

the Itchen and elsewhere. But one only needs to read the books of Skues thoroughly to know of his great interest and his powers of observation. He set a standard I have found hard to follow, and I suspect this is the case with many other authors who write about nymphing methods in practice at the present time.

What started in the south-country chalk streams of England and was described by Skues as "minor tactics" has now spread throughout the world, and the use of the nymph in one form or another takes place in all classes of water. Indeed, one could say that nymphing now represents the "major tactics" and the dry fly the minor. For my own part, I much prefer nymphing to any other form of trout fishing. From the time I caught my first fish on a nymph I had evolved, I have been fascinated by this technique and with all that must go with it.

One could say that the chalk and limestone streams are ideal waters for such fishing, and so a little information about those we have here in the south country might be a good idea. These are all spring-fed, meandering types, where the fall in level down the valley is never more than about 5 or 6 feet to the mile. Some have controls in the forms of hatches, dams, or weirs to hold up heads of water and so lessen the speed of flow. Other parts are quite natural, with alternate deeps and streamy shallows. All grow a wealth of aquatic plants that act both to conserve and check the flow of water and to be harbor and sanctuary for trout and the general food animals, which of course includes the insects. The weeds, as we call these plants, often grow so that they direct the flow into small channels or runs where the fish can position themselves and wait for food to be carried to them by the currents. In some cases, where growths are prolific, the weeds have to be cut and whole stretches prepared for fishing. Throughout most of the year, especially during the trout-fishing season, the water remains at a constant level and is perfectly clear. For the greater part it is possible to see through it and down to the chalk and gravel bed to depths of 6 feet.

So in many respects the chalk-stream fisherman has a great advantage over others who have to fish fast-running rivers and those where color in the water makes it impossible to see much beneath the surface. But it is the plentiful and varied insect life that makes the fishing so attractive. Without these creatures to induce fish to feeding in mid-water and at the surface, no nymph or dry-fly fishing as we know it could take place. The great majority of the insects that attract fish are small, with a body length of not more than half an inch. Consequently, any artificials evolved and used in deception must be in accordance. This means that delicate tackle can be used in presentation, but of this more later.

My home river is the Hampshire Avon, and I have spent most of my lifetime along its upper reaches as keeper and manager. But I also know all the other classic streams in the south very well, and I have had the pleasure of fishing the nymph in them. These are all much alike in general character, so what I write about my home stretches can be taken as being suitable for the others too.

Even though we have a great variety of insects in our streams, a large number of them can be ruled out from the nymph fisher's point of view. Many are acceptable in nymphal form by both trout and grayling, and indeed by other fish too, but any artificials made to look like them by the flytier cannot be fished in the way the trout expect to see the naturals, nor can the same sport be obtained even if such methods are adopted.

Trout holding and feeding in weed lanes.

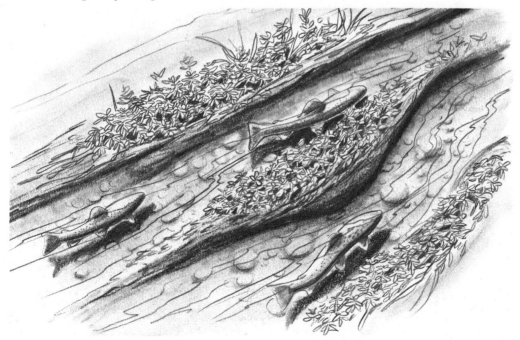

Nymphs that provide food for trout can be placed in four categories. All come under the heading of Ephemeroptera. There are those that live in the riverbed, those that exist for the most part under stones and debris on the bottom, those that crawl about on the gravel and vegetation, and those that can swim freely. Although it is possible to make artificials for all these, the difficulty comes in presenting them in a lifelike manner. Only those that can swim freely can really be imitated successfully.

This of course reduces the number considerably, but even so there are plenty left to meet the requirements of the nymph fisherman. What is more, in creating artificials to represent nymphs of the swimming group, those that have the greatest attraction for fish are being considered. It is indeed this swimming group that figures most in any autopsies one might carry out, and this alone is sufficient proof that they are taken whenever the opportunity occurs.

Since I started fishing with the nymph I have evolved patterns to imitate all members of this swimming group and, indeed, had success with them. But I found there was no need for any exact likeness of one or another and that if most of the details and characteristics of several could be incorporated in two patterns the fish could be taken consistently on them. General shape and coloration, together with the right size, is of greater importance than an exact copy. My two universal patterns, as I call them, are the Pheasant Tail and the Gray Goose. The Pheasant Tail serves for the dark-colored nymphs and the Gray Goose for the lighter ones. The description of the materials and the method of tying can be seen in my book *Nymphs and the Trout*. Both artificials have proved to be effective throughout the season. Range in hook sizes can take care of the actual sizes of the naturals. Often when one fails to attract, the other is successful. But when no response to either is obtained I considered myself beaten.

Successful nymphing, however, is not just a matter of having artificials that have been proved effective. Good eyesight and a knowledge of where to expect fish in feeding places are two things necessary for nymphing in the clear chalk-stream waters. Although it is quite easy to see into the water, the trout can merge so well with the bottom and the vegetation growing from it that very close scrutiny is required. Again you have to remember that fish have good cause to be cautious and that there are times when they can see out from the water far better than you can see into it. Should they see you first and become alarmed, your chances to get one or another are gone. The rules on most of the chalk-stream fisheries state that only upstream nymphing is permitted. This means that only fish square across the river or upstream of you may be fished for. A second ruling is that only those you can see directly or judge to be of takable size by indications such as a rise form, bulge, or other displacement of the water should be cast to. Though fish can be caught by fishing nymphs downstream, it often means that fish much smaller than the size limit allowed are hooked and have to be returned.

Brown nymphing in shallow water—showing plainly.

Providing that you are cautious in moving along a bank and that you scan the water thoroughly, there is no great difficulty in locating a majority of the fish that are in feeding positions. It is movement that you look for. Perhaps this is no more than just the waving of the ventral fins or the even wagging of a tail. It may be a fish tilting upward to the top, or even breaking the surface. It could be a fish moving to right or to left to show a glint of light on a side, and it might be just a flash of white as jaws open and close on a luckless nymph just taken. There could be a kind of bulge in the surface, or a wave to one side or the other. In very shallow water you might see fish delving to the bottom with the tail and perhaps dorsal showing plainly above the surface. And, of course, there might be rise forms, for fish will often take nymphs as these are about to change to duns and when they are floating just beneath the surface film.

The important part is knowing precisely where to look. In this respect an angler who knows his river has a great advantage over a stranger. But if you remember that most fish take up feeding positions where they can expect their prey to be brought to them by the currents, you can locate these places before looking down into them. Most of these are quite easy to recognize since they carry the various flotsam. But take note of where these converge into narrow lanes or runs between weed beds or other obstructions, where the water perhaps sweeps around a bend on your side or the opposite one. Look well into these places first and then look a second time.

Seeing a fish and knowing it is on the feed is half the battle. The next part comes when you position yourself so that the artificial can be placed both accurately and delicately. You should try to avoid any possibility of line or leader casting a shadow across the lie of the fish. At the same time, try not to drop the nymph too close to where the fish is visible or where the distortion caused by its entry will make it difficult to see any movement the fish may make in taking. The ideal presentation should be about a couple of feet up-

Ideal presentation of nymph—a couple of feet upstream from trout.

stream, in line, or just to one side or the other of the head of the fish. There the nymph should sink and drift with the stream.

After making your delivery you will know roughly just where the nymph is drifting. It is time then to watch closely for a movement of the fish to show it has taken. This can occur in several different ways: perhaps just a move forward and a check, or maybe a slight turn to one side or the other; perhaps a lift in the water or a sudden swirl. But in every case, if you are really intent on watching the fish you will see the jaws open and close and the white flash that comes when this happens. At the same time, there will come a check in the drift of the floating leader and it will pull down into the water. This is the time to tighten and to tighten quickly.

Where a fish is not plainly visible, or is impossible to see at all, then the indication of a take can be registered by closely watching the floating leader. (A short part of the line and about two thirds of the leader should be treated lightly with a good floatant so that both can ride high and be plainly visible on the surface.) Delicacy and accuracy are required in placing the nymph, and then you should concentrate on the point where the leader goes beneath the surface. It is never possible to be quite sure initially, when fishing blindly, that it is a fish that causes the leader to check in its drift and draw down—this could be caused by a strand of weed or by the nymph's touching the bottom—but it is this movement you must observe. My advice is to tighten quickly should this check and draw occur, and not stop to think, Is it or is it not a fish? If it was indeed a fish, then a far more noticeable and decisive movement to the leader will be made. This usually occurs when the fish has discovered he has been deceived and shakes his head with mouth open to eject the artificial. Some fish might be hooked even at this late stage, but by far the greater number will have gotten rid of the nymph before you can lift the rod tip and tighten.

I would like to make it quite clear at this stage that fishing a nymph in the upstream manner is much the same as fishing a dry fly. Fish do not hook themselves, nor do you feel anything with the rod when they take. It is up to you to judge the precise moment to lift your rod tip to tighten and so bring about a connection. With the dry fly you see a rise form (and in many cases the neb of the fish as it takes) and can act accordingly. With the nymph there is nothing so definite. As I have said, when you can see a fish, all you need do is watch as its mouth opens, and tighten to hook just as it closes. But when the fish cannot be seen, the tightening should be done just as the check in the drift occurs and the leader draws.

Much also depends on the flow of water in which the quarry is positioned. Should this be fast, the take can be fast too. A quick take also means that there can be a quick discovery that the artificial is inedible, and so your reaction must keep pace. In slow-running water the take is far more leisurely and deliberate, and often you have plenty of time to be deliberate too. There is the slow move to intercept, an almost lazy opening and closing of the jaws, and then a moment or so as the fish resumes his feeding position. This same leisurely take occurs when fish cannot be seen and the need for speed in the hooking is not so essential. Even so, it is not wise to delay the strike once the leader has been seen to check and draw.

If artificial nymphs are constructed so that they can sink quickly, as mine are, most of the fish are deceived just by the sinking and the movement given to the artificial by the stream, but sometimes, in slow-running water, fish will disregard the nymph if it is just cast and allowed to drift. When this happens it is because the fish fail to see a movement of the nymph that is suggestive of life and therefore are not interested. It is a simple matter to impart movement by using the rod, and in recent years this technique has become known as the "induced take." The phrase "induced take" is one that was used by the late Oliver Kite, one of my pupils for several years, when he wrote his *Nymph Fishing in Practice*. The induced take is indeed an apt description and one likely to be remembered. The movement of the nymph by use of the rod attracts the eyes of a fish on the feed.

When fish are lying in feeding positions they see many things other than food animals floating by, and all these are disregarded. But should it happen that something like a nymph, floating inertly, suddenly starts to swim in one direction or another, then the eyes of the fish are immediately attracted to it and the thought must be registered that it is a living creature and therefore edible. Success with this technique is in knowing just the right moment to impart the lifelike movement. This is just as the artificial drifts close enough to a fish for the movement to come as a kind of surprise. But to do it properly

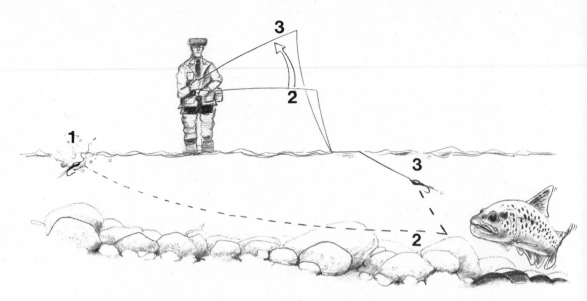

Induced-take method: (1) a weighted nymph is cast upstream and allowed to sink; (2) as the nymph approaches the feeding trout's position, the rod is held low and the slack taken up; (3) the rod is lifted just as the nymph gets to about a foot from the trout, causing the nymph to rise upward.

some preparation is required. First there is the delicate delivery far enough upstream for the nymph to sink down to the level of the feeding fish. Then comes a quick gathering of all slack line and leader with the rod held low, followed by an even lift of the rod tip just as the nymph enters into a radius of about 1 foot from where you can see, or think, the head of the fish is positioned. Where a fish is visible you can see his reaction, but if one is not visible, just watch where the lift of the rod tip has caused the leader to drag and create a V wake. Be ready to flick the rod tip smartly upward should the leader check or the V wake reverse. A word or two of extra advice, though: Do not lift quickly, but just enough to cause the wake of the leader to appear and to bring the rod into a comfortable position in the hand for quick hooking. If done at the right moment, a drag of about 1 foot or so is quite sufficient. Again you must remember that you have to hook the fish, for though an occasional one might hook himself, most sense or feel the drag on nymph and leader and quickly open the mouth to eject.

The lift to move the nymph should be just an even one and not a series of jerks as is sometimes practiced in sink-and-draw methods. The object is to try to make the nymph glide, as though swimming, and to keep a tight line all the while. To be able to control and move a nymph properly you must have sufficient leverage, and so it is a disadvantage to use a short rod. The trouble with short rods is that before you have been able to lift the tip high enough to impart, say, a 2-foot drag, there is no leverage left to use for tightening should a fish take. In fact, the rod passes that comfortable position in the hand when just a flick of the tip will set the hook. But again, if you have too long a rod then some of the speed so necessary in hooking is lost in the transmission of power from butt to tip, or so I find. The ideal length for a rod is from 8½ to 9 feet. The rod should be supple in action and have a fast but gentle tip. With this rod you should use a lightweight line and a leader tapered to a long and fine tippet.

The whole outfit should be of a delicate nature. There is seldom any need to cast a long distance, and nothing is gained by doing so. Even if a fish is deceived and takes, it is doubtful if your reaction can be quick enough to hook it beyond a distance of about 20 paces. Should a fish be hooked, chances are that the weight of the long line, plus the flexing of the rod, is too much for really fine tippets to withstand. Stalking to within easy and comfortable reach of, say, 15 to 20 yards is by far the best procedure to adopt when light tackle is used. This distance can give you all the advantages you require and also the greatest pleasure in your fishing.

A line that floats well is a must for nymphing and, as I have said, the lighter this can be for easy manipulation, the better. I much prefer the double-taper types, which run to a fine point. With double-taper lines the belly is then clear of the water with the weight actually at the rod tip. Only the light part and the leader have to be lifted for hooking, and speedy action results. The fineness and strength of the leader tippet should correspond closely with the size of nymph being used and of course with the size of the fish you expect to take. For instance, it is hopeless to expect to land really big trout where there are snags and weeds if you are using a tippet of, say, 1-pound test. But at the same time it is unwise to expect fish to take a very tiny nymph tied on to a thick, strong leader.

Today there are many fish in our chalk streams that are much larger than those in the days of Skues. At that time, and indeed during my own early life, very few big trout were introduced and one's fishing depended almost entirely on the wild-bred stock. Though 2-pounders were not uncommon, any over that weight were considered exceptions. The average could be said to be between 1 and 1½ pounds, but now numbers are introduced that are double, even triple, the weight of the average wild fish, especially rainbows, which during the past thirty years have been put into the majority of our classic waters. With these, and the large browns put in from stock ponds, an entirely different concept of nymph fishing has arisen, for these fish are much easier to deceive and in many cases will accept artificials readily that in the past would have scared a wild brownie. Perhaps in a way this is just as well, because though they will take the small nymph patterns eagerly they will also take patterns that are much larger and can be used on much stronger leader points.

Of course, these large fish are easier to see than their smaller wild brethren and for the most part, especially those being cast to for the first time since introduction, are not very difficult to deceive. Many have not been in the running stream long enough to have learned much about the varying insect life or about other creatures that may move in mid-water. And so they become easy prey. Often, too, fish that have been introduced have no real sense of self-preservation and consequently are not easily scared by approach or faulty presentation. As I have said, such fish can bring about an entirely wrong conception of nymph fishing, and there are many who say that nymphing is too easy. I agree that it is, but so also is dry-fly, wet-fly, or any other form of fishing where big stock fish are being introduced frequently.

For nymphing to either trout or grayling in our waters, there really is no need for a large number of artificials. Those I use and have described have served me well, and each is simple to construct. I have no desire to evolve or indeed to have others. The Pheasant Tail and the Gray Goose continue to be just as attractive now for trout as they were when I first made the patterns years ago, and the bug for grayling never fails. So I go nymphing with just the three types, knowing that with one or the other I have a good chance to catch fish if they are on the feed. Confidence in what you have to offer goes a long way to success, but, even more, you need to have confidence in your ability to make your artificial look and behave like a natural.

FOUR OF MY FAVORITE NYMPH PATTERNS

Though evolved originally for river fishing, the Pheasant Tail and the Gray Goose are also very effective in still waters. The Killer Bug was designed mostly for grayling but, together with the Bow-tie Buzzer it can be used with deadly effect in all ponds, lakes and reservoirs.

The Pheasant Tail

This pattern has been proved everywhere throughout the world and will, I feel sure, continue to hold pride of place as an effective artificial.

I feel the success of the pheasant tail is indeed due to the fact that it might well, in the different sizes, be mistaken by fish, for one or another of at least a dozen nymphs, of various genus and species.

Now as to the dressings. The materials used are quite easy for most, who are interested, to obtain. To represent the olives, etc., my pattern of the pheasant tail can be constructed on three different hook sizes, No. 00, No. 0 and No. 1, and I make no claim that the use of pheasant tail fibres for a body of nymphs, or flies, is original. But what I do claim is the manner of base building, ballasting, and the tying in of the pheasant-tail fibres, with fine copper wire, of a colouring to suit and tone in with the general dressing.

First grip the selected hook firmly in the vice and then give the hook an even covering from bend to eye with fine red-coloured copper wire. The wire we use is little thicker than a human hair and this one can obtain at little cost from various sources. It is used for the windings in small transformers, dynamos, or electric motors. After the hook has been covered and the wire locked so that it cannot spin around the hook shank, wind the wire in even turns to the point where the thorax of the nymph is to be constructed, and there build up a hump. Then wind the wire back to the hook bend and let it dangle. Wire is much easier to use than silk as it will not spin off or loosen if the tension is relaxed.

The wire with its red colour forms the base for the dressing and at the same time gives additional weight to the hook. I dispense entirely with the use of silk and use the fine wire to tie in the dressing. The wire is now dangling from the hook bend. Take four centre fibres of a browny-red cock pheasant tail feather. Hold the fibres by their tips and then tie them on with the wire so that the fine ends stand out about one eighth of an inch from the hook bend. They form the tails, or setae of the nymph. Then spin the four fibres of the pheasant tail on to the wire so that they are reinforced, and then lap fibres and wire evenly to the hook eye. Hold the wire firmly, separate the fibres from it and then wind the wire to the point behind which the thorax is to be made. Bend the fibres back and fasten for the first lap of the thorax, then forward to the eye of the hook again. Fasten here securely with half a dozen turns of wire and then cut away spare fibres.

Our finished effort should have a very pronounced thorax which suggests the bulging wing cases, and a body which tapers neatly to the tail. With the tail fibres spread, all is complete.

The Grey Goose

This pattern also is of simple construction and should be made in three different sizes as suggested for the P.T., No. 00, No. 0 and No. 1. I use fine copper wire in the construction of all my nymphs but use different colours according to the demand. For the base of this pattern The Grey Goose, I use a golden coloured wire and also this same colour for tying in the dressing. For the tails, and the body and thorax, I use herls from the wing feather of the ordinary farmyard grey goose. Only a few of the wing feathers are suitable and only the parts of these which have a lightish grey, green, yellowish appearance. The construction is somewhat similar to that of the pheasant tail. Take out four herls from the wing feather, tie these in so that the tips can form the setae for the nymph, and then dress in the same manner as with the P.T. At the butt end of the herls the colouring is darker, as with the pheasant tail fibres and this, lapped backwards and forwards, can bring about a well defined thorax and wing cases. As with the first artificial, the colour of the wire is one of the features. The gold shows through the dressing and is very marked, at the head end.

Both of these dressings change their general colouring when wet.

The Killer Bug

I now come to the dressing of what has come to be known as the Killer Bug. Once again this is of very simple construction, so simple indeed that anyone looking at it could be forgiven for thinking it could not possibly deceive a fish. These we construct in sizes varying according to the requirements, from sizes

No. 3, No. 4, 5 and 6 for lake and sea trout, to others on hooks of size 8 and 10 for use after salmon. Generally however it is the former, and smaller sizes, which are in greatest demand.

To make this bug, grip the hook firmly in the vice and then give the hook a double even covering of wire, colour of this not important but normally we now use red. This can be much heavier wire than used in the construction of the nymphs. When the double covering has been done leave the wire dangling at hook bend. Then start at the eye end of the hook and lap in securely a length of wool. The colour and the texture of this is important. I call it wool, but actually it is a mixture of wool and nylon, produced and carded for mending purposes. The manufacturers of this product give their name as Chadwicks and they list the colour as being 477. Actually it is a natural and not very easy to obtain. However, this is by the way. After locking in the end of the wool, give an even winding to the hook bend, back to the eye, and then once more to the hook bend, so that in fact the base is covered with a triple layer. Then, holding the wool tightly, use the wire to tie it in securely at the hook bend with about four turns. Then cut off both wool and wire neatly. The colour of this bug changes completely when it is wet and I feel sure it is this, that causes its attraction for so many kinds of fish. Though I have constructed these bugs with many other colours of wool, none have been so effective.

The Bow-tie Buzzer
I now come to the last of my creations and the manner of its tying. I use but

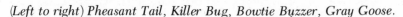

(*Left to right*) *Pheasant Tail, Killer Bug, Bowtie Buzzer, Gray Goose.*

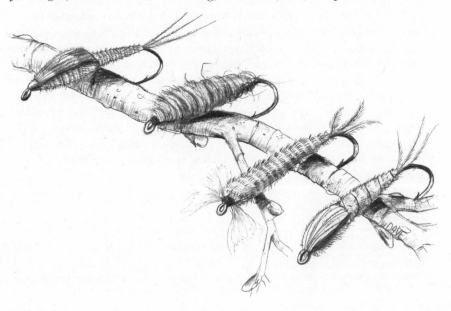

one hook size. This is size No. 3. Grip the hook firmly in the vice and then, using a fine gold coloured copper wire, spin on a single even layer along the hook from eye to bend and leave the wire dangling. Then tie in a strip of silver foil, or tinsel and spin this evenly on the hook up to just behind the eye. Fasten and cut the remainder free. Then select four or five fibres of red cock pheasant tail. Tie these in so that the fine ends can act as a short tail. Then wind fibres and wire together in neat spacings which show the foil in ribs, to the hook eye and there extra windings can be done to form the thorax. Fasten in securely with three or four turns of wire and the tying is complete. The red feather, gold wire and silver base all blend to give the right colouring and translucency. But this is only the first part. Though the actual nymph is constructed one of the main features is missing. This is the white fringe, or celia.

I tried incorporating this in dressings but without much success until I hit on the idea of making it entirely separate. I knew it to be important, very important, that some kind of movement could be simulated and so instead of tying in a white fringe at the head of my nymph, I arranged it so this could be carried on the end of the leader, or cast. It is very simple really. All one needs to do is to thread the nylon point through the eye of the hook, make a slip knot in it, and then attach a tiny piece of white nylon wool. This can then be cut down to the correct size with a pair of sharp scissors and if knot and nylon is quite secure, it cannot be pulled through the hook eye.

*Vernon S. "Pete" Hidy was born in Ohio, where he learned to fish excit-
ing meadow streams with worms and crawfish tails for bass, perch, catfish, and carp. After college he moved to Pennsylvania and learned to
fish for brown trout in the streams of the Pocono and Catskill mountains.
There he met his mentor, James E. Leisenring, as well as Reuben Cross
and Harry and Elsie Darbee, all remarkable flytiers who shared their
knowledge and skills with him.*

 *After World War II he and his wife, Elaine, moved to Oregon
because it is a big exciting country with fine streams for trout and steel-
head. There he became the founding president of the Flyfisher's Club of
Oregon and served as the editor of the* Creel, *the club's annual maga-
zine, for five years. He is the co-author with James E. Leisenring of* The
Art of Tying the Wet Fly and Fishing the Flymph *and the author of*
Sports Illustrated Fly Fishing *and* The Pleasures of Fly Fishing.
He also edited the fishing classic A Leaf from French Eddy *by Ben Hur
Lampman, a famous Oregon writer whose hobby was fishing.*

 *Pete Hidy has carried a camera on trout streams for many years; he
used the best of his photographs to illustrate* The Pleasures of Fly Fishing. *He is a member of the Flyfisher's Club of London, the Angler's Club
of New York, the Federation of Fly Fishermen, the Boise Valley Fly
Fishers, and an honorary life member of the Flyfisher's Club of Oregon.
When asked to comment on fly-fishing techniques, he has a standard answer: "Try to become a versatile fly-fisherman, try to please the trout,
and, above all, be kind to dry-fly purists."*

10
Soft-hackle Nymphs—the Flymphs

V. S. Hidy

SOFT-HACKLE NYMPHS, when they are fished and tied to represent hatching mayflies or caddis flies, offer anglers some delightful sport. The word *nymphs* is deceptive here because the hatching insects are no longer nymphs. A more accurate word is *flymphs*. Why a new word? Because these are all *hatching* insects. They are in the brief but dramatic stage of metamorphosis (a Greek word meaning "change of shape") when they are changing from wingless nymphs to flies with wings.

Both the tying and the fishing of flymphs call for some simple and rather obvious techniques. These techniques have been developed and perfected during the last century by some ingenious and skillful anglers, a list that includes T. E. Pritt and G. E. M. Skues of England and James E. Leisenring of Pennsylvania. Before describing their contributions, we should consider two popular and effective soft-hackle flies.

The Brown Hackle and the Gray Hackle have always been reliable general-purpose flies, and some may say they represent nymphs when fished wet down and across the stream. These flies can represent mayflies as well as beetles and other terrestrial insects that drop on or are blown on the water. Trout take them most often, however, as the leader swings downstream with the current and the fly rises to the surface *in the manner of a hatching insect*. Of course, when trout are feeding selectively they may ignore these flies.

To understand the rationale of flymph fishing, one must understand what is happening beneath the surface prior to and during a hatch—what changes are taking place in the insects and how the trout are responding.

Before the hatch begins to reach the surface, the insects have become active down among the grasses and moss beds. Hungry trout cruise there for nymphs and are alert to any movements or other signs of insects. When the

165

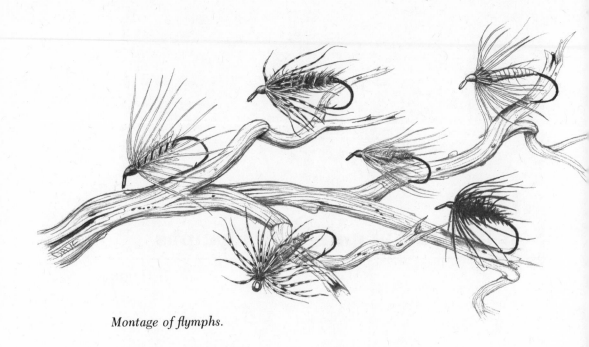

Montage of flymphs.

hatch begins, the more advanced, mature nymphs leave their cover and rise to the surface. The trout start to swirl for them, and this signals the beginning of a hatch. If the hatch is brief or limited by a scarcity of insects, the angler may find that all the desirable trout are feeding beneath the surface throughout the hatch. This means that those who are fishing only dry flies, or are waiting for the spinner fall after a hatch of mayflies, may hook few or no fish.

Some anglers are content to cast an ordinary, thorax-type nymph to these swirling trout, and they may catch some fish. Fine; they have an acceptable technique. The flymph fisherman, however, bases his strategy on our knowledge of the changing appearances of the insects during their brief but dramatic metamorphosis—as the trout sees them.

Here is what the trout sees: First, each hatching mayfly nymph and mature caddis pupa is shedding its nymphal shuck, and there is a thin film of air beneath the shuck that creates a subtle translucence. Second, the new, unfolding wings have a hydrofuge (water resistance) that creates a film or a small bubble of air.

Suggesting these hatching insects with the delicate film or bubble of air takes us beyond the conventional wisdom and into the world of mimicry. When properly tied, such flymphs mimic the film of air and/or the bubble of air that trout see during the insects' metamorphosis. After you catch a trout, or after the fly becomes soaked through by repeated casting, you should dry it thoroughly with a piece of Kleenex to restore its maximum appeal. Again, although trout will take a fly that is torn to bits, you have the option of tying on a fresh new flymph, as many of us do.

For the benefit of theorists and entomologists, we may now add mimicry

A flymph imitation of a hatching mayfly showing the film of air, or hydrofuge, along the body and the bubble of air in the hackle that simulates the water-resistant, unfolding wings explained in the text.

to the list of qualities many anglers believe can excite trout and determine the success of an artificial nymph: color, undercolor, natural-color harmony, translucence, texture, size, shape, proportions, delicacy, and vitality. That is theory. We all know, of course, that trout can be caught with only one or two of these characteristics, as shown by the nymph imitations of two English anglers, Stewart and Kite.

Over a century ago on the chalk streams of England, W. C. Stewart stressed action and behavior to create vitality. He tied his nymphlike flies by twirling the stem of a soft hackle with the tying silk and winding it around the front section of the hook. Trout were attracted to the lifelike movements of the hackle fibers and the rise of the fly and one or two dropper flies along the surface.

In recent years another English angler, Oliver Kite, developed and publicized his "induced-take" method with a hook dressed only with a dozen or so turns of fine copper wire to represent an insect's thorax. Kite based the design on his theory that "a trout will take the nymph, any nymph, if it is made to behave in the correct manner." When you read about Kite, however, you will find that in the dressings of his favorite patterns he clearly specifies the colors of the tying silks, body materials, and hackles.

Flies tied with soft hackles were probably used by the first fly-fisherman centuries ago. It has been during the last century, however, that the distinctions between soft-hackle wingless flies, soft-hackle nymphs, and soft-hackle flymphs have been made. In 1885, English angler T. E. Pritt wrote, "It is now conceded that a fly dressed hacklewise is generally to be preferred to a winged imitation. Trout undoubtedly take a hackled fly for the insect just ris-

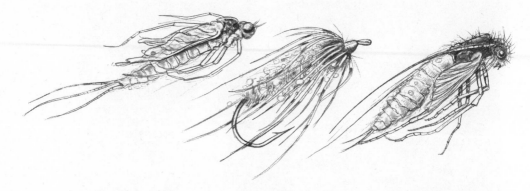

Artist's concept of mayfly and caddis-fly emerging stages with flymph imitation: (left to right) caddis pupa, flymph, mayfly emerger.

ing from the pupa in a half-drowned state; and the opening and closing of the fibers of the feathers give it an appearance of vitality, which even the most dexterous fly fisher will fail to impart to the winged imitation."

Starting in 1910, the legendary father of nymph fishing, G. E. M. Skues, wrote several brilliant books and gave his classic definition of a nymph long before many English anglers recognized nymph fishing as an important technique. Skues's definition clearly specified that all artificial nymphs must have a thorax representing the unopened wing case and a few very short fibers to represent the nymph's six legs. (Every angler should read Skues's books: *Minor Tactics of the Chalk Stream* [1910], *The Way of a Trout with a Fly* [1921], and *Nymph Fishing for Chalk Stream Trout* [1939]. He wrote others, but these are his classics.)

In America, meanwhile, from 1910 to 1940, Pennsylvania's James E. Leisenring had been reading Skues's books. And he, too, liked to experiment. For over thirty years he tested various techniques and types of flies on a variety of trout streams in our eastern and western states from April until October, before writing his book *The Art of Tying the Wet Fly* in 1941.

When the trout preferred, Leisenring would fish dry flies. He also tested and caught trout on Skues's thorax-type nymphs. Best of all, however, he liked to tease and deceive rainbows and brown trout by tying and fishing his soft-hackle flies to simulate hatching mayflies and caddis flies. His skills with this technique made him famous. The technique became known as "the Leisenring lift."

For this technique Leisenring used flies he tied with subtle, beautiful, tapered spun bodies, some ribbing, and two turns of soft hackle. He enjoyed studying insects and tying a specific pattern to match any mayfly or caddis fly. He used short-shanked hooks, sizes 12 to 16, for his caddis-fly imitations, and regular-length hooks, sizes 10 to 18, for his mayfly imitations.

Fishing a flymph requires nothing more than easy, accurate casts of 30 to 60 feet with the fly lighting in or just beyond the current, if there is a current. In moving water, mending your line can be important in achieving a natural, drag-free drift. At times in slow water, however, a small amount of drag is ac-

Accurate spot casts are necessary when trout are cruising or swirling for flymphs among patches of moss as shown here on a backwater slough adjoining Silver Creek.

ceptable because the hatching insects often move at angles in, out, or across the currents as they hatch.

Studying the behavior of trout can show you how trout feed prior to and during a hatch. With today's fine Polaroid glasses you can easily observe trout feeding on flymphs. In larger pools you can see several trout competing for a few hatching insects, often swirling savagely when the hatch is just beginning. By contrast, you may be able to observe what happens when a large trout establishes his territory in a desirable position, say, behind a rock where he can feed without competition on the insects arriving with the currents. When you find such a trout, observe how he times his leisurely rises. I have often seen them rising and swirling just beneath the surface at intervals of a few seconds. Naturally, I try to time my cast to fit into the trout's feeding rhythm. At such times, when the light is right and you can see the trout clearly, and when you are using a sharp hook, let the trout take the flymph and return to its feeding position. This is an exciting experience because a good rainbow will literally go wild when it feels the tug on its jaw while it is relaxing and waiting for the next insect.

Long easy casts with some mending of the line are recommended for fishing flymphs in main currents of larger pools such as this. If the trout are swirling for the hatching insects, cast your fly a few yards upstream from the largest swirl and let the current take it to the feeding fish.

Trout will take a flymph at times when you are not sure where your artificial is, for example, in a swirling eddy or even in quiet water at dusk when you cannot see clearly what is happening out there. You try, therefore, to see your line's direction and develop a sixth sense for where the fly is and where it is going. This can be exciting fishing after the sun goes down. The bigger trout move and feed more boldly, often taking a flymph with quick, twisting swirls that snap your tippet. As experienced anglers know, dusk is the time larger caddis flies hatch. Trout like to take them in or just below the surface film.

Leisenring developed and perfected his lift technique by trying to please trout swirling and feeding just beneath the surface or, quite often, by teasing and coaxing trout to feed during a lull. When he saw a good trout swirling, he would move to a position from which he could cast upstream and somewhat beyond the trout. Next he would give his line a tug to straighten the leader. Then, as the fly approached the fish, he would slowly raise the rod tip. Leisenring called this "making the fly become deadly" since it caused the soft-hackle fibers and the fibers of the fur or herl bodies to quiver and move as the fly approached the trout. It was rising to the surface and escaping at the same instant. The trout would often take it at once, sometimes later, after turning and following it for a closer view.

Few anglers could match Leisenring's empathy for the trout. His virtuosity and skill as a flytier and angler led him to try to *please* the trout. "You must tie your fly and fish your fly so the trout can *enjoy* and *appreciate* it," he would say to those who asked to inspect his fly book and inquired about his fishing tactics.

Successful flymph fishermen should keep in mind that trout prefer insects that are alive. Living insects have an iridescence of color and some undercolor that vanishes when they die. One should therefore select hackles and body materials according to their ability to make the artificial act and look alive.

Collecting, blending, and preparing materials will surely make you a more skillful and versatile angler. Durable tapered bodies are made from fur or blended dubbings spun between two pieces of silk thread as shown in the photograph. (E. H. "Polly" Rosborough's big twisted noodles are fine for large nymphs but too coarse for flymphs.) Desirable hackles are those from the necks of partridge and starling. Desirable hen hackles are honey dun, blue dun, brown badger, and grizzly.

The most desirable body materials for flymphs are furs of the muskrat, mole, artic fox and gray or red fox, and mohair, which is fur from the Angora goat. Above all these, however, are the four colors of fur from the head or the mask of the English hare. Trim the fur from a hare's mask with small scissors and divide it into four sections, face, cheeks, poll, and ears, as shown in the photograph. After you spin some bodies and tie some flymphs with material from a hare's mask, you will find it is very appealing to trout.

On some streams such as Idaho's Silver Creek, cloudy days, with or without scattered showers, may provide exciting flymph fishing because caddis flies often hatch then. On bright sunny days, caddis flies seldom hatch until dusk and some of the larger ones come out after dark. The bigger trout expect these and will take larger caddis imitations before dark.

The Clark spinning block simplifies the spinning of bodies. The spun bodies are easily stored on cards of light paperboard or similar heavy paper cut in pieces about 3½ by 5½ inches. These should be notched with twelve cuts on each side slightly less than ½ inch apart. Bodies should be spun on waxed thread; they will not unravel if left on the card a day or two.

Use only natural fur for bodies; fresh furs are more effective than old dry furs. Do not use synthetic body materials. In recent years fly-tying material dealers claim there is a shortage of furs. True. Muskrat, mole, beaver, and fox furs are hard to get and more expensive than in the past. As a result, they try

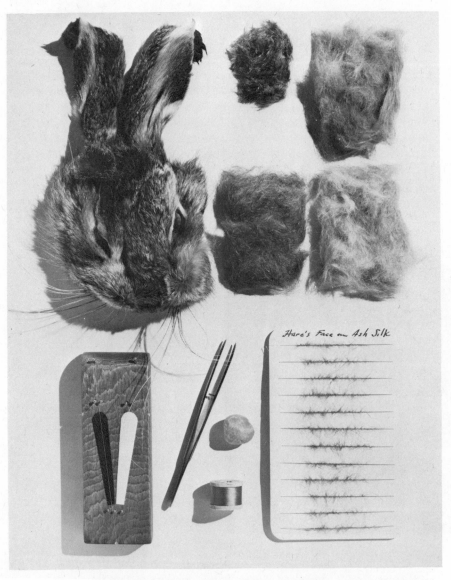

Basic material and tools: Hare's mask before trimming. The trimmed fur from a mask should be separated as shown in the piles of fur from another mask: clockwise from top: dark ear fur; poll from behind ears; light brownish fur from cheeks; medium brownish fur from face.

Tool on left is a spinning block for easy spinning of dark fur or light furs. Tweezers are used for placing fur on waxed thread. Lump of wax is shown above a spool of tying silk. Spun bodies are stored on notched cards shown here and described in text.

to sell you Orlon, nylon, and a variety of acrylics that are fine for dry flies, streamers, and steelhead flies but useless for flymphs. Natural furs have more desirable textures and more subtle, natural colors, and they have the water resistance that provides the hydrofuge mentioned earlier. Synthetics do not.

Flymphs may be tied on any hook, but some hooks are more effective than others. There are three hooks, all with turned-up eyes, that I use and recommend as ideal for flymphs. First, Mustad's 94842 TUE is fine for a light-wire hook. Next is a heavier-wire hook ideal for mayfly flymphs and available from E. Veniard Ltd., Thornton Heath, England. This hook, which I prefer for mayfly flymphs, has round wire (not flat like the first Mustad) with a slight limerick bend that is hardly noticeable. Finally, as an ideal hook for the shorter bodies of caddis flies, I suggest the hook Veniard calls its *wide-gape, up-eye trout hook*. It's a dandy! Veniard's also sells Pearsall's silk thread in desirable colors.

Up-eye hooks such as the above somehow look better in the water as they rise toward the surface. Also, the wire in the hook's eye is tapered for a desirable professional finish. Cheap hooks are worthless.

Now you know the materials, the strategy, and the rationale of flymph fishing. If you persevere in mastering this technique, you may become Leisenring's equal in the art of deceiving trout *up close*.

FOUR OF MY FAVORITE FLYMPH PATTERNS

Caddis:
Partridge and *Hare's Ear*
Sizes 14, 16; fur from hare's poll or face spun on ash silk; gold wire ribbing; one or two turns of partridge neck hackle slightly longer than hook.

Mayfly:
Honey Dun
Sizes 12, 14, 16; fur from hare's poll or face on ash silk; gold wire ribbing; two turns of honey dun hen hackle.

Blue Dun
Sizes 12, 14, 16; muskrat fur on primrose silk; olive-yellow thread ribbing; two turns of blue dun hen hackle.

Iron Blue Dun
Sizes 16 and 18; mole fur on crimson silk with two turns of silk showing before body is tied; no ribbing; two turns of starling neck hackle.

Charles "Chuck" Fothergill has been a flytier and fly-fisherman for thirty years. These avocations became his vocation in 1970, when he opened his retail store in Aspen, Colorado, specializing in fly-fishing, backpacking, and cross-country skiing. He's a licensed fishing outfitter and has taught fly-fishing and tying for many years.

Chuck's commitment to trout conservation is well known through his activities in Trout Unlimited, his daily contact with anglers from across the country, and his various articles in national periodicals.

His home is on a private ranch near Carbondale, Colorado, which boasts a fantastic population of large trout, at which several national fly-fishing schools have been conducted, and where he can be found experimenting with new fly patterns and techniques in his free time.

11
Advanced Nymphing Techniques

Chuck Fothergill

THERE ARE MANY WAYS to fish a nymph that are more productive, and more difficult, than the chuck-and-chance-it, across-and-down method used by most anglers. In this chapter I will touch on three different types of nymphing that have proved highly productive for me and that the average fisherman would do well to master.

THE OUTRIGGER TECHNIQUE

The "outrigger" technique is a nymph presentation to those fish located near the bottom of a river, that layer of water in which the larvae of insects spend most of their lives and where trout do most of their feeding.

A brief but definitive description of this nymphing technique might be the "upstream, dead-drift, tight-line, high-rod, weighted-nymph technique." I have used this method with success for many years but had never given it a name or heard it labeled by anyone else. Recently, angling professional Lefty Kreh mentioned that he was looking forward to coming to Colorado and joining me on the river to nymph-fish using the "outrigger" technique. This description made me wish I'd coined the term. (Photograph 1 gives you an immediate association between the technique and Lefty's terminology.)

The Tackle

I like a rod 8 to 9 feet in length, of medium action, with a relatively full flex, but neither overly weak nor overly strong in the butt section and not soft in the tip section. I want a rod with an even distribution of power from the butt to the tip-top. A rod too soft or too stiff in either section can cause intolerable problems when casting with abnormal amounts of weight on the fly and/or leader.

Trout feeding on bottom nymphs.

I like a double-taper line sized to match the rod, or even one size larger than matching.

My leaders average from 13 to 15 feet in length and are the knotted compound type with stiff nylon butt sections and limp nylon tippets.

My reels are all of the single-action type. Weighted flies and strip lead weights round out my equipment.

Outrigger technique: (a and b) rod, line, and leader held high as weighted nymph taps bottom; (c) lead strip shown tapping rock tops (x) and holding lead deep.

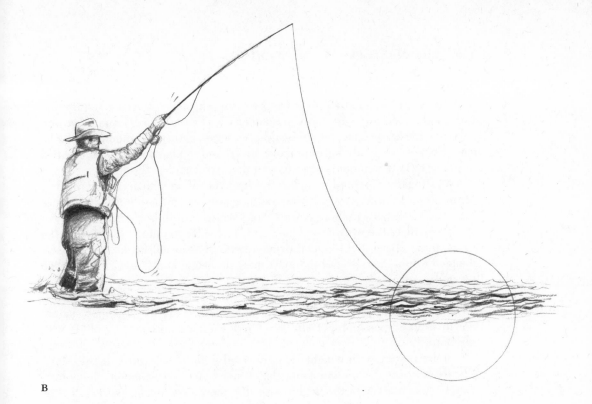

B

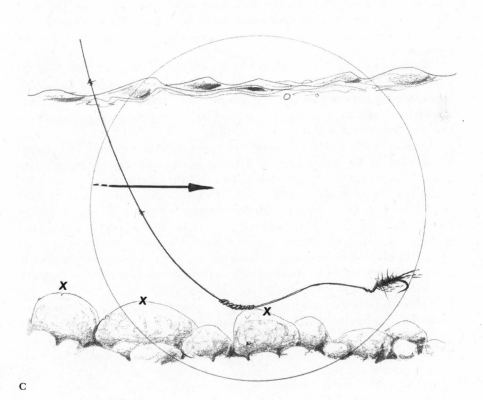

C

The Cast

The greatest drawback to outrigger nymph fishing is the care required to execute a satisfactory cast. Basic fundamentals of casting technique must prevail, but the crisp, graceful, free-and-easy false casts, so common to all who cast dry flies, suddenly become more forced and deliberate with the addition of minor to major amounts of weight to the leader and to the fly.

Casting the weighted nymph is less forgiving of error than casting the dry. More power is necessary to throw the increased weight and permit it to turn over before gravity pulls it down. More pause is required after the power stroke, to allow the weight, the line, and the leader to unfurl. If we make the usual quick, sharp, tight-looped dry-fly casts, disaster will strike and we'll be doomed to untying some of the most intricate "wind knots" ever experienced by anglers anywhere.

Casting with lead must be executed as smoothly as possible; no snaps, jerks, or bounces are permissible. The tight-looped dry-fly cast must surrender to a more open loop because the top of the loop must never collide with the bottom.

False casting with weights is performed with as few throws as possible. The fly must not dry out any more than is necessary, and it should sink immediately on contact with the water. Also, the more casts made, the greater the possibility of tangling the leader.

On most rivers, the outrigger technique requires no more than the standard up-and-across cast. Presentations are made anywhere from directly upstream to directly across stream, but the quartering upstream throw is most common.

Because this dead-drift method of nymph fishing requires that there be no line drag, the initial step toward preventing it is incorporated in the cast itself, executing what has been recently named the "reach cast." This cast alteration is made when the water between you and your fly target is moving faster than the flow into which your nymph will fall.

A straight-line cast would result in an immediate downstream belly in the line formed by the faster current. This would immediately cause the fly to drag, which would result in no takes. To avoid this, throw an upstream belly in the line before it lands on the water. This will allow at least a short dead drift of the fly before a downstream belly begins to form on the water. Here's how it's done: As your presentation cast is shooting through the guides toward its target, merely push your casting arm and rod tip as far upstream as possible and apply a slight upstream snap of the rod tip to form more completely an upstream curvature to the line. The section of the line midway between you and your fly will now have landed upstream of the fly itself.

All casts, whether reach, straight-line, quartered, directly upstream, or whatever, will be complete only when the line being held in the free hand is placed under the index finger of the casting hand. This index finger now becomes a control center throughout much of the drift of the line downstream because it holds the line firmly against the rod grip. This pressure on the line allows you to maintain the "tight-line" aspect of outrigger fishing (as well as most other types of fly-fishing).

The Drift

The difference between the moderately successful angler and the very successful angler utilizing this special technique of nymph fishing lies in the ability to allow the fly to reach fish in a natural manner. Following are the various manipulations an angler might go through to put himself in the category of the very successful angler.

The Depth of the Fly. Most of the time it is very important that the artificial nymph sink to the water depth at which the fish are feeding on natural nymphs. I demonstrated this principle while fishing with a friend on the Roaring Fork River in Colorado. With a favorite pattern tied to my tippet, and one strip of lead (approximately 3/32 inch wide and 1½ inches long when taken from the package) wound tight and flat around the leader 18 inches above the fly (see photograph 2), I made about a dozen drifts through a run I knew to hold fish but did not get a strike. I then fished the same water after adding another full strip to the leader about 6 inches above the first strip. Still no strikes. As I added the third lead strip to the leader, again 6 inches above the previous strip, I mentioned that this additional weight should put me very near the bottom and I could now expect some action. After two casts I set the hook into a small rainbow. I made another half-dozen casts and took a respectable brown.

My friend went through the same procedure—not as an experiment but to acclimate himself progressively to all the weight he had to cast. He had a

Lead stripping for weighting the leader.

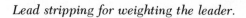

few leader tangles but was also rewarded by catching and releasing several fish during the course of the day. His experience has been repeated by many fishermen who were willing to overcome the awkward transition from casting only a dry fly to casting with considerable weight on their leaders.

There is an optional method of sinking the fly to a given depth at a given point in the stream, and that method is to throw a longer cast upstream. As the fly travels back down, it is progressively sinking deeper. Where a 30-foot cast might sink 3 feet at a given point with three weights, a 40-foot cast might sink to the same depth with only two weights. The option is there, but the longer cast may be more difficult to make and may "line" more fish upstream than you wish to alarm. Personally, I prefer to make shorter casts with more weight.

The outrigger technique is well suited to pocket fishing, where short casts over a multitude of varied current speeds is the order of the day. These pockets of holding and feeding water usually vary in size from that of a

Fly line showing leader butt above the water's surface.

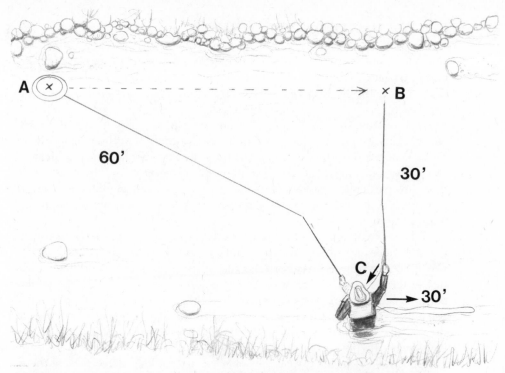

(A) *Cast 60 feet up and across presentation;* (B) *nymph drifts downstream 30 feet across from angler;* (C) *30 feet of line is stripped in to maintain tension.*

bathroom sink to that of an automobile, and their waters move much more slowly than the currents surrounding them. Accurate casts followed by instantaneous line control are musts.

Line Control

Stripping the Line. Previously I mentioned the necessity of placing the line under the index finger of the casting hand at the end of the presentation cast. This is essential when the current speed brings the line back to you faster than you can keep it taut with only a hand-twist retrieve. It's a simple thing to do and a must in maintaining line control. (The drawing shows that a 60-foot cast up and across a 40-foot-wide river results in the fly being only 30 feet away from you by the time it drifts back directly across from you near the opposite bank. This means that to maintain taut-line control throughout this drift you must strip in 30 feet of line.)

With the line under your finger, the strip is made with the free hand, grasping the line just below the index finger, pulling the line down to your side, and dropping the line onto the water. I personally don't like to "coil" the line in my free hand, as the coils seem to persist in tangling around each other.

Mending the Line. As the line is stripped to keep it taut, it is sometimes necessary to remove any belly formed by different current speeds. The usual situation is one in which the current between you and the fly is faster than that in which the fly itself is moving. A belly starts to form in the faster current, so that the fly is dragged out of its natural current lane into the faster current.

To remedy this condition, lift the rod tip and flip it upstream with enough force to pick the line from the water's surface and throw it upstream. There is now a short time span in which the fly can travel in a natural manner as the fast current again forms another downstream belly. In many rivers there are particularly fast sections that require constant mending throughout the entire drift of the fly. It may not be unusual to make five or six mends during one drift.

The downstream mend is not normally required as often as the upstream, but it is necessary where the fly's current lane is faster than the water between you and the fly. Rather than the fly being dragged swiftly and unnaturally downstream, the slower intermediate current causes the fly to slow down or actually stop in its fast current. Neither dragging nor stopping offers fish a drift pattern that they can accept as natural. To mend this condition, lift the rod tip, but this time throw the tip and line downstream to put the line belly below the fly.

Always bear in mind that your object is to maintain a free float of the fly while keeping complete control of the line. Stripping and mending go a long way toward achieving this control.

Rod Lift. Another tackle-handling procedure that can be used to maintain line control is to raise the rod as the fly is drifting back downstream. Drag is caused by water pushing on the line. If we reduce the amount of line on the water, drag is automatically reduced and a dead drift is encouraged. (Photograph 1 shows the procedure. Very little line is on the water to be affected by the current. When working short casts, have the line itself completely off the water and, if possible, even a short section of the leader butt also off the water.)

There are drawbacks to holding your rod in this elevated position. For one, your arm can become very tired! It happens to all of us, but the more we fish the more tolerant our muscles become. But the primary drawback occurs on windy days when line and leader are blown uncontrollably and we are forced to lower the rod tip to just above the water's surface. Drag under these conditions is seldom avoidable.

The Strike

When a trout takes a nymph, natural or artificial, he does so in a relaxed and unemotional manner. He sees the nymph, moves to head-on acceptance, and opens his mouth and then closes it. The fish doesn't charge the insect. Because the event is accomplished quietly and systematically, the strike to the artificial fly is extremely subtle and can easily go undetected unless the angler is ever watchful for the slightest change in the float speed of his line. It's necessary to remember that we don't see the fly, we don't see the fish, and we don't feel anything as the strike is made. The lack of a truly obvious response from the fish is what makes this method of fishing more difficult than others but, at the same time, more challenging and interesting.

It is absolutely necessary that the line float high if each hesitation is to be detected. I keep my line well dressed with a good silicone-based line dressing, and I also dress about 2 feet of the leader butt. The line must be of a very light color; mine are what the respective manufacturers refer to as either ivory or peach. The combination of high flotation and a light-color line that we watch through Polaroid glasses offers the maximum opportunity to observe what is taking place at the leader-line connection.

Make an imaginary short cast upstream, say 30 feet (12 feet of leader, 20 feet of line, and 8 feet of rod). Employ all the variables mentioned previously in casting and drifting, but don't forget that no matter what manipulations are gone through, one fact must be recognized and one action must be practiced faithfully: Since the strike response will probably be extremely short-lived, 100-percent dedication to watching the end of the line must be practiced as long as the fly is in the water. The hesitation in the line is subtle, sometimes indefinite, and of very short duration. If you glance away for any reason, you may miss a strike. If you wish to observe the natural beauty surrounding you, do so when the trout has no opportunity to take your nymph.

Assume that your cast was well executed and your line handling perfect. As you watch the leader-line junction, it stops. This is the object of all your efforts! Set the hook. The line is tight, the rod is downstream of the line so the striking effort need be only to snap your wrist backward. You expect an argument at the end of the lead, but it doesn't come. The line is tight, the rod tip high, but the fly seems inert. It is! You hooked a cottonwood branch wedged between two rocks. Disappointing? Yes. But you did the right thing. You had faith that the line pause was caused by a trout, and you reacted accordingly. Never, never assume you have hooked the bottom. Always assume that each line pause will result in a hooked fish and that each cast will bring a fish to play. This is the way to think all day long on the river—even when the catching is slow!

If a strike is perceived and the hook set, but no contact is made, allow the fly to continue its journey downstream. Many times I've had two strikes on the same drift. Often the second strike produced a fish, whereas the first may have been caused by a rock (but no one could ever convince me of that!).

One last hint: You might occasionally be able to hook a fish if, just prior to lifting the line from the water, you snap the rod back in a simulated striking motion. At times a trout will take the fly when the line starts to tighten downstream and it planes up toward the surface. Even though fish caught in this manner are not hooked as a direct response to outrigger nymphing, the technique does offer an occasional bonus fish.

The Pickup

When attempted with a lead-bedecked leader, fancy roll pickups and severely obvious change-of-direction casts will only create frustration, spawning the demon "wind knot." Lifting the line from the water at the end of the drift is a deliberate action made before starting the next series of false casts.

When a drift is complete and the line is tight in the current downstream, do not go into a backcast. This can be fatal—many times the line will be pulled directly into the rod, causing no small amount of havoc. As the first stroke of the false casting series, the line from this downstream position should be thrown upstream. It is the natural thing to do and requires very little change of direction prior to the next presentation.

To sum up: Be patient, be persevering, be persistent! Outrigger nymphing is not easy and can cause some initial frustration while the technique is being perfected. One fact is clear, however, and must be remembered: You are representing the underwater stage of life of an aquatic insect and fishing this representation in the level of the river in which the fish feed for most of their lives. The odds are with you, and you can't ask for more than that.

FISHING THE WEEDS

Trout often congregate in weedy areas to feast on the nymphs and crustaceans that live in, on, and among the vegetation there. The following technique describes how to fish a nymph in this type of cover.

Fifty feet from my back door is a small trout stream; 30 feet beyond the stream is a large pond. Both these waters are home to trout of up to 4 pounds. The water is private, seldom fished, and provides great challenge to nymph fishermen from midsummer through fall, owing to the great abundance of weeds.

The Tackle

Use a floating line to keep as much tackle as possible above the weeds. Use a *knotless* tapered leader, because knots have a way of reaching out and snaring every weed in the county.

Nymph tied with clear nylon loop weed guard.

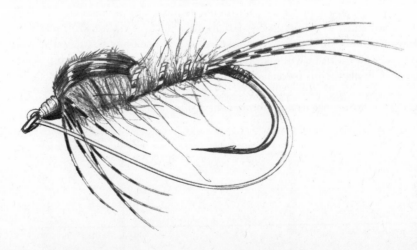

Nymph is lifted up off weeds in lake as trout approaches.

The flies used should be dressed with a monofilament weed guard tied in at the tail, curved downward around the hook bend, and finally tied in at the head of the fly. This little guard offers resistance to weeds and pushes them away from the point of the hook.

The leader tippet can be considerably larger than that used generally with a dry fly. Its visibility to the trout is lessened because it is under water, and its additional strength will help save fish and fly if a hooked fish dives into the weeds for safety.

Presentation

Lakes and Ponds. Fish inhabiting weedy still waters have life pretty much as they would ask for it. Insects and crustaceans usually abound and are easy prey. I've watched many a fish of gargantuan proportions swim lazily and methodically back and forth across a small area of water, casually picking off scuds, mayflies, and damselflies in the larval stage. I've watched trout tailing over weed beds as they've buried their heads in the weeds to dislodge nymphs. The trout's methodical procedure in consuming this food parallels the manner in which artificials should be presented.

Because most scuds, freshwater shrimps, and insect larvae in lakes live essentially "in" the weeds, the fly should be allowed to sink into the weeds after a cast is made. A weighted nymph is most helpful. When you sense that the fly is down among the weeds, strip the line or jiggle the rod tip just enough to move the fly 2 or 3 inches; then let it settle again to another resting position on the weeds. This subtle motion will give the fish the impression that a live insect is available, but the restrained tug on the fly will cause alarm. This process should be repeated until another cast is to be made, a fish strikes, or, heaven forbid, the hook gets caught in the weeds. In any event, the hook should be checked before each cast to assure that it's weed-free.

If one particular method isn't working, variations of retrieve are always in order. Maybe two tugs and a pause should be tried. Maybe one long and a short and then a pause. Experiment. Change the sizes and colors and configurations of the nymphs you use. The possibilities are innumerable!

Streams. When nymph-fishing a weedy stream, I prefer to cast the fly across and slightly downstream. This technique, though quite different from my normal upstream presentation, allows the smooth bend of the hook to go downstream ahead of the hook point—a distinct advantage when trying to avoid being hung up on the weeds.

As long as the fly is moving with the current, or you hold it back by not allowing the line to progress downstream, the possibility of snagging a weed is minimized. It's the upstream cast which permits the hook point to aim downstream that catches weeds instead of fish.

When weeds are of the long trailing variety, a direct downstream slack line is useful. The fly may be stopped dead in the current and allowed to sway gently with the motion of the long weeds. The resident rainbow may believe the fly is a real thing attached to the weed and move in to take it.

Striking and Playing

With your line extended essentially taut in front of you on a lake, or pulled tight downstream by the current, the strike to a fish should be made very gently. In both instances the fish nearly hooks himself. The last thing you want is for the fish to power-dive farther into the weeds. A strong strike reaction on your part will cause a strong dive reaction on the part of the fish.

After striking gently, raise the rod tip high overhead. You want the leader to pull the fish's head upward to as vertical a position as possible. The less chance the fish has to lower his head and seek sanctuary in the weeds, the greater the opportunity you have to land him. This procedure is not unlike playing a fish in most other less-complicated circumstances, but its importance over weeds is considerably magnified.

When a strong fish does tangle himself, your fly, and your leader in the weeds, the best approach is to allow the line to go completely slack. With no pressure against his jaw, the fish will frequently relax his defenses and swim out to open water, where you can again tighten the line and recommence the argument.

ERRATIC NYMPH ACTIONS

At times, trout are not inclined to rise or feed. The following different presentations will sometimes cause these reluctant fish to strike.

Although the main emphasis of the outrigger technique and my personal preference in fishing the nymph is centered around a dead-drifting fly, there are occasions when an angler will get more strikes by giving a nymph various degrees of motion. At these times, we no longer wish to imitate the helpless nymph awash in the current. We want instead either to represent the fast-swimming action of some natural nymphs or to attract the fish's attention by imparting an unnatural motion to the fly. The latter technique is not unlike fishing a lure with spinning tackle.

I can recall one instance in southern Colorado when all my dead-drift efforts were fruitless. After one cast, I allowed my line to drag below me in the current while I was digging into my vest for a match. My rod tip was bouncing around in the process and, as it did, I had a strike. I allowed my next cast to swing directly below me, where I jerked it erratically upstream. Success! I set the hook and was into the fish. The balance of the day proved unsuccessful during the drift itself but productive using an upstream jerk.

Effective erratic retrieves at a given time or place are often discovered by accident. There are no magical formulas that I know of, such as a given series of fast-short or slow-long tugs with specific pauses. If fish are not moving to natural presentations, experiment and use your imagination until a successful formula is achieved for that day, place, or type of nymph.

An example of a retrieve first discovered by imagination was an attempt to match the emergence of the giant *Pteronarcys* stone fly (commonly referred to as the willow fly and the salmon fly) on western rivers. This nymph crawls to the riverbank, climbs a branch of a nearby willow bush, and proceeds to transform into the adult stage of its life cycle. To imitate its journey from its regular, swift-water home to the riverbank, this is the procedure:

Using a sinking line, cast across-stream and allow the line to tighten below you. The planing action of the current will tend to lift the fly, so submerge your rod tip close to the river bottom directly downstream from where you are standing. Your fly will now be as close to the riverbed as you can get it. If you slowly move your rod tip toward the bank you will, to some degree, imitate the action of the natural larva crawling to the bank to emerge. Should there be fish in the shallow bank water below, your efforts can be rewarded!

Normally, traditional methods produce the best results, but don't shortchange yourself. Depart occasionally from standard procedure to investigate the potential of diversity.

FOUR OF MY FAVORITE NYMPH PATTERNS

Gold-ribbed Hare's Ear Nymph
If I had but one nymph pattern to fish with year-round, this would be it. It's easy to tie, but I would emphasize the following points of its construction:

(1) Avoid using the cream-colored underfur of the hare's mask; keep the body dark.

(2) Keep the rib subtle; I much prefer the gold wire to a wider tinsel.

(3) Make the body shaggy; pick out the hairs with a bodkin point if necessary.

(4) Be sure to use a tacky wax on the thread before dubbing the hare's hair and fur. The wax will help retain the hair on the thread to promote the shaggy appearance required.

Best sizes: 12 to 20
Hook: Mustad 9671
Thread: Brown
Tail: Brown partridge hackle
Rib: Gold wire
Weight: Lead wire
Underbody: Brown yarn
Body: Hare's hair and fur
Legs: Brown partridge hackle

Renegade

Although more of an attractor-type wet fly than a true nymph imitation, this pattern is extremely effective every month of the year. I like to keep the hackles relatively sparse, and always recommend that the body be reverse-ribbed for maximum durability.

Best sizes: 8 to 16
Hook: Mustad 9671
Thread: Black
Aft hackle: Brown
Rib: Gold wire
Weight: Lead wire
Underbody: Black yarn
Body: Peacock herl
Fore hackle: White

Muskrat

This simple pattern of brown and gray has proven itself for years on countless rivers and lakes. Its coloration and simplicity may be the reason for its productivity. The rib is subtle but provides sparkle and segmentation.

Best sizes: 12 to 18
Hook: Mustad 9671
Thread: Tan or gray
Tail: Brown hackle fibers
Weight: Lead wire
Body: Muskrat fur
Hackle: Brown

Hare's-ear Stone-Fly Nymph

As a general stone-fly imitation, this is my favorite. I like to bend the hook before tying to give the fly the appearance of the swimming nymph. The thorax is of lighter color than the abdomen, to represent the natural, and the yarn wing case provides much more durability than standard feather cases. The yarn can be marked with a permanent-ink marking pen for more natural appearance.

Gold-Ribbed Hare's Ear.

Renegade.

Best sizes: 4 to 8
Hook: Mustad 79580
Thread: Brown
Tail: Pheasant-tail fibers
Rib: Gold wire
Weight: Lead wire
Underbody: Brown yarn
Abdomen: Hare's hair and fur (dark)
Thorax: Tan mohair or Seal-Ex
Legs: Brown partridge hackle
Wing case: Brown yarn

Muskrat.

Hare's-Ear Stone Nymph.

S. A. Neff, Jr., lives in Sewickley, Pennsylvania. He is an angler, flytier, rod designer, photographer, lecturer, and collector of angling memorabilia. For over fifteen years he has seriously pursued rising trout, and his searches have taken him from the limestone-rich Henrys Fork in Idaho to the magnificent Gacka River in Yugoslavia. His angling presentations have been viewed in the eastern United States, Canada, Ireland, and the Soviet Union.

While living in Ireland, Sid Neff developed a keen awareness of the traditions in fly tying and appeared in many fishing films on Irish TV. Although his fly designs are contemporary, the materials are the traditional silk, fur, and feathers. His flies have been exhibited in shows at the Museum of Natural History and the National Art Museum of Sport, both in New York City, and he has flies in many private collections.

For five years Sid was art director of Trout magazine, published by Trout Unlimited. He has had photographs and articles in Trout, Trout & Salmon (England), Fly Fisherman, Pennsylvania Angler, and Americana Magazine. His collection of fishing tackle, gathered from many places and from many generations of anglers, spans a period of over 150 years, and will be represented in a new Time-Life series, The Encyclopedia of Collecting.

12
Mini-Nymphs

S. A. Neff, Jr.

MINI-NYMPHS ARE THE NYMPHS (or other underwater stages) of insects that, when mature, are miniature versions of all the classic insects. They are found in all four of the major orders of aquatic insects—Ephemeroptera, Trichoptera, Plecoptera, and Diptera. I would be hard pressed to name a clean trout stream that does not have a population of tiny insects. In fact, on many of our eastern streams the populations of the larger insects have been so depleted (owing to various forms of misuse) that the trout must depend upon the tiny insects for much of their food. Over the past five years, a much-deserved recognition has been given to many of the tiny-insect species. One can hardly pick up one of the serious fishing magazines without finding an article touting the virtues of fishing a tiny-insect hatch.

As the seasons in various trout states were extended, anglers have encountered insects in the summer and autumn months that were totally foreign to them. The best example of a "new summer insect discovery" is the *Trichorythodes*. It was found first in the Cumberland Valley of Pennsylvania, and as its reputation spread anglers began to "discover" it all over the country. Along with the tongue-twisting *Trichorythodes*, names like *Cloeon*, *Centroptilum*, and *Chimmara* have become almost as common as Hendrickson and Green Drake. Because of the diminutive size of these insects, many anglers have some difficulty in fishing imitations dressed on size 22 to 28 hooks. Those anglers who do fish the tiny-insect hatches usually fish flies that float on the surface and completely ignore an extremely important phase of the hatch—the emerging nymph. Granted it is much easier to fish a size 24 dun *on* the water than a size 24 nymph *under* the water, but I can think of many instances in the past fifteen years when the nymph saved the day. This chap-

193

ter will help the angler solve some of the problems encountered in fishing the nymphal stage of the tiny-insect hatches.

Through experience I have not found the chuck-and-chance-it style of fishing a tiny nymph too rewarding. Nor have I found the tiny nymph to be an effective tool on very large, rough freestone rivers. The insects (and their imitations) we will examine here are those found on limestone waters and gentleflowing freestone streams.

THE TINY INSECTS

Long, difficult-to-pronounce Latin names of insects tend to discourage many fishermen. Since this is not a chapter solely on aquatic entomology, I will not go into specific names and identification. Many of the tiny insects have no common name, however, so I will identify the genus whenever I think it is necessary along with a general description of the insect.

The limpid currents of alkaline rivers such as the Letort Spring Run, in Pennsylvania, present many challenges to the angler fishing with tiny nymphs.

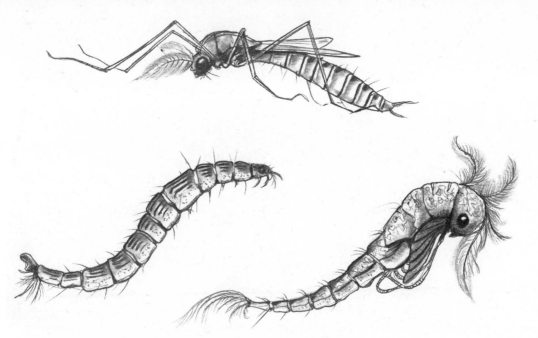

Three life stages of the chironomids: adult, larva, and pupa.

Chironomids

Chironomids closely resemble mosquitoes, except they lack a biting device. They are the most hardy of the trout-stream insects, having a much higher tolerance of contaminants and pollutants. I have seen good populations of chironomids providing food for the trout and rising fish for the fly-fisher in many streams where mayflies and caddis flies can no longer exist.

The chironomids have a four-stage cycle: egg, larva, pupa, and imago (adult); our interest here, of course, is in the larval and pupal stages. A tiny wormlike larva hatches from the egg and, depending on the species, either burrows into the mud or silt in the slow-moving sections of the river or attaches itself to a weed stalk near the bottom. The burrow dwellers leave their homes and migrate to the faster sections, where they form a cocoon and begin their pupal stage. In this stage their form changes drastically, from a long cylindrical worm to a pupa with a round, elongated abdomen and a thick thorax containing the legs and wings of the adult insect. Emanating from the head are featherlike plumes that will be used for gathering oxygen prior to emergence.

The larval worms range in size from 3 to 8 millimeters and in color from dull yellow to brown, along with shades of olive and gray. Some species that inhabit the slow-moving areas are red, hence the name bloodworm. Although the form changes with the different stages, the color does not change except in the case of the red larva, which becomes brown or very dark gray in the pupa. Upon emergence, the adults of all species remain the same color as the pupa.

Because of the chironomids' diminutive size and inaccessibility, trout rarely bother with them in the larval stage, except when the larvae migrate

Brown in typical position to feed on emerging surface-film midge pupa.

from the pools to the riffles. This migration is generally accomplished with the larvae drifting just under the surface and usually takes place in the early spring, when the water temperatures go into the high 40s and low 50s.

When I experience a rise to these migrating larvae, I usually pick out the biggest risers and offer them a larva fly fished in or just under the surface film on a dead drift. Because I have no way of knowing the exact color of the natural larvae, I begin with a gray fly and if it is refused I change to olive, to yellow, to brown, and finally to red.

Because of its availability, the emerging pupa is the most important stage to the angler. When the pupae escape from their cocoons, they swim up to the surface. For a few moments they hang perpendicularly in the film and take in air. Their feathery plumes are air-gathering devices. At the beginning of the emergence, the trout intercept the pupae swimming up from the bottom. When the hatch is in full swing, the trout swim just under the surface, feeding on the countless hanging pupae. As in the case of the migrating larvae, the rise to the emerging pupae is quiet and deliberate. Identifying the color of the emerging pupae is rather easy—capture the adult and match your pupal imitation to it. The color of the adult rarely varies much from that of the pupa.

Ephemeroptera

The next group we will examine is the order Ephemeroptera (mayflies). This group is comprised of at least twelve genera having species that fit into the category of mini-insects. The nymphs of these genera can be put into two basic groups: fast-swimmers (or agile darters) and crawlers.

The swimmers and darters have a long torpedolike abdomen, a rounded thorax, a somewhat humped wing case, and a small round head. Their slender legs, used only in climbing and grasping, are held against their sides as they dart about. In motion they look more like tiny fish than insects.

Swimmers and Darters. The swimming and darting group includes the genera *Baetis*, *Cloeon*, *Neocloeon*, *Centroptilum*, and *Paraleptophlebia*. Their colors range from olive (in the *Baetis*) to almost black (*Paraleptophlebia*). In size they vary from 3 to 6 millimeters. The crawler nymphs are short and flat, with broad legs that enable them to move about in the silt. Generally they are covered with fine hairs which collect silt. Unlike the agile swimmers, whose

Slow-flowing limestone rivers are ideal for fishing tiny nymphs. Ned Maguire, a noted Irish angler, casts to a nymphing trout on the River Suir.

speed is their defense, the crawlers must depend upon camouflage for protection against predators. Due to their bulkiness, crawlers swim with a labored wiggle rather than an agile dart. The genera in this group are *Ephemerella*, *Trichorythodes*, and *Caenis*. In color they range from mottled olive to almost black, and in size from 4 to 6 millimeters.

Unless the angler has considerable experience in entomology, it is difficult to make specific identifications of nymphs. However, this type of information is not absolutely necessary for successful nymphing. I do think the shape and general color of the artificial are important. If you are fishing to an emergence of olives with a short, fat nymph, your chances of success are greatly reduced. Over the years it has been my practice to carry a set of generic nymphs dressed in appropriate sizes, in all color ranges, and in appropriate shapes. When I am on strange water or when I encounter an emergence with which I am unfamiliar, I wade into one of the food flows and gather some of the naturals with a small mesh net. Since I don't kill fish or condone the use of a stomach pump, this is the only sure method of quickly identifying what the trout are eating. One can also gather nymphs from the weeds and stones in the shallow water, but immature nymphs of larger species are often collected and may make proper identification difficult.

As the season advances, the lighter-colored species appear, duns ranging from a medium-olive color to a very pale olive (with a bluish wing). These tiny duns appear from June through September. I've seen them rise from the rivers in the Catskills to the rivers in the Rockies. The nymphs vary in color from light olive to medium brownish-olive and in size from 3 to 5 millimeters.

In the East I have rarely seen the tiny pale duns in large enough quantities to be of much importance; however, on the weed-filled western spring creeks, and especially on Henrys Fork, they are responsible for some of the most exacting fishing of the season. They provide the angler with an opportunity to catch a very large trout on a very small nymph.

The duns of the *Cloeon, Neocloeon,* and *Centroptilum* appear in the summer months and are of the same size as the pale *Baetis.* They range in color from pale olive to dark amber, and the wings are shades of blue. The nymphs are pale olive to dark amber and are 3 to 5 millimeters long. These insects are more frequent in the West, although I have occasionally encountered good hatches in the East.

The last genus in our group of swimmers and darters is the *Paraleptophlebia.* The emergence of this genus coincides with the *Baetis* in late April and May in Pennsylvania and New York. On some waters it far outnumbers the olives. Although the duns are similar to the *Baetis* in size, they differ greatly in color, going from dark amber to dark brown. The coloration of the nymphs ranges from very dark amber to almost black.

Like the olives, the small red quills emerge in the first half of May. On some streams I have seen them almost daily from late morning until late afternoon. These tiny dark Ephemerids have provided some of my most memorable early-season angling on the freestone streams in north-central Pennsylvania.

The rise to the inert *Paraleptophlebia* nymphs is often mistaken for a rise to a dun, and the angler goes over to a dun imitation. This mistake can be costly, because for every dun a riser takes at this stage in the emergence, it is taking a dozen nymphs. In fact, I have found the risers, at times, to be far more interested in both the active and inert nymphs than in the duns, until the emergence is almost over.

Crawlers. In the group of crawling nymphs we have some of the most important summer insects for both the eastern and the western angler. Of the three genera mentioned earlier, the *Ephemerella* and *Trichorythodes* are the most familiar to the summer angler.

The *Ephemerella* genus is the most varied of all the Ephemerids, with both large and tiny members. The latter vary in color from the blue-wing pale wateries to the sulfurs to the blue-wing olives. This genus is distributed around the world.

In the East and Midwest there are three species that are important. Although similar in size they vary greatly in color. The best known is the sulfur, which appears from May until the end of September. While I've found the sulfur-colored blue-wing duns on both freestone and limestone waters, they prefer slow-moving limestone streams like the Au Sable in Michigan and the meandering meadow streams in the Cumberland Valley. As the season advances, this insect decreases in size from 6 to 4 millimeters. The coloration varies from dark mottled amber to mottled brown.

The other two species of crawling nymphs important to the eastern angler are the blue-wing olive and tiny red quill. Although I have found them on all types of water, they are far more prolific on freestone streams. They differ from the sulfurs in that their season is relatively short—usually throughout June.

Of the two, the blue-wing olive is more common than its darker red quill cousin. I consider it the most intriguing hatch on the Beaverkill. Like its European counterpart, it frustrates anglers season after season. I have watched many anglers make a common mistake when they encounter rising trout during a blue-wing olive emergence—they fish a fly that represents the dun. At least for the first half of the emergence the trout are interested not in the dun but in the emerging nymph. The emergence behavior of the *Ephemerella* nymph differ from other Ephemerid nymphs in that they emerge *before* they reach the surface. As I explained earlier, they swim in a wigglelike motion toward the surface. When they are about a foot from it the dun emerges and, protected by a bubble of air, swims quickly to the surface. This is the stage that confuses most fishermen. I have found an emerger nymph dressed with a soft fur wing or a soft spider to be very effective.

In the West, the species of tiny *Ephemerella* duns are pale yellow in color with a bluish wing. Because they emerge generally through the morning hours they are called the pale morning duns.

Of the last two genera in the crawling group, the *Trichorythodes* is far more important than the *Caenis*. It has been found during the summer months on most of the limestone streams and many of the slower-moving freestone rivers. The emergence generally takes place between seven and ten in the morning.

It has been my experience that the nymphal stage is not nearly as important as the dun or spinner stage. The large trout occasionally come up at the peak of the emergence and then go down and wait for the spinners to fall. At the peak of the spinner fall, they return to the surface. Despite this, I have found three instances where the nymph can be extremely effective: first, during a hatch, when a riser is located in a rise position and a fly fished on the surface would drag, a nymph under the surface will usually swim more naturally and therefore be more effective; second, on very small limestone streams before and during the first half of the hatch, I use a sinking nymph in the riffles or at the heads of the pools; and third, on lakes such as Mebgan, where

The shape of the artificial nymph should be similar to that of the natural nymph. Top, *crawling type, swimming type, fur-wing emerger type;* bottom, *tiny crawler type.*

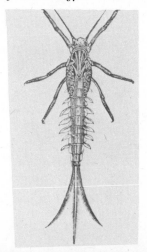

the trout are always cruising, the fish may swim past a dun or spinner imitation on the surface, but swim a nymph past them and they are yours. I've never seen a nymph work more effectively than it does on this type of water.

Caddis Flies

The multiplicity of caddis-fly species in North America almost rivals that of the chironomids. Identification of the caddis is not as easy as Ephemerids, nor do I consider it as necessary. Except where I fish to a specific emergence, I dress a series of generic representations.

The caddises have a complete cycle: egg, larva, pupa, and adult. Therefore, it is feasible to have representations of both underwater stages. As many readers well know, most genera of caddis flies are housed in cases in the underwater stages. Attempting to imitate and fish the cased caddis in small sizes is just not practical. It is wise, however, to have some larval imitations that are reminiscent of the worms in the cases. These worms range in color from dirty gray to yellow to orange to olive and bright green. I dress them on size 18 to 24 hooks.

Some species of caddis do not build cases in the larval stage. They are called free-ranging or free-living larvae and are darker in color than their housed cousins, usually brown and olive. The artificials should be dressed in the same sizes as the cased larva. Both free-rangers and case builders seal themselves off during pupation, but upon emergence the angler must deal with them to achieve consistent success.

During the pupal stage the insect is transformed from a cylindirical worm into a pupa with a well-defined abdomen and thorax; the hind legs extend to the end of the abdomen. When the pupa leaves the cocoon, it swims rapidly to the surface and breaks through the film, and the adult emerges and flies off.

In dressing representations of the larger species of caddis pupae, I faithfully represent all the parts (wing cases, hind legs, and so on). In the small sizes, however, I have never found this necessary. The important thing is to get the proper form and relationship of the abdomen and the thorax and, of course, the proper color range. The colors of the emerging pupae differ little from the larvae, and again I have a set of generic representations. While the

Top, *caddis larva;* middle, *caddis pupa;* bottom, *ovipositing adult female caddis.*

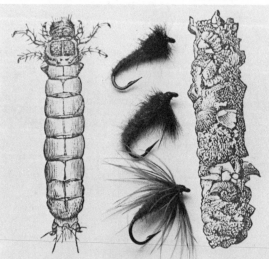

color of the abdomen may be yellow or even bright green, the thorax is in the brown range—going from medium to dark brown to olive brown. Six to eight generic representations of both stages should equip the angler for almost any caddis activity. The generic set I carry has proven successful not only on the streams in this country but also on the classic waters of western Europe and the less-well-known rivers of Yugoslavia. On numerous trips west, I have found some tiny-caddis activity on the spring creeks in the Yellowstone valley, on Henrys Fork, and on Silver Creek, but I have never seen these hatches approach the consistency of the tiny-mayfly hatches.

TACKLE

Now a word about tackle and its uses, since most of the casts are aimed at specific feeding trout. The characteristics of the rod used in this type of fishing are very important.

I use four cane rods: 6 feet 4 inches for small woodland streams; 6 feet 9 inches for eastern limestone streams; 7 feet for western spring creeks and when wading large limestone rivers; and 8 feet for large limestone rivers on windy days or where wading is out of the question. The first three rods fish a No. 4 double taper. The nylon used is extremely important when fishing with small flies. If the tippet is too short or too thick, the tiny flies will not swim correctly, but if the nylon is too light, the chance of hooking and landing a large trout is nil. The tippet should always be at least 30 inches and no heavier than .005 (6X). With flies smaller than size 20, it is absolutely necessary to use nylon of .004 (7X), and when the trout become superselective, especially on flat water, I go down to .003 (8X). The French are producing some excellent nylon under the names Nylorfi and Luxor GT. Both have a good breaking-strain-per-diameter ratio.

Many fishermen hold their rods almost straight up when playing a fish. This is a mistake with light tackle. The higher the rod is held, the higher the fish is in the water and therefore the more he can use the current to resist the angler. Lower the rod and the trout will go down. A fish near the bottom can be maneuvered much more easily than one in the surface current.

The longer a trout is played, the greater the risk of a mishap. Unless the hook is lodged in the bony part of the mouth, even tiny hooks can wear a hole and come out. Another danger is that the nylon will wear by rubbing against the edge of the trout's mouth. I have lost several fine fish when they simply wore the nylon until it broke. If I could have conquered them five minutes sooner, I would have pictures of them instead of memories.

FIFTEEN OF MY FAVORITE NYMPH PATTERNS

To sum up patterns, here are some of my most successful underwater representations:

Chironomid Larva

Hook:	Sizes 18 to 26
Nylon:	Prewaxed 6/0; match body material color
Body:	Dirty yellow, cream, and red: dyed swan herl and ribbed with matching nylon. Amber, brown, gray, and olive: natural and dyed European squirrel, Australian opossum, and muskrat
Head:	Match body material with nylon

Chironomid Pupa

Hook:	Sizes 18 to 26
Nylon:	Prewaxed 6/0; match body material color
Abdomen:	Dirty yellow and cream: dyed swan herl and ribbed with matching nylon. Amber, brown, gray, and olive: natural and dyed European squirrel, Australian opossum, and muskrat
Thorax:	Fine ostrich herl dyed to match abdomen colors
Head:	Very short; match body material with nylon

Swimming Nymphs

Dark Olive (Baetis)

Hook:	Sizes 18 to 22
Nylon:	Prewaxed 6/8; medium olive
Tails:	Three wood-duck fibers tied short
Abdomen:	Water rat (or muskrat mask) dyed in picric acid and spun very sparsely on nylon; two thirds the length of the fly
Thorax:	Same material wound on to form an egg shape
Wing case:	Hen blackbird secondary section (or secondary with similar color and texture). (For the emerger, omit the wing case and add a short tuft of fur from the base of a rabbit's ear.)
Legs:	Pick out a few guard hairs from sides of thorax
Head:	Medium-olive nylon

Light and Medium Olive (Baetis and Cloeon)

Hook:	Sizes 18 to 24
Nylon:	Prewaxed 6/0; light olive or primrose
Tails:	Three wood-duck fibers tied short
Abdomen:	Heron or goose dyed olive (in picric acid) and ribbed with nylon of matching color, or gray European squirrel dyed olive and spun very sparsely on nylon; two thirds the length of the fly
Thorax:	European squirrel dyed olive and wound on to form an egg shape
Wing case:	Hen-blackbird secondary section. (For the emerger, omit the wing case and add a short tuft of fur from the base of a rabbit's ear.)
Legs:	Pick out a few guard hairs from sides of thorax
Head:	Light-olive or primrose nylon

Pale Watery (Cloeon, Neocloeon, and Centroptilum)
Although the duns are pale-colored, the nymphs tend to be much darker. I have found them in the gray to olive-gray range. When you use the olive nylon the nymph will appear gray when wet and will go toward olive if bright-yellow nylon is used.

Hook:	Sizes 20 to 26
Nylon:	Prewaxed 6/0; olive or bright yellow
Tails:	Three wood-duck fibers tied short
Abdomen:	Natural European squirrel or water rat spun sparsely on nylon; two thirds the length of the fly
Thorax:	Same material wound on to form an egg shape
Wing case:	Starling primary section. (For the emerger, omit the wing case and add a short tuft of fur from the base of a rabbit's ear.)
Legs:	Pick out a few guard hairs from sides of thorax
Head:	Olive nylon

Amber (Centroptilum and Paraleptophlebia)

Hook:	Sizes 18 to 24
Nylon:	Prewaxed 6/0; amber or bright yellow
Tails:	Three wood-duck fibers tied short
Abdomen:	Beaver mask bleached in peroxide or natural amber Australian opossum spun sparsely on nylon, or herl from a cinnamon turkey primary and ribbed with amber nylon; two thirds the length of the fly
Thorax:	Same material wound on to form an egg shape
Wing case:	Woodcock secondary section (grayish-brown). (For the emerger, omit the wing case and add a short tuft of fur from the base of a rabbit's ear.)
Legs:	Pick out a few guard hairs from sides of thorax
Head:	Amber nylon

Dark Red Quill (Paraleptophlebia)

Hook:	Sizes 18 to 20
Nylon:	Prewaxed 6/0; claret
Tails:	Three wood-duck fibers tied short
Abdomen:	Equal parts of brown Australian opossum, claret beaver, and black rabbit (or beaver) spun sparsely on nylon; two thirds the length of the fly
Thorax:	Same material wound on to form an egg shape
Wing case:	Black bantam hen secondary section. (For the emerger, omit the wing case and add a short tuft of very dark gray rabbit's fur.)
Legs:	Pick out a few guard hairs from sides of thorax
Head:	Claret nylon

Ovipositing Spinner (Baetis)

Hook:	Sizes 18 to 22

Nylon:	Prewaxed 6/0; dark tan (or pale orange)
Tails:	Three natural blue dun cock hackle fibers tied short
Abdomen:	Amber beaver (bleached) and red squirrel in equal parts, spun sparsely on nylon
Thorax:	Same material wound on to form a hump
Hackle:	Natural blue dun hen wound on spider fashion
Head:	Dark-tan nylon

Crawling Nymphs

Blue-wing Olive and Pale Morning Dun (Ephemerella)

Hook:	Sizes 18 to 22
Nylon:	Prewaxed 6/0; olive
Tails:	Three wood-duck fibers tied short
Abdomen:	European squirrel dyed olive (in picric acid) and wound on much heavier than the swimming nymphs; guard hairs should be picked out to simulate gills; abdomen and thorax are of equal length
Thorax:	Same material wound on to form an elongated egg shape
Wing case:	Hen blackbird secondary section
Legs:	Pick out a few guard hairs from sides of thorax
Head:	Olive nylon

Blue-wing Olive (Ephemerella)

Hook:	Size 18 to 22
Nylon:	Prewaxed 6/0; medium brown or dark orange
Tails:	Three wood-duck fibers tied short
Abdomen:	Brown Australian opossum and European squirrel dyed red-brown, equal parts; guard hairs should be picked out to simulate gills; abdomen and thorax are of equal length
Thorax:	Same material wound on to form an elongated egg shape
Wing case:	Dark woodcock or hen pheasant secondary section
Legs:	Pick out a few guard hairs from sides of thorax
Head:	Medium-brown nylon

Blue-wing Olive (Ephemerella)

Hook:	Sizes 18 to 22
Nylon:	Prewaxed 6/0; dark brown
Tails:	Three black hen hackle fibers tied short
Abdomen:	European red squirrel and mole mixed in equal parts to a rich dark gray; guard hairs should be picked out to simulate gills; abdomen and thorax are of equal length
Thorax:	Same material wound on to form an elongated egg shape
Wing case:	Black bantam hen secondary section. (For the emerger, omit the wing case and add a short tuft of fur from the base of a rabbit's ear.)
Legs:	Pick out a few guard hairs from sides of thorax
Head:	Dark-brown nylon

Little Morning Dun (Trichorythodes)

Hook:	Sizes 20 to 24
Nylon:	Prewaxed 6/0; medium brown
Tails:	Three wood-duck fibers tied short
Abdomen:	European squirrel dyed a rich brown; guard hairs should be picked out to simulate gills; abdomen and thorax are of equal length
Thorax:	Same material wound on to form an elongated egg shape
Wing case:	Dark woodcock or hen pheasant secondary section
Legs:	Pick out a few guard hairs from sides of thorax
Head:	Medium-brown nylon

Emerging Blue-wing Olive Dun (Ephemerella)

Hook:	Sizes 18 and 20
Nylon:	Prewaxed 6/0; light olive
Tails:	Three natural blue dun hen hackle fibers tied short
Abdomen:	European gray squirrel dyed bright olive (in picric acid)
Thorax:	Same material wound on to form a hump
Hackle:	Medium- or dark-blue dun hen hackle wound on spider fashion
Head:	Light-olive nylon

Caddis Larva

Hook:	Sizes 18 to 24
Nylon:	Prewaxed 6/0; match body material color
Body:	White, yellow, and bright green: natural and dyed swan herl and ribbed with matching nylon. Brown, amber, and olive: natural Australian opossum, bleached beaver mask, and European gray squirrel dyed in picric acid
Head:	Dark-brown nylon

Caddis Pupa

Hook:	Sizes 18 to 24
Nylon:	Prewaxed 6/0; match body material color
Abdomen:	Cream, yellow, and bright green: dyed swan herl and ribbed with matching nylon. Brown, amber, dark gray, and olive: natural Australian opossum, bleached beaver mask, mole, European squirrel dyed in picric acid; abdomen should be thick and two thirds the length of the fly
Thorax:	Usually of a dark contrasting color: brown, dark olive, or dark gray; red squirrel, European gray squirrel darkened in picric acid, and mole, wound to the same thickness as the abdomen
Wing case:	Short tuft of fur from the base of a rabbit's ear tied in on the underside of the fly and extending slightly beyond the abdomen
Legs:	Optional (two fibers from a dark breast feather of a hen pheasant)
Head:	Nylon to match body-material color

*Charles E. Brooks was born in Venice, Illinois, and spent his boyhood
and early teens in the Missouri Ozarks, near the Current River. He became a flytier at the age of nine and a fly-fisherman at ten. After serving
as a bombardier in the Air Corps during World War II, he spent one
season as ranger in Yosemite National Park and reenlisted, retiring as a
major in 1964. Since then he has researched and fished the trout streams
in the West Yellowstone area, where he and his wife live, and has fished
widely over the Midwest, Far West, Alaska, and the Rocky Mountains.*

His three books on trout fishing, Larger Trout for the Western Fly
Fisherman *(1970),* The Trout and the Stream *(1974), and* Nymph Fishing for Larger Trout *(1976) are all oriented toward larger trout and
emphasize the use of the underwater fly.*

13
The Maxi-Nymphs

Charles E. Brooks

MANY ANGLERS REFUSE TO BELIEVE that the huge size 4, 4XL nymphal imitations I use have any counterpart in nature, yet big stone-fly nymphs do exist by the tens of millions in the streams I fish, and their huge imitations are day-in, day-out the most effective takers of big trout when fished properly.

In the Madison River, some few miles from my door, there is a 70-mile-long uninterrupted stretch in which the real giant stone-fly nymphs exist in such numbers that they outweigh the total of *all* other nymphal-larval forms. These naturals also have a four-year underwater life span and are thus available as food for trout all year, any year, in sizes and quantities that dwarf any other species. The angler who chooses to fish the smaller caddis and mayfly imitations in waters of this type is dealing himself a weak hand and facing long odds.

The actual nymph in question is *Pteronarcys californica*, the underwater form of the so-called salmon fly of the Rocky Mountain West. These flies are also known as trout flies, mountain flies, red flies, river flies, and willow flies. The nymph is named after the willow fly, that is, willow-fly nymph, but is sometimes also called a hellgrammite. This latter name confuses them with the larva of the dobsonfly (*Corydalis cornutus*), a midwestern to eastern species, totally unrelated.

Willow-fly nymphs exist in fast rocky streams throughout the Rocky Mountain West and Northwest, and Ernie Schwiebert makes the flat statement that in these rivers they are the most numerous nymphal form. Therefore they are of the utmost importance to the fish and the fisherman, and he who ignores their use is also ignoring their importance.

In lesser numbers, large stone-fly nymphs are also found in the proper

water types in the upper Midwest and in some faster, rocky eastern streams such as the Delaware. They are the most important nymphs in any waters where they exist.

In fishing any imitation, it behooves the fisherman to know something more than just what the natural looks like. Since both nymph and fish are usually invisible to the angler, knowledge of their habits and habitat is important, as is the ability to recognize fish-holding water.

When speaking of the big stone-fly nymphs, Richard Muttkowski in *The Ecology of Trout Streams in Yellowstone Park* says that "generally trout and stoneflies are intimately associated. Where one is found, the other will be also." In most areas, big stone-fly nymphs are found in fast, rocky water. These large creatures *must* have crevices between rocks as hiding places, and they must have fast, well-oxygenated water. Thus they will be found in riffles, runs, rapids, and cascades with gravel-rubble to rubble-boulder bottoms.

Trout will be found in these areas too, but the size of the trout you find is directly related to the depth of the water and the size of the boulders protruding above the surrounding bottom. For trout of 1 pound or more, look for water over 30 inches deep and rocks more than 1 foot in diameter rising above the general bottom level.

If the water is moving very quickly—4 to 8 miles per hour (6 to 12 feet per second)—you will probably be unable to see the boulders because the bubbles in the water cause refraction. But you can tell where they are by looking for what Dan Bailey calls "standing waves," waves that break continually in the same place. Your rock will be some little distance upstream of the wave. Normally, there will be many such standing waves in a particular run or rapid, and thus one fishes the water rather than to a particular spot.

Nymphs living in this fast water are crawlers and clingers, so the method of fishing is on the bottom, dead drift, simulating an insect that has lost its grip and been swept away by the current. You cast upstream in order to get the nymph down quickly, but you actually fish the nymph after it is across and drifting down, and you fish to the end of the drift and let it hang a few seconds on a tight line in order to allow the nymph to come as high in the water as it will. This serves two purposes: It will give a following fish more time to take, and it will make it easier to lift line and leader from the water for the next cast.

Hewitt's stern but indisputable dictum that one must fish the right nymph in the right place with the right motion, and that success is proportional to the manner in which these requirements are met, is as valid here as in any method. Dead drift is the right motion because even if these nymphs could swim, as some proponents claim, no nymph alive can swim in currents of 4 to 8 miles per hour, the kind of currents in which these giant stone-fly nymphs will be found.

So two things must be done: You must get your nymph to the bottom, and you must fish it dead drift but with control. Get it to the bottom quickly so that you will be able to *fish* more of the drift. This means an upstream cast, a fast-sinking or Hi-D line, a short leader, and a weighted nymph. Some people believe you can accomplish the same thing with a floating line by using lead on the leader. This is even more of an atrocity than casting the sinking-line combination, and those who have tried to demonstrate this method to me in stone-fly water have been forced to admit that it just won't work.

Therefore, the proper tools are the above-mentioned type of sinking line, size 7 or 8, a rod of 8 to 9 feet, a leader of 4 to 6 feet, tippet size .010 or .012 inches, and a heavily weighted nymph. Let's examine the reasons for each of these pieces of equipment.

Montana Stone Nymph and natural (Pteronarcys californica).

Giant stone-fly nymph and imitations: (left to right) Charles Brooks Stone-Fly Nymph design; giant Pteronarcys californica *nymph; standard Stone-Fly Nymph design.*

A fast-sinking or 7 or 8 Hi-D line gets the fly down quickly, more quickly than, say, a 5 or 6 would. The answer here is weight, the larger numbered lines going down faster. A 9, 10, or 11 line would go down still faster, and if you can handle such a brute of an outfit, do so. A longer rod allows easier control of your nymph by letting you hold more line off the water and by enabling you to manage slack line better. A 10- or even 12-foot rod would be better still, and again, if you can handle it, do it.

The short leader is to keep it and the nymph from being floated up off the bottom by updwellings that always exist in powerful currents over rough bottoms. The tippet size is to keep from breaking the fish off on the powerful strike needed to set the hook against the curve that will always be in the line no matter how much skill and experience the angler has. This curve is caused by the fact that the weighted fly is moving in the much-slower friction layer at the bottom, while the line is cutting to the surface through very fast currents.

The curve will be from 4 to 8 feet, fly to apex of bow, varying directly with the current speed. In order to set the hook, you must strike with great quickness and power so as to overcome the resistance of the water to the line and move the fly the ½ inch needed to set the hook. In effect, the line is around a movable pulley—a slow pull will cause the pulley to move, but not the fly. Because of inertia, a strong, fast, heavy pull causes the fly and not the pulley to move. So you need a heavy leader because the powerful jerk that must be used would break a finer leader if the fish were broadside in the current or moving upstream, and such is almost always the case.

The correct fishing method is to first locate a piece of deep, fast, rocky-bottomed stream with a choppy surface in which both stone flies and trout are known to dwell. Position yourself *solidly* at or just above the upper end of the stretch and commence by casting a short line up and a little across. Make several casts of this length before lengthening line. Thorough coverage of the *bottom* is the aim. Keep repeating each series of casts until you cannot cast farther or until your casts are reaching all the fishable water. Then move downstream 20 feet or so to a new casting position and repeat the pattern.

Line control is attained by raising and lowering the rod, not by retrieving slack. As the fly sinks and comes downstream, it will come closer at a point just opposite you and then will begin getting farther away as the current carries it downstream. To control the line, raise the rod tip so as to keep a slight droop in the visible line, and move the rod at the same speed and direction in which the fly is moving. If you straighten the visible part of the line, you have lifted the fly off the bottom and spoiled the drift. If the droop is too great, you won't feel the strike. As the fly comes opposite, you should have the rod tip at its highest, then lower it as the fly moves away downstream, always striving to keep just a slight droop in the visible part of the line.

If you miss many strikes, and you will, don't lose heart. Begin to strike harder and faster, jerking the rod upstream and pulling strongly and swiftly with the line hand. When you become proficient in this method, you will still fail to hook two out of three, unless it is one of those exceptional days when you can do no wrong. And the more you fish this method in the proper waters, the more exceptional days you will have; in general, your trout will be larger than the stream average, and some will be very fine indeed.

Another of the large nymph imitations I fish is actually a representation of a larva, that of the riffle beetle. There are many genera of these insects in the United States and they are found in trout streams everywhere, but anglers know little or nothing about them.

In spite of the name "riffle beetle," they inhabit many kinds of water and are often found in deep pools with sand or sand-silt bottoms or around weed beds. They are viciously carnivorous.

Riffle-beetle larvae live in the water for two years before pupating into the adult beetle and are taken eagerly in the larval stage by trout. They have two habits that can be imitated profitably by the angler. In smooth waters—pools, eddies, glides, and flats or the tail of broads—they drift along just under the surface, looking for prey. The proper method here is a dry-fly-like drift, using a floating line, with a quick twitch every ten seconds or so to simulate the action of a tiger pouncing on its prey. This method can be used in any smooth-surfaced stretch, especially around weed beds. The leader must be greased and the nymph tied unweighted on a fine-wire hook.

Riffle-beetle larvae vary in size not only between species but in different growth periods, and you should have the fly in sizes from 8, 3XL to 4, 4XL for both this and the following method.

The second method requires a weighted nymph that sinks rapidly. It is fished along the bottom, dead-drift in slow waters with a smooth surface and with a crawling hand-retrieve along the bottom of somewhat faster waters. A sink-tip line works well with this method most of the time.

Some anglers are surprised to learn that the big size 4, 4XL pattern will work in the smoothest of waters for the most sophisticated of fish. This past fall, two friends of mine took a young inexperienced angler to fish on one of our fine western spring creeks. The regular methods of fishing small to tiny dries or small nymphs in the surface film did not work, and several hours of casting produced nothing.

Meanwhile, the younger fellow had gone upstream looking for greener pastures. In the early afternoon he returned, saying that he had solved the problem and he could catch any fish in the stream that he could see. One of the men promptly pointed out an 18-inch trout lying on the smooth bottom a few yards away and invited the youngster to catch it.

The neophyte chunked out a size 4, 4XL Riffle Devil, heavily weighted, a few feet upstream of the trout. The current rolled the fly down along the bottom and past the fish, which whirled, leaped upon it savagely and was hooked and landed. Then the young fellow made good his boast by hooking every fish pointed out to him the rest of the afternoon.

I have had the same experience with this fly fished in the same method in nearby Duck Creek and have also had excellent success with fish of 2 or more pounds using my Assam Dragon Nymph in the same manner.

This latter nymph is an impressionistic version of a dragonfly nymph, and I use it in two colors, a light tan and a dark brown, to simulate two color variations of the same species. Dragonfly nymphs are entirely carnivorous and will always be found where other aquatic insects are found except in rough-bottomed fast water. They can survive very well in such waters, being powerful swimmers, but crevices among the rocks offer too many secure hiding places for their prey. Therefore, look for them in all smooth-bottomed waters, especially in pools, ponds, and lakes. They crawl and they swim, or sometimes clamber among weeds, but except when doing the latter they are always along the bottom, and that is the place to fish the artificial.

It doesn't matter how one gets the nymph to the bottom, but I prefer a Hi-D line and weighted nymph in order to get it down quickly, in both lakes and streams, so I have more fishing time and less waiting time. Once it's on the bottom, fish it with a hand-twist retrieve and a 6-inch twitch every few seconds. The latter movement simulates the nymph pouncing on its prey and will often provoke a reluctant fish into striking. Always fish the cast out completely.

The Assam Dragon is one of the best nymphs to use in lakes, and many friends report that they take their largest trout using this nymph in the manner described above. The brown or tan versions imitate several species of dragonfly nymphs. Others of this order are almost always some shade of green. These are usually found in and around weed beds, although the tan or brown nymphs will also be found in weedy areas. Over the years, I've not encountered many smooth-bottomed, smooth-surfaced waters where the tan or brown colors would not serve.

The large mayfly nymphs of *Hexagenia* and *Ephemera* are the largest of their kind in the United States. The so-called Michigan caddis is in reality a mayfly, *Hexagenia limbata*, and the nymph is sometimes tied on a size 2 hook, although that's much too large. A size 6, 3XL or 8, 2XL will do nicely most of the time.

These nymphs are found in areas of slower water with fine-gravel, silt, or sand-silt bottoms. They are burrowers, tunneling into the soil and passing it through to extract food in the manner of an earthworm. They are rarely found out of their burrows on bright days, but on dark days, after sunset, or before sunrise they come out and move around on the bottom, and these are the times to fish them. The artificials are especially useful on cloudy, rainy days.

They are slow movers and crawl slowly or swim just above the bottom, and the artificial should be hand-retrieved not faster than ten completed hand twists per minute, either on the bottom or just above it. Any tackle and casting method that allows this type of handling is all right to use.

With these big mayfly nymphs and the dragonfly nymphs mentioned earlier, it doesn't matter whether you cast up, down, or across as long as you can exert perfect control over the fly and keep it on or near the bottom, moving slowly. Both the mayfly nymphs just mentioned and the dragonfly nymphs mentioned earlier have a two-year underwater life.

Siphlonurus, another large mayfly nymph, dwells in similar waters but nearly always in or around weed beds. Basically it is a climber and crawler, but it also swims slowly between fronds and in channels along and spaces between weed beds. Once again, any tackle that will allow handling the nymph as described above is satisfactory.

Since *Siphlonurus* crawls, swims, and clambers it can be given more types of action than the other two, but every action must be slow. Thus, it can be hand-retrieved along the bottom, at mid-water, or at any depth around weeds. It can be lifted nearly to the surface and allowed to drop back easily to simulate its crawling and climbing around weeds. It and the other two big mayfly nymphs should all be kept moving constantly but slowly.

The hit to these mayfly types will be different from that with the other larvae discussed earlier. The stone-fly and dragonfly nymphs and the riffle-beetle larvae will be smashed solidly, and you will feel the hit *if* you have your line under control. Line control is a must in nymph fishing if one is to succeed.

These mayfly nymphs do not have any escape techniques such as rapid darts to evade or to seek cover, as do riffle-beetle larvae and dragonfly nymphs, nor do they have fast currents to whirl them away as do the stone-fly nymphs. The trout instinctively sense this, and where they pounce upon these three types they take the mayfly nymphs with an easy sipping motion, unless there is competition from another fish.

The difficulty of sensing the take is one of the most difficult things about fishing these mayfly nymphs. Since all are slow-water types, casting, handling the retrieve, and controlling the line are not hard, and anyone can do it with a little practice. But detecting the take is a problem and most everyone has to find his own way to solve it.

A floating or sink-tip line in waters less than 4 feet deep will usually work well enough, and *if* one has positive control, the above-surface portion of the line will usually give some indication of the take. In very deep pools, ponds, and lakes, however, a sinking line is required, and detecting the take here is never revealed by motion; you must feel it to know that it has taken place. Here again there are many different ways of doing this, but the method that has worked best for me is to keep the rod pointed straight down the line, to allow absolutely no slack, and to keep the line under the forefinger of the rod hand. The strike is made by jerking with the line hand and allowing line to slip through the fingers if one comes up solid. There is no perfect way to feel that kind of take, but over the forty-odd years I've used this method, it has been the most successful.

Mayfly nymphs hatch into adult mayflies and thus give the nymph fisherman an excellent opportunity and exciting sport during the transformation. One should either know the time of hatching or be able to detect it early in the period. At this time, the action of the artificial is changed to a smooth, even lift by whatever type of manipulation you can manage in order to get the desired rising-to-the-surface effect. Takes will be more frequent during such periods, and they will be stronger, producing a definite surface-line movement or a pluck that one can feel. The very largest trout will often be on the feed at this time, because of the size of the nymphs and the fact that they are more visible and more easily obtained.

After the hatch is well under way you might have better success by fishing the nymph in the surface film, dead-drift with light twitches. I have received many hard strikes with this method, and the fish average larger than at most other times. Never use more than a 7½-foot leader for these big nymphs.

The best method for catching large trout is like the old recipe for rabbit stew: First you must find the fish. That means, for the most part, avoiding shallow stretches and areas of no cover (depth and a choppy surface are the best kinds of cover). Then the nymph used must be of a large type found in such waters and its size must be representative of the natural *at that time*. The rest is simply practice and perseverance. Or, in the words of one famous angler, "Just one more cast."

FOUR OF MY FAVORITE NYMPH PATTERNS

The patterns I use most are described, along with tying instructions, in my books *The Trout and the Stream* and *Nymph Fishing for Larger Trout*. Here are four of my favorites.

Montana Stone Nymph, size 4 4XL.

Montana Stone (sizes 4, 3XL and 4, 4 XL)
The natural of this is 1½ to 2 inches long in the weeks just before hatching.

Tail: 6 fibers of raven or crow primary, tied forked

Body: Black fuzzy yarn or fur

Rib: Brown flat nylon monofilament

Hackle: One brown dyed grizzly and one regular grizzly, hackle fibers stripped off one side of each; tied on base of thorax and wound together two separated turns

Gills: Gray or white ostrich herl wound at base of hackles

Thread: 3/0 black monocord; the hackles must be firmly bound *onto* the thorax before winding or they will come loose.

Assam Dragon (sizes 6, 2XL and 4, 2XL)
The strip of seal fur is tied on at the bend and wound like chenille, leaving room behind the eye for two turns of hackle. The only place I know where this fur can be obtained on the skin is Kaufmann's Streamborn Flies, P.O. Box 23032, Portland, Ore. 97223. Bleach fur in peroxide to get tan color for the Light Assam Dragon.

Body: Natural brown seal *fur on the skin;* a strip ⅛ by 4 inches is needed for each fly

Hackle: Large brown dyed grizzly tied reversed (curved forward)

Riffle Devil (sizes 8, 3XL to 4, 4XL)
This is tied exactly like a Woolly Worm, then the rear ¾ of hackle is trimmed to taper to the front three turns, which are left full length. Weight all the above nymphs with enough turns of 0.030-inch lead wire to cover ¾ of the hook shank.

Body: Olive chenille, large. (Nearly all genera of this insect are olive-green in the larval stage.)

Hackle: A *very* long brown or furnace-wound palmer

Assam Dragon Nymph, size 4 2XL (Libellula genus of dragonflies).

Riffle Devil, size 4 4XL (Dytiscus and other genera of riffle beetle larvae).

Genie May (sizes 8, 2XL to 6, 3XL)
Use gray body material, ostrich-herl rib, and olive-green dyed grizzly hackle and tail in the same manner to tie the Gray May (*Siphlonurus*).

Tail: Hackle fibers, grizzly dyed dark orange
Body: Mottled brown yarn or fur
Rib: One thin strand of purple yarn and one gray ostrich herl wound together
Hackle: Grizzly dyed dark orange tied in at base of thorax and wound two separated turns

Genie May Nymph, size 6 3XL (Hexagenia *genus of mayflies*).

Brian Clarke is perhaps the best-known exponent of still-water nymph fishing in the United Kingdom.

His book on the subject, The Pursuit of Stillwater Trout, *laid down the first complete methodology for the technique to appear in print. It was described as "historic" by* Trout and Salmon *magazine and was compared by other reviewers to the work of Skues, for its depth of thought and observation.*

In addition to his contribution to this and other books, Brian Clarke has written numerous articles on fly-fishing technique and fish behavior for publications in Europe, is Fishing Editor of the London Sunday Times, *and is well known as a speaker on all aspects of fly-fishing on rivers and lakes.*

He is married, with three daughters, and lives in Hampshire, England.

14
The Nymph in Still Water

Brian Clarke

BACKGROUND

IT IS ONE OF THE WORLD'S GREAT TRUTHS that no one is making rivers anymore. It is another—and fundamentally more saddening—truth that men have dedicated themselves for centuries to the relentless desecration of those clear streams that once they had.

Over the past thirty years, these two basic facts have led to the greatest revolution in fly-fishing that the United Kingdom has ever known, and they will inevitably lead to a similar revolution in the United States: the emergence of fly-fishing on *lakes* as the most widely practiced form of the sport.

The revolution in England began after World War II, when chains of water-supply reservoirs were built to slake the ever-growing thirst of industry and the cities. Many of those lakes—covering anything from a few thousand square yards to many square miles—were stocked with trout as public policy; and the simple fact that they were there and accessible saw the first burgeonings of the mass-following sport we know today.

In the 1960s and 1970s smaller, privately managed fisheries that offered exclusivity in exchange for higher rod fees began to break out like an aquatic rash around the country. Now every city and major town (at least in the southern half of the country) has first-class trout fishing within easy reach, and at an affordable price.

In an area as small as England and Wales, some 250 major lakes and almost as many smaller ones are now available for trout fishing. Since 1945, one estimate has it, enough additional fishing has been provided for a quarter of a million new rods. I have had no difficulty persuading my many American friends that conditions are ripe in the United States for a similar explosion.

As the interest in fly-fishing increases and as the available waters become fewer and more heavily burdened, the American fly-fisher is certain to relieve the strains in the only way he can. He is certain to exploit the lakes and reservoirs that already exist, and to create the only form of fishing that he *can* create: smaller lakes and pools that simply need to be dug from the ground.

It will not escape him, as it did not escape his friends in Britain, that while big lakes are located where the good Lord wanted them, and supply reservoirs are created where water is needed, smaller fisheries of a few acres or so can be developed where the *fishing* is needed, *when* it is needed, to a quality that is needed. It also will not escape him that with an eye sensitive to the natural environment, and with careful husbandry, waters of great charm and beauty can be created, waters in which any artificiality need be no more apparent than the occasional stocking of a regularly fished stream, waters that will demand of him the highest skills if he is to succeed consistently.

WHY THE NYMPH

Two basic techniques for extracting trout from lakes have been developed in the United Kingdom. The first, and longest practiced, is the lure, streamer, or fancy fly, fished quickly. The second—and most recent on any kind of scale—is the imitative artificial nymph.

In the first technique the lure is cast out, allowed to sink to the depth at which it is believed the fish are residing, and then stripped back toward the rod at various speeds until it is (or, more commonly, is not) hit by a passing or following trout. It is a style of fishing that catches great numbers of fish for the few who do it well. It is also a craft (and it *is* a craft, demanding considerable skill) that lacks all the subtlety and finese, all the beguilings and intimacies, that are the special satisfaction of fly-fishing as it has been developed on rivers. By the thousands, British anglers are beginning to turn from this style of lake fishing to the nymph.

Nymph fishing for trout in lakes has been practiced by a small but steadily growing band of aficionados for many years. But the real breakthrough came in the early and mid-1970s and coincided with the publication of a book I wrote on the subject, *The Pursuit of Stillwater Trout*. It is a matter of record that that modest treatise, within two years, had broken all records for an angling book sold in the United Kingdom and had been translated into at least one foreign language.

I make these points not to boast but to illustrate the great thirst for satisfaction and fulfillment that many thousands of fishermen in Europe obviously felt, even though they were catching fish with the lure. In all my correspondence, and in the great bulk of the correspondence that has appeared in the fishing press, one thing has remained constant: the release that so many anglers have felt from the bondage of powerful rods, heavy lines, and gaudy lures of feather and tinsel, often on multihooked rigs.

I was never a very successful lure fisherman at any time. There were two reasons for this, I think. The first was that I am an ordinary, domesticated sort of chap, with a job, a home, and a family, and a garden that reproached me every time I looked its way. So, for a thousand and one domestic and financial reasons I just couldn't get to the water often enough to see any pattern either in my own failure or in the success of others. I simply never knew where to start, because I couldn't see why any fish would be silly enough to attempt to eat a "fly" that looked like a cross between a canteen of cutlery and an extravagant lady's hat. And so my fishing never acquired that most essential of metaphorical backbones—a sense of purpose.

Now, I do not like being devoid of a sense of purpose in *anything*, much less in something as profoundly important as the catching of trout. And it was the sheer frustration of not being able to employ sensibly what time I *did* manage to get at the water that made me do the one thing I should have done in the first place: sit down and think things through in a rational way, and consider whether there was not a more intelligent approach to things than cast, pray, and retrieve. That made me search about for a fish-catching alternative to the lure and the tandem hook.

Happily, an alternative *did* exist. I discovered the nymph. Within the limitations imposed by a chapter as brief as this, I will outline the thought process behind my personal approach to a nymph-fishing technique for lakes. It is a process that in a single season led to an increase in my average catch of 500 percent. And it is a process that led to an immeasurable increase in the pleasure I obtained from the sport.

THE PRINCIPLES OF NYMPH FISHING FOR TROUT IN LAKES

There are three overriding factors on which practical nymph fishing on lakes is based. The first is that nymph fishing is by definition an imitative art; that is, in practicing it we are setting out to imitate both in appearance and in movement the aquatic insects we know lake trout eat. And we are setting out to present our imitations in such a way that the fish can *see* them. (To be sure, not even the most perfectly designed artificial, delivered to the water with the most spiritual delicacy, will catch a fish that cannot see it!)

The second key factor in nymph fishing is that, other than in the most persnickety sense, there is no current on a lake and therefore no natural movement of the water to assist or hinder the movement of the artificial. All movement of the natural nymph must be created by the angler in the way that he retrieves his line after it has been cast out.

Much less obvious and much more complex is the third factor. It concerns the way that lake trout generally react to the angler's artificial nymph, and it is reached by a process of deduction. Lake trout, unlike river trout, must find their food. There are no cozy lies to which sleeking currents bring a procession of offerings to be accepted or rejected on a whim. The lake trout must hunt for his food, and when he has sighted it he must swim up to it at a speed somewhat in excess of the speed at which the potential victim is moving, before he can overhaul and consume it. Thus it is a reasonable assumption that, in hunting food, no fish will expend more energy in pursuit of a potential victim than it will replace by consuming that victim. And practical observation confirms—though common sense would in any case dictate it— that trout feeding in earnest will move to acquire an item of food only as fast as they have to and no faster.

The third key factor in nymph fishing, therefore, is that a fish intent on intercepting a slowly moved artificial nymph, which presumably it believes is food, will move slowly-plus-one to catch it, *and that therefore there will be only the most gentle, most minimal impact upon the line to which the nymph is attached.* A savage take will be the exception. In the majority of cases the take will not be felt by the angler at all.

Everything that the still-water nymph fisherman does, and all the equipment he uses, is designed in light of these fundamental premises and the facts that flow from them:

1. The fact that nymph fishing is imitative and that the angler should therefore have at least a minimal knowledge of what a natural nymph is if he is to be consistently successful.

2. The fact that the angler himself must impart any movement suggesting life in his artificial.

3. The fact that most of these movements will be slow, because most insects are capable only of slow movement.

4. The fact that there will be little impact for the fisherman to *feel* when a slowly moving trout makes the acquaintance of a slowly fished nymph.

5. The fact that the fish will eject the artificial quickly, if given the opportunity, the moment it decides that fur and feather dressings with nasty big

Trout in lakes cruise in pursuit of nymphs.

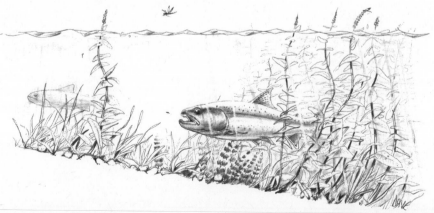

hooks inside do not coincide with either its gastronomic preferences or a wholly reasonable desire for a long, tranquil, and unbludgeoned existence.

EQUIPMENT FOR STILL-WATER NYMPHING

Because he cannot rely on feeling the take of an accepting trout, the nymph fisherman must seek another means of alerting himself to the sport's most electrifying moment. And because a slight movement of the leader or line needs a much less violent pull to create it than does a heave that the distant angler can feel, the nymph fisherman designs and uses his equipment in a way that will record *visually* all but the most tentative inquiries.

For this reason, nymph fishing on still water is primarily a technique for the floating line. Line can be seen on the surface: below, except in the most extraordinary circumstances, it cannot. (Under some conditions—for example, at the time of a wholly inescapable breeze—a sinking or sink-tip line *must* be used, and then the angler will have to rely on feeling what takes might come his way. But since these circumstances will occur on only a small proportion of outings, we will ignore them here.)

Let us look at the key elements in the equipment the nymph fisherman must use on still water: the fly at the business end and the rod, reel, line, and leader that enable him to present it for the scrutiny of the trout.

The dedicated nymph angler can resolve the question of fly pattern quite simply. He can perform autopsies on the fish that he takes or he can observe living specimens as they swim. If he does both these things, he will know what foods are available to the trout, which creatures from this range the trout actually prefers, and how all the relevant creatures move—information that will help greatly in teaching him how he should try to retrieve his artificials.

The state of the art is now so advanced in England, however, that lack of even this basic knowledge need not prevent anyone from practicing this type of fishing in the United States, with success. The fact is that most underwater insects are brownish or greenish, coupled with shades of off-white or silver. And I have given at the end of this chapter a few dressings that I am certain will take fish from almost any American lake holding trout—or, indeed, from almost any lake in the world that trout inhabit. This tiny group of artificials suggests a whole range of aquatic insects and, provided they are moved slowly, they will deceive trout.

As for the mechanical aids to the business, the most distinctive element is the leader. A specialized rod, reel, and line are not too important. The only essential requirement of the rod is that it have a quick action (so that fast, subtle takes can be hit quickly) and that it will throw 20 yards or so when the occasion demands. More is not often needed, provided the fish are not scared off; and anyway, 20 yards is about the maximum range at which delicate movements of the leader can consistently be seen.

The rod that I normally use for still-water nymphing is made of hollow glass and is about 9 feet long, rated AFTMA 6 or 7. I use a high-quality, floating, full-length double-tapered line to match it, and any reel that is light and will carry enough line and backing to accommodate the longest run of the largest fish I am likely to encounter. It is only the *leader* that really matters.

The greatest depth of water in which it is practicable to fish with a nymph is about 15 feet, and it is a happy coincidence that most of the insects which lake trout pursue and eat reside within this limit. Fish can, of course, be moving anywhere within that depth—from right on the bottom to just below the surface. Unless they are right on the surface (and if the food they want is on the surface we will be able to see them rising to it) a leader will be needed that is of sufficient length to enable every level of water to be explored on the way down, and that means one capable of bridging the gap between the line floating on the surface and the trout that might be feeding on the bottom.

Because a sunken leader going down from a floating line descends in a generous curve, the leader will need to be much longer than a depth of 15 feet would seem to suggest. To fish the bottom in water 10 or 12 feet deep, a leader must be about 20 feet long. To fish water 15 feet deep it will need to be up to 30 feet long. And even when you are fishing on the surface to trout that are rising, the leader will need to be up to 16 feet long because most still-water rises to the surface occur in calm water, when it is necessary to put a reasonable distance between the fly that the fish sees and the heavy fly line that enables it to be delivered.

To anyone used only to river nymphing or to the use of streamers on lakes, the length of such leaders will seem staggering. In spite of their length, however, such leaders are easy to cast, except into a stiff breeze. The biggest problem to overcome is the psychological one of believing that the feat is impossible—at least from *this* bank of the river Styx!

All you have to do to cast a long leader is ensure that enough fly line is out through the top ring to flex the rod before the cast is attempted. Once the rod has begun to flex under the weight of the aerialized line, the leader will follow. And it will turn over cleanly if the "shooting" of the line is gradually decelerated by the free hand as the cast is nearing its intended distance.

When fishing to deep trout, the line and the leader are cast out and the nymph is allowed to sink slowly down, exploring all the way to the bottom. Then it is retrieved at a very slow pace—typically at a maximum rate of 1 foot every 3 or 4 seconds. When fishing to rising trout, the fly is cast out and retrieved just below the surface, where the trout can be observed taking their food.

THE TAKE OR STRIKE

As I have already indicated, the take or strike of a fish to the nymph is usually a delicate affair: so delicate, in fact, that without the utmost concentration on the part of the angler, it will be missed. In particular, nothing will be felt of the take of a nonrising trout, nine times out of ten.

The only indication that the still-water nymph fisherman gets is a movement at the end of the leader where it cuts through the surface film on its journey to the depths. Sometimes the leader end will stab smartly down; on other occasions it will twitch, move slightly to one side, or be drawn across the surface of the water, away from the rod. If there is a cross-breeze, and a slight curve or belly develops in the line, the delicate draw of an accommodating fish may only be recorded by either a lessening or an increasing of the degree of curve.

Sometimes there might be nothing there when the rod is raised; or the hook might simply be caught on a weed or a rock. But often there *will* be a fish; and the primary rules of nymph fishing are that the angler's eyes should never leave his leader end and that, while the fly is in the water, he should tighten at anything that looks foreign to the normal state of the line, the leader, or the water around them.

RISE FORMS

All the variations in the take that I have so far indicated are the things one looks for when "fishing the water" in search of trout that cannot be seen. But sometimes—*blissful* sometimes!—the fish can be observed rising to insects in or immediately below the surface film. The movements or rise forms that such fish make on still water are the most important clues any angler will get in his quest for fish, and it is essential that he knows how to interpret them.

The logic of understanding rise forms takes us back to one of the key premises upon which nymph fishing is based: Trout are not interested in using up energy for the sake of it. When feeding in earnest they will move quickly only when they *have* to move quickly, to catch something that *itself* is moving in a hurry. When taking something that is stationary or moving slowly, the trout will normally move slowly too. In other words, there is a direct relationship between the speed at which a feeding trout will normally swim and the speed at which its intended victim is moving.

But there is also a direct relationship between the speed at which a trout swims and the effect its movement has on the water around it. When a fish swims, it does so by thrusting its body from side to side. Each time it thrusts, it displaces water on either side of its flanks. If it swims quickly, the powerful thrusts of its body will displace water violently. If it swims slowly, the movements of its body will displace water more gently.

We can now see that there is a direct relationship not only between the movement of the trout and the movement of the creature it is pursuing, but also between the movement of the water and the movement of the trout. And we can also see that by using his wits and powers of observation, the alert fisherman who takes the trouble to learn which creatures move at which speeds can look at the movement of the water (the rise form) and relate it to the movement of the trout. The angler can also relate the movement of the trout to the speed of movement of the small group of appropriately moving insects in the water. Then, eureka! He knows which artificial he should be using (one suggesting the group of insects that the trout's movements tell us it is probably eating) and how he should be retrieving such a fly (the way the natural creature transports itself).

"Boils" or swirls close to the surface *but not breaking it* suggest that the fish are having to chase fast-moving or awkwardly moving nymphs and pupae 1 or 2 feet down. High-speed fish movements that *break* the surface film and cause spray to fly suggest the presence of nymphs or pupae hatching *in* the surface film or fast-moving adult flies (like egg-laying caddises) *on* the surface film.

A fish making a porpoising, head-to-tail rise is certainly feeding on more slowly moving creatures *immediately below* the surface film (why else would its back show *above* the water?). A fish taking in flies with a tiny sipping or kissing noise, and making only a dimple on the surface, is taking dead or dying flies trapped in or on the surface film. (We know the victim is at the surface, because the sipping noise can only be an intake of air—and air is only at the surface; we know the creature must be immobile because of the utterly unhurried, pinpoint nature of the rise form we can see).

Even when no such distinct rises can be seen or heard, the truly observant angler can use his appreciation of water displaced by swimming fish to locate the whereabouts of specific trout when others around him notice nothing at all. This is particularly so in calm water when, in an otherwise flat-calm mirrored surface, patches of light reflection appear in areas of dark or patches of dark reflection appear in areas of light. The reflection of a straight tree trunk on a nearby bank may suddenly acquire an S bend, or the sharp reflection of a hill or building may blur at just one point. Each of these occurrences would betray the presence of a trout moving below the surface and causing the slight displacement of water that the surface reflections reveal.

In rippled water as well, nymphing fish can sometimes be located if they are anywhere near the surface. Typically, areas of calm water 1 or 2 feet across will appear like oases in the ripple, indicating that fish have turned sharply beneath the surface, displaced water violently, and sent upthrusts bulging to the surface. In rippled water, too, crisscross patterns will sometimes appear, suggesting that the back of a fish has broken the surface unseen and caused circular ripples that cut across the pattern of wavelets established by the breeze.

Sir Winston Churchill once said that there was no finer investment than putting milk into babies. For the nymph fisherman (whether on still water or not) there can be no finer investment than sustained, practiced observation: than in learning to use his eyes and in understanding what they see.

From the foregoing, it will be clear that the catching of trout on still waters, using the approach I have set out here, is a highly sophisticated business: a pursuit that calls upon many of the technical skills demanded by nymph fishing on rivers and several additional skills besides. It also makes a considerable number of mental demands on the fisherman: intense concentration in spotting the takes and strikes; acute observation and deductive skills in interpreting the rise forms and the behavior of unseen fish; some knowledge of aquatic insects and the basics of imitative fly dressing; an understanding of the effects of weather and weed growth on the margins of lakes. And much more.

All these things, and other matters I have not touched on here, have put back into lake fishing many of the refinements and subtleties that fast-sinking lines and multihooked streamers had taken from it. Most important of all, perhaps, they have put back into the sport a sense of purpose that for so many was missing before: a quiet confidence that so-and-so is the fly to use, moved in such-and-such a way, at such-and-such a depth, *over there*, because everything that can be seen and deduced tells us either that it must be so or at least that it is very probably so. Not quite a formula for certain success but certainly a formula for some success—and inner satisfactions, as well.

As I said at the beginning, fly-fishing on lakes *is* going to come to the United States, and on a big scale. It is as inevitable as the dawn, without ifs, buts, or maybes. And when it does come, the American angler will soon tire of heavy gear, chuck-and-chance, and fly-box hypnosis. He, no less than his British counterpart, will seek the satisfactions that are there for the application of effort.

The serious nymph fisherman may not yet have landed on the shores of the New World's lakes. But he cometh.

SIX OF MY FAVORITE NYMPH PATTERNS
for American Lakes

The first two dressings suggest chironomid (midge/mosquito) pupae, which are present on almost every still water. One pattern is a general representation of some of the larger species; the other suggests smaller, specific species. If nothing is rising, I would fish the larger pattern anywhere in the world, with more confidence than any other dressing I know.

Large Chironomid
To fish, allow to sink in free fall when no fish are rising. Watch the leader—takes often come as the fly is sinking. Retrieve slowly, inch by inch.

Hook:	Size 8
Silk:	Brown
Body:	Cock-pheasant tail fibers wrapped around the hook shank from halfway around the bend to ¼ inch behind eye
Rib:	Fine copper or gold wire
Thorax:	Hare's body fur, dubbed to form a ball immediately behind the hook eye (a few turns of lead wire beneath the thorax will help sink this fly quickly when the trout are believed to lie deep down).

Small Chironomid

Fish as with Large Chironomid, when fish are deep down. When trout are rising, this is likely to be the most successful pattern of all. Retrieve in long, slow pulls just beneath the surface. Beware of occasional heavy strike to this pattern.

Hook:	Sizes 14, 12, 10
Silk:	As body color
Body:	Black, red, fawn, or olive floss silk or feather fiber, in same proportion to hook length as with Large Chironomid body
Rib:	Fine silver wire
Thorax:	Peacock herl, to form a small ball immediately behind eye of hook; tie in a tiny tuft of white floss silk on top of hook, to project ⅛ inch from front end of thorax over hook eye.

Damsel Nymph

Fish with long, slow draws of 2 feet at a time, close to bottom unless fish are known to be higher in the water.

Hook:	Long-shanked, sizes 12 and 10
Silk:	Olive
Tail:	Three olive cock hackle tips, or ostrich-herl tips, projecting ¼ inch behind hook bend
Body:	Olive seal's fur
Rib:	Fine gold or silver wire
Thorax:	Olive seal's fur, with gray-brown feather fiber tied in along the top for wing cases
Head hackle:	Soft olive cock, longish in fiber, tied sparsely

Caddis Larva

Fish along bottom with very slow, smooth pulls.

Hook:	Long-shanked, sizes 12 and 10
Silk:	Brown
Body:	Cock-pheasant tail fibers, or peacock herl, over closely wound weighting of copper wire, to within ¼ inch of hook eye
Rib:	Copper wire
Head:	Yellow or buff wool
Head hackle:	Brown, gingerish, or honey soft cock, tied sparsely

Caddis Pupa

To fish, allow to sink 2 to 3 feet, then draw up to the surface in steady, slowish, smooth pulls.

Hook:	Long-shanked, sizes 12 and 10
Silk:	Brown
Body:	Cream, olive, or orange seal's fur, to ¼ inch behind eye
Rib:	Fine silver wire
Thorax:	Dark-brown feather fiber

$\longrightarrow$

Nymph patterns for still water: top center, Large Chironomid; second row, Small Chironomid, Dayfly Nymph; lower center, Damsel Nymph; bottom row, Caddis Pupa, Caddis Larva.

Wing case: Pale-brown feather fiber, tied along top of thorax

Head hackle: Honey or rusty hen, tied sparsely, as beard

Dayfly Nymph (Frank Sawyer's Pheasant Tail Nymph)

To fish when no fish are showing, allow to sink 3 or 4 feet, then retrieve in brisk draws of 1 foot or so, every few seconds. When fish are rising and dayflies are on the surface, retrieve just below the surface in twitches and draws.

Hook: Sizes 16, 14, 12

Silk: Brown (Sawyer uses copper wire, which incorporates intrinsic weight and durability into the dressing.)

Entire fly: Three or four cock pheasant tail fibers. Tie in points to project to rear, just beyond hook bend; wrap around body until a little behind hook eye, then form ball to suggest thorax by winding three or four turns around remaining space on the shank. The wing cases are suggested by doubling and redoubling the remaining ends of the fibers along the top of the thorax.

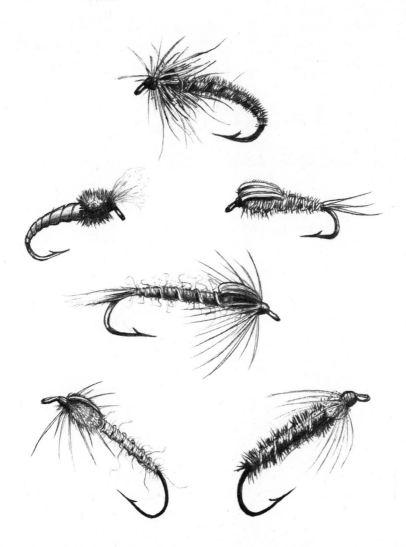

Byron Dalrymple was born in Michigan and attended that state's univer-
sity. He subsequently spent four years in New York City and five years
in Hollywood, writing music for radio and films.

Since 1944, when he turned professional writer, he has authored
2,700 articles, appearing in all major outdoor magazines and many gen-
eral publications such as the Saturday Evening Post, Collier's, *and* Lib-
erty. *Recent assignments have been given him in* Outdoor Life, Field &
Stream, Sports Afield, Southern Living, American Rifleman, Holiday,
American Hunter, National Bassman, *and* Fly Fisherman.

He wrote regular columns for eight years in Argosy, *five years in*
Sports Afield, *fifteen years in* Fawcett Yearbooks, *and is currently in his*
ninth year with Outdoor Life.

As a co-owner of War-Dal Productions, he produces films, mostly
outdoor, for major corporations for distribution on national TV.

Byron Dalrymple has just completed his eighteenth book. Total
copy sales are over the 2,000,000 mark. He presently lives in Kerrville,
Texas.

15
The Use of Nymphs
for Fish Other Than Trout

Byron W. Dalrymple

LOOKING BACK OVER more than four decades of fly-fishing, intermingled with many other angling approaches, I often reflect that I was probably fortunate to have been launched totally as a self-starter. No instruction books. No mentors. I'd had experience as a kid with a cane pole and graduated to a cheap, poker-stiff solid-steel casting rod about as handy a tool as the lightning rods would be that marched along the ridge line of the farmhouse where I was reared.

I had caught suckers, sunfish, several bass, and a pike or two from a nearby river. It was my opinion that they were all pretty darned-fine fish. At an age when many a modern youngster with fly-fishing in his family background has graduated from his third summer fly-fishing school, I finally had the exhilarating experience of watching a gentleman operating with a fly rod on a trout stream. I didn't know much about what he was up to, but I had to try it.

The tackle I got together was a cut-rate hodgepodge. I had nobody to ask about rudiments, so I just got tangled up in it as best I could. My fly selection was made by poking around in a Northern Michigan store that had a few, saying, "I'll take one of those, and that one over there, and that skinny black one."

The skinny black one I remember best. In a mid-thirties Ford I traveled an old logging trail to reach the North Branch of the Au Sable River. I cast the skinny black fly into the current of what was then a truly superb neo-wilderness trout river. I was so utterly ignorant that I was not the least bit surprised to begin catching trout. I am not certain—and have no intention of researching the matter and perhaps ruining the romance of those times—whether fishermen called such flies "nymphs" in those days. If they did, I haven't the faintest idea what nymph pattern it was.

I got out of the woods late in the aftrnoon and reached a lake near the main road, where in a primitive fashion I was camped, and started wading and fishing the lake shore, still using that treasure of a skinny black fly. I'd wade out a few steps, drop the fly as far off as I could, let it settle, then twitch it. God has never since created bluegills that were as big or as eager, or that fought so stubbornly. I vividly recall every detail of both fishing experiences. I distinctly remember not comparing the trout and the bluegills. Which was the better fighter? Which was the better *fish?* They were both just fine with me. I had no preconceived notions of caste.

There was another, older camper on the lake, who had also been catching trout but enjoyed sharing his time with the bluegills too. I was watching him one day when a third fisherman drove in, apparently seeking a campsite. He looked disdainfully at the man intent on the bluegills and said, "Why do you waste time on those things when there are trout just over the hill? No bluegill could ever remotely compare to a trout."

The older man paused and looked at him, smiled a wry little smile, and replied quietly, "Well now, maybe you ought to ask the bluegills about that. They might disagree."

It was several years before I realized I had been "nymphing" for both fish. The experience fixed in my mind the idea that these flies—the nymphs— were without question among the most deadly of artificials. I still had not read much of the nonsense about how difficult nymph fishing is, and so I just went along catching trout—and other species too—without any inhibitions.

What I did slowly become especially conscious of was the fact that the nymph was exceptionally productive for a wide *variety* of freshwater fish. It is interesting to comb through fishing literature referring to nymph fishing and to realize that practically nothing has been recorded pertaining to the useful- ness and productiveness of these flies for anything other than trout.

It is a curious fact that among those spiny-rayed fish that are predomi- nantly minnow feeders there are times when even *they* gorge on nymphs. All fish are opportunists in foraging. I recall using mayfly nymphs sold by bait stands catering to ice fishermen to catch yellow perch in winter. The true sun- fish of sporting size—bluegill, redear, yellowbreast, green—though they dif-

Bluegill protesting stubbornly. These fish are not very selective, but small flies enhance hooking and also appeal. They move up slowly and suck them in.

fer in amounts of insect material taken on the average, all eagerly accept living nymphs. Crappies, inveterate minnow feeders, do likewise.

In northern Wisconsin on certain lakes where extensive hatches of large mayfly varieties occur, there are astonishing feeding sprees on the rising nymps and the emerging insects by—would you believe it?—walleyes. I used large Montana-style patterns similar to the Montana Nymph and to Dan Bailey's Mossbacks, swimming them just below the surface amid swirls of feeding fish, and enjoyed a unique experience, considering that, on the average, 99 percent of an adult walleye's diet is fish.

Smallmouth bass are setups for nymph fishing because in most of their habitats nymphs are one of their prime sources of protein. Largemouths are not quite so eager, simply because this bass is not the least bit discriminating in its tastes. Anything that moves is fair game, as long as it's a mouthful. Live hellgrammites are renowned smallmouth bait and are fair for juvenile largemouths, but imitations of outsized hellgrammites or other giant nymphs have in my experience proved close to worthless. Such large simulations, fished slowly as they need to be, just aren't very convincing.

One of the all-time classics of non-trout nymph fishing was concocted years back by the Wisconsin writer-angler Mel Ellis. He and some cronies, working the shores of the Door Peninsula when enormous Lake Michigan mayfly hatches were in progress, are credited with being the first to successfully take large carp on nymphs. I don't know how many fly-fishermen have ever had a carp of sizable proportions tethered to a crimped fly rod. They are awesome fighters. Presumably only under heavy-hatch circumstances are carp likely to gather for this annual harvest. The point is, however, that practically all waters produce living nymphs of one kind or another, and the majority of freshwater fish feed upon them to some extent, even though the literature is so heavily tilted toward trout that few fishermen are aware of this.

As everyone knows, many non-trout species are readily caught on surface flies. But they can be taken on top only under certain conditions and only for brief periods. Because living nymphs are a normal and natural forage, flies that simulate them are superior in productivity for more hours in the day and more months around the year. They have an edge on standard wets because they are closer imitations of the naturals. They easily beat out streamers for all species of broad-spectrum diets because the minnow feeders will resort to nymphs, but the species that are predominantly foragers upon insect forms ingest very few small fish.

I have made a lifelong hobby of gathering fishing experiences with the off-trail species and of fishing just for the challenge in unorthodox ways for the more common ones. During a recent taped interview about fly-fishing, I was asked to name my single biggest "catching" thrill. The interviewer suggested—nudge, nudge—that it was probably with a trout. Explosive dramatic trout incidents of course began crowding my mind like a string of popping firecrackers.

There was the rainbow, nymphing in a deep pool backgrounded by a boiling smoke pot on the Firehole River, a brute with a tail as broad as an old-fashioned backsmith's apron. It picked up my wispy offering, a Gold-ribbed Hare's Ear Nymph, tore the pool to shreds, and went its way, leaving me limp-lined and sweaty. There was the bulge-bellied brook trout on the slow-curling tamarack-tinged Black River in Michigan that whacked a Strawman Nymph—a fly then causing talk across the country—and actually jumped, even though sixteen books on my shelf claim brook trout never do.

There was the mean-jawed brown in a quiet glass-clear run of New Mexico's Chama. There seemed no way on earth to cast to that trout—current too slow where he lay, too clear, too shallow, the bottom gold-colored sand to throw back the slightest shadow of line or leader—but I made the cast over the grass of the bank and stopped it short, jerking the leader around at right angles so that as the line fell upon the grass the nymph slid with only a diminutive dimple into the water. The brown shot out and seized it. An insoluble problem solved in an unorthodox way.

But, I reflected, it was the interviewer who had put trout into my mind. I could more honestly say that my biggest thrill came when I was on the beautifully crystal-clear, swift Pedernales River in Texas, its towering rock-bluff banks footed by venerable cypresses almost as tall, its fame linked to Lyndon Johnson. I was fishing a Montana Nymph, or maybe it was a Black Montana stone-fly Nymph, or maybe a Woolly Worm (which books say is a wet, not a nymph, even though trout *think* they are nymphs and that's why they're so sensationally productive). I'm uncertain, and it isn't important. I had endlessly experimented here—on this river reminiscent of a fine Western trout stream but home to a scattering of bass, freshwater drum, and channel cats—and now at last there was a gentle tap and I was fast to the target of my efforts, one of the last-named, the fish I had been determined to take on nymphs. A sleek channel cat of possibly 3 pounds was slashing the current, streaking across and among the rocks.

Don't scoff. Just go do it first! It is illimitably more difficult to deliver clear-stream channel cats to the skillet via the nymph route than it is to fill an ice chest with trout on the same. But it can be done. These catfish, the most streamlined of the tribe and addicted to clear, clean waters, are all but impossible to inveigle on lures of any kind. But living nymphs are a staple fare of these bottom-feeders, as a survey of stomach contents will easily prove. Thus the nymph is the only practical artificial for them. This was one of the finest thrills I have ever experienced, one repeated a number of times since.

There come to mind two other non-trouts that are peculiarly suited to nymph fishing: the Rocky Mountain whitefish and the grayling. Whitefish are not easy to hook because of their small mouth and their peculiar take. One of the prime items of whitefish diet is the nymph. Many varieties inhabit whitefish streams. The fish grub for them with their tough snouts among the stones.

One summer on the Madison, fishing the last couple of miles before it leaves the park, I finally got an infallible whammy on whitefish. Some were large—2, maybe 3 pounds. Those who have fished dry for whitefish know they can be exasperatingly selective. I became so frustrated that I said the hell with them, tied on a good-sized stone-fly nymph pattern, and began shooting it across and down into a particular eddying pool where I had lost an outsized brown a few days before. I had assumed the nymph was too big for whitefish to pester it. But instantly there was a *tap, tap, tap.*

I kinked a shoulder setting the hook on nothing. The second time I knew this must be whitefish. I had been bringing the fly in when the bumps occurred. I simply let it drop back slack to get rid of the fish, picked up, and—WOW! I was into a fish that raced off with tremendous power. Of course it turned out to be a big whitefish. This intrigued me. I began casting, bringing the nymph upward until I felt the pestering taps, then dropping it back slack and quickly, firmly picking up again. On at least two out of three tries I was into a whitefish. I have tried the technique numerous times since, especially when whitefish are surface-feeding and difficult. It works astonishingly well.

Grayling offer hooking problems too. In my estimation this handsome aristocrat attracts far less attention nowadays than it deserves. It is available in more waters of the West than most anglers realize, presently in at least nine states. Grayling, which have long intrigued me, fool a fisherman often when rising. They have the odd habit of coming back time after time when missed on a dry fly. And commonly they're missed over and over. The cure I discovered long ago is to use nymphs, not necessarily deep, and with a method almost identical to that noted for whitefish. Grayling can thus be caught easily while surface feeding, and they are not very selective. They can also be nymphed into the creel as easily when they aren't showing at surface, by using small nymphs and casting upstream, allowing a standard natural drift and watching the line intently for a pickup.

The nymph fisherman plying his craft with the non-trouts faces one handicap: He fishes much of the time in lakes. Where the panfish such as sunfish and crappies, rock bass, and warmouths are concerned, this is no insurmountable problem much of the time. But it can be difficult with bass—in fact, sometimes simply prohibitive—for the fish lie too deep and in too much debris. It can also present problems with grayling, also commonly found in lakes.

Weighted nymphs are an assist, of course. They are also an abomination to cast, just as an added split shot is. Nonetheless, with proper rod and line it can be done. Sinking lines also help. I personally think advertisers have in some instances far oversold the sinking line for lake fishing. Some would have you believe 30 to 40 feet is nothing. I much prefer to stick to a floating line and long leader, so I can watch the line more closely and have a better feel.

A particular grayling experience emphasizes this point. On a Montana lake I discovered that there were some beautiful grayling congregated in mid-

Crappie Jig-Nymph

summer in spring holes possibly 12 feet deep. I stumbled upon the grayling when I ran the boat over one of the holes. In the crystal-clear water they showed plainly, but getting a fly down to them presented difficulties. A sinking line, which I tried, frightened the fish.

It may bring a smile to some readers—or maybe heart stoppage to others—when I divulge that I scrounged around through my tackle and found several extremely small lures that are known in the South as crappie jigs. The explicit definition of "nymph," most will agree, has yet to be written. Purists may niggle about that, but they talk only to each other. These tiny jigs had chenille bodies, split-shot weighted heads, and a small feather thrusting out over the hook. Were they nymphs, weighted nymphs? Well, a weighted nymph has a wingless body and a tail, and some have chenille bodies.

Properly defined or not, I was about to fish a weighted nymph on a floating line. The color: gray-white. Admittedly, casting was not pleasant, more lob than cast. But I shot the lure across the spring hole to the far side, having anchored the boat outside at working distance. Down went my "nymph" like a pebble. I twitched it gently. The line tip, already pulled under somewhat, shot out straight away, and I set the hook. True as I tell it, in twelve casts I hooked and played down ten grayling, all in the 16-inch class. Whether or not this was nymphing, apparently the grayling thought so.

Because I dislike casting weighted flies, or using a split shot as has been done often enough successfully, much of my non-trout fishing in lakes and ponds is executed by the countdown method—so many seconds per foot. On our Texas ranch we have a small lake that I built with a concrete dam on a clear hill-country stream. I have experimented endlessly in it. It contains five varieties of sunfish, plus largemouth bass. I take great delight in fishing for the sunfish, almost always via the nymph route. I cast to a rock wall or the edge of a weed bed and count while awaiting the wafting down of the fly.

It is of particular interest that as a rule the green sunfish strike in the shallower areas, at about 2 feet down. The bluegills usually lie somewhat deeper along cover. The redears or shellcrackers must be picked right off the bottom, in 6 or 8 feet of water. The yellowbreasts, a species that considers clear streams of moderate current optimum habitat, are invariably medium to deep and where there is some current.

For those who wish to branch out to nymphing species other than trout, among the so-called panfish the group of true sunfish, plus the rock bass and warmouth bass, are the prime customers. These are the ones that depend chiefly upon insects for food. Among the minnow feeders, the crappie and

For the nymphing panfisherman, the Deep South is a paradise. This getting-ready scene is at a small lake near Ocala, Florida.

yellow perch and the small freshwater sea-bass relatives—white perch, white bass, yellow bass—are seasonal possibles, particularly when hatches are beginning or about to begin. The yellow bass, which is a closer-to-shore fish than its white relative, is surprisingly open to nymphs fished along rocks near lake shores or among near-shore reed beds, where they congregate in schools.

It would be an error, however, to envision panfish nymphing as in the same technical and selective field as nymphing for trout. Frankly, I don't fret the least bit about specialized patterns, or for that matter about which standard trout patterns I try. These small, abundant, wide-ranging, sporty, and active fish are not very selective. Certainly you will discover at times and in certain waters that a particular nymph seems to be preferred. But by and large almost any will do. There are scads of so-called panfish flies, some of which apparently hew to the nymph classification, or nearly so, and all catch fish. Because I have long been a trout fisherman, I simply select somewhat automatically from among trout flies those that appeal to *me* as possibles for *them*.

For all the sunfish and their close relatives, small designs always produce best. A big rock bass, warmouth, or green sunfish—they have large mouths—

will whack a big stone-fly nymph pattern, or those types I think of as large typicals, such as Bailey's Mossback nymphs. But for the bluegill, yellowbreast, redear (shellcracker), and the longear sunfish where it grows large enough to count, the small flies they can move up to and gently suck in are far and away the most productive. I have watched hundreds of them do this and know precisely how they do it, taking their time. Use either the true patterns or reasonable facsimiles among the nondescript panfish flies everywhere available. Some of the well-known standards are March Brown, Hare's Ear, Light Cahill, Caddis Larva, Black Midge. I suggest these not as unalterably "best" but simply as a guide. A jillion designs in small nymph-type flies will fill stringers with panfish.

Keep in mind that the angler must *activate* the lure. It has always struck me as unfortunate that practically all writing about nymph fishing deals with (1) swift trout streams and (2) the fact that the flies must be fished so that they drift naturally. It may be that this was never intended, but that is the impression an average inexperienced or prospective nymph fisherman certainly gets.

The fact is, it's not even always correct in swift streams. Some of the most startling results can be had—as readers of this book of course know—by fishing a nymph across and down, letting it sweep around like any other wet fly, and then swimming it alertly on the uptake. Further, in slow streams such as those occupied by large yellowbreast sunfish, this is the only way to elicit strikes, and in a lake or pond a nymph is picked up by any fish regardless of species, either as it sinks or as it is gently twitched on the retrieve.

As for channel cats, my experiments convince me that patterns are not very important but that making absolutely certain the fly is right on bottom is mandatory. A channel cat is not going to move up to it. In addition, the fly must be "worked" by the angler, slowly and in a natural manner, not simply drifted. A catfish has an altogether too finely honed sense of smell to be fooled by an inert drifting object. Motion, however, creates a tempting illusion. Small sizes, at least in my experience, are not as effective as medium ones.

With grayling and whitefish, the former in both lakes and streams, patterns are certainly of some importance. There is no reason to believe they require specialized patterns, however. They and the trout invariably present in the same waters feed on the same varieties of living nymphs. The several

Warmouth darting out for a Stone-Fly Nymph.

Stone Fly nymphs, the several Caddis patterns, the Muskrat patterns, the Hare's Ear, and the various Mays do the job without any great fuss. I always listen to what the natives and the guides say about trout flies on those waters and go that route. I really have no idea how many if any fishermen still use the rather old designs of the several R. B. nymphs and the Hewitt nymphs, or variations on them. They were and are hard to beat. Ditto for the old R. B. Caddis. My learning experience, I hasten to remind you, dates back substantially. Some of those oldies are habits hard to break.

Nymphing for bass is a different game. I live presently in Texas, which some say has become the largemouth capital of the United States. I have fished for largemouths literally border to border and coast to coast and have spent endless hours observing my own bass in our ranch lake. I am only lukewarm about nymphs for largemouths. I've had days that were sensational. But on the whole they just don't care much for small offerings, and the giant-size replicas are usually spurned with what I'd call a bassy smirk. Nonetheless, largemouths are worth trying occasionally. Size 8 is about it in a Hellgrammite nymph. Try also the several Stone Flies and the Zug Bug.

Smallmouths are a different picture. By no means has enough research been done on nymphing for this fine fish. The trout fisherman comes to the endeavor with a handicap. He is programmed to the selectivity of trout, their penchant for spending certain periods feeding exclusively on one item, and their various other whimsies. Smallmouths have an exasperating habit—but still an Achilles' heel of sorts—of feeding during a session on anything that comes along, top to bottom.

Early and late in the day, early and late in the season—these are the rules for fly-fishermen after smallmouths. And, stream fishing is without any question the focus for the nymph fisherman. The swift places that often hold trout such as rainbows are seldom hangouts for the bass. They are distinctly cover fish, just like the largemouth, the cover being rocks, undercuts, even deep shade. They hang at the head or foot of a pool, or move into long riffles to feed. But they obviously won't feed over sand or scoured rock because little is there except what floats by.

Wherever you catch them active, however, they may be taking a variety of forage. Surface-lure anglers who never see a smallmouth break still have them bat lures eagerly all day on occasion, yet stomach analyses may show crayfish, minnows, and nymphs. They are extremely shy and are seldom loners. Two or three, maybe more, will usually be in a location. Leaders as fine as for trout are needed. A gentle cast is mandatory. The size of the fly is important, but I'm not convinced that the pattern is—as trout fishermen would be inclined to believe. The very small nymphs are usually spurned, and extra-large ones get the same treatment. This is a fact of life about smallmouth fishing even with plugs and spoons. Largemouths, as I've noted, like a mugful. The smallmouth, living in a spare habitat, is suspicious. The middle road is the way to go, with nymphs in sizes certainly not larger than 6 to 8 on the average.

Stream fishing in wadable water for smallmouths is reminiscent of trout fish-
ing, but a distinctly different approach is called for. This scene is in
Michigan's Upper Peninsula.

Fish the fly just as for trout. The upstream cast with a natural drift is all right. So is across and a down-current sweep. Don't be afraid to move a nymph, but don't exaggerate the movement, either, especially in the slow stretches. And if you happen to have been a largemouth-bass fisherman, one method or another, forget about that fish. This one is different, as different as bucks and does, as deer hunters so often find to their chagrin.

Obviously a treatise on nymphing the non-trouts cannot be even close to definitive in these few pages. We're talking about too many fish personalities, too many types of water. But the value of including these species that many trout anglers may instinctively consider less consequential is to point out that fishing is many-faceted and that there are challenges and enjoyments in all kinds.

During the days when this chapter was put together I made a trip to Devils River, a tributary of the Rio Grande near the Texas-Mexico border, where I fished one of its tributaries, Dolan Creek. It is so unbelievably clear that depth is deceptive. Great rock bluffs tower along one side. Springs of crystal-clear water gush hundreds of gallons into its course every few yards along the foot of the bluffs. Current is swift. The incongruity of this piece of beautiful "trout water" in the border desert is striking.

I waded the broad stream, fishing the edges, the shade of boulders, the deep slots eroded in the rock bottoms. I was intent on catching what is unquestionably the rarest of the so-called panfish within U.S. borders: the Rio Grande perch, a rugged, sunfish-shaped member of the Cichlid family of the tropics. A fish common to Mexico and ranging northward only in a few streams and ponds of central and southern Texas, it is not a perch at all, of course. Average weight is ½ to as much as 2 pounds.

Rio Grande perch can be awesomely perplexing. In this showcase they were doubly so. After hours of concentration I finally hooked three, using a very small, near-white nymph design reminiscent of a caddis.

I don't propose to claim this *fish* was on a par with a Firehole brown. But I will claim that the *challenge* was provocative—and that I've tangled with Firehole browns six times as heavy without half the stress and strain. It seems to me sometimes that the lore of trout fishing becomes too endlessly convoluted, that too many trout fishermen become inbred. There's a vast fishing world "outside" inordinately suited to nymphing, and you don't have to forego the one to enjoy the other.

FOUR OF MY FAVORITE NYMPH PATTERNS

It is difficult to pick four favorite nymphs; many nymph-type flies tied for panfish and bass are unnamed or obscure, so a choice, to make any sense, has to be made from trout patterns. Obviously these work just as well, as my chapter notes. The non-trouts, as stated, are by no means as selective as the trouts. Four that are extremely productive are the *Gold-ribbed Hare's Ear, Muskrat, Caddis Larva,* and *Bailey's Mossback.*

The rarest U.S. panfish, the Rio Grande perch, is not a perch, in fact, but a member of the tropical Cichlid family. It is found in the United States only in central and southern Texas.

Editors' Note: Excellent ties for both the *Gold-ribbed Hare's Ear* and the *Muskrat* patterns are given by Charles Fothergill at the end of chapter 11. Sid Neff, chapter 12, gives a fine tie for the Caddis Larva pattern, although for bigger fish, larger hook sizes should of course be used. A standard tie for *Bailey's Mossback* follows:

Bailey's Mossback

Hook:	2X or 3X long
Tail:	Two goose quill barbules, short, forked
Body:	Raffia, nylon or hair; topside dark, underside light
Covert:	Dark raffia, nylon or hair
Legs:	Goose quill barbules: 2 long slanting to rear; 2 shorter at center thorax, 2 forward above covert
Variation:	Substitute turkey or pheasant barbules for legs.

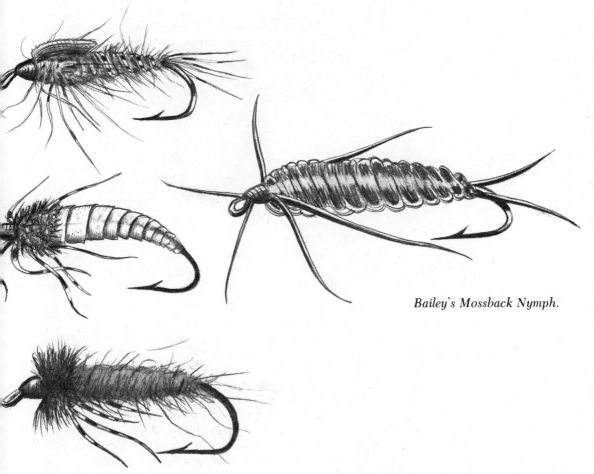

Bailey's Mossback Nymph.

Top, Gold-Ribbed Hare's Ear;
middle, Latex Caddis Larva;
bottom, Gray Nymph.

Steve Raymond was born in Bellingham, Washington, and is a journalism graduate of the University of Washington. As a small boy he began fly-fishing in British Columbia and has been an addict ever since. He is a member and past president of the Washington Fly Fishing Club and serves as vice-president of the Museum of American Fly Fishing. He has served as a director of the Federation of Fly Fishermen, was secretary of that organization in 1970–71, and was named the Federation's "Man of the Year" in 1977.

He is presently Environmental Editor of The Seattle Times and was editor of The Flyfisher magazine for six years. He has appeared on ABC-TV's American Sportsman series and has contributed chapters to two anthologies, Fishing Moments of Truth and the first work in this series, The Masters on the Dry Fly. He is author of two books, Kamloops and The Year of the Angler, the latter a winner of several state and national awards.

16
Non-Nymphs or Pseudo-Nymphs

Steve Raymond

WHERE THEY ARE PRESENT, scuds and sow bugs are usually a far more important part of a trout's diet than all the nymphs or pupae that have been exalted in fly-fishing literature or immortalized in the creations of fly-tiers. In a way, that seems a little strange. You'd think anglers would recognize that scuds and sow bugs are often available to trout when nothing else is, and that flytiers would devote more time and thought to the imitation of these ubiquitous little crustaceans. But they haven't.

Perhaps one reason is that scuds and sow bugs—unless you look for them—are usually out of sight underwater and many fly-fishermen apparently just don't think about imitating what they can't easily see. Adult mayflies, caddises, stone flies, and midges serve as constant reminders of the presence of subsurface nymphs and pupae, so they get all the attention.

Another reason might be that scuds and sow bugs are usually so abundant that offering the trout an imitation has seemed like trying to lure a cow to a single blade of artificial grass planted in a pasture. But the odds really are not that bad, as a fly-fisherman with a good scud or sow-bug imitation will quickly discover.

True, they are not nymphs—they are not even insects—but they share the habitat of nymphs, behave in similar ways, and require similar methods of fishing. So it seems logical and convenient to lump them into the general category of nymphs, at least for the purposes of fly-fishing, and that is why they are in this book.

Compared with the diversity of crustaceans found in salt water, those inhabiting fresh water are relatively few. And of those few, only the scuds and sow bugs are of general interest to anglers. But before we go any further let's clear up one common misconception: Freshwater shrimps and scuds are not

245

the same thing, even though scuds are almost universally referred to as shrimps. The true freshwater shrimp, or prawn (*Palaemonetes*), is much larger than the scud, not as widely distributed, and not as important, either to trout or to trout fishermen. So for the sake of accuracy and to avoid confusion, even though it violates common usage, in this discussion we will stick to calling scuds by their rightful name.

For the record, let's put the scuds and sow bugs in their proper places on the taxonomic ladder:

Class: Crustacea
  Subclass: Malacostraca
    Division: Peracarida
      Order: Isopoda (aquatic sow bugs)
      Order: Amphipoda (scuds)

The scuds include three genera—*Gammarus, Hyalella,* and *Eucrangonyx,* in descending order of size—of which the first two are most important. The sow bug, *Asellus,* is nearly as important as the scud.

Other freshwater crustacea, such as fairy shrimps and opossum shrimps, also contribute to fat trout and other species. But they present such problems of imitation—both in fly tying and fly-fishing—that they are generally of little interest to fly-fishermen.

Another crustacean, the crayfish, is an important source of food for bass, panfish, and trout. There are at least nine genera and more than 250 individual species in North America. The four most common genera are *Cambarus, Orconectes, Pacifasticus,* and *Procambarus,* of which *Pacifasticus* is most widely distributed. Unfortunately for anglers, crayfish are largely nocturnal in their habits and are not readily available to fish during the day. Night fishermen using weighted deer-hair imitations sometimes do well on bass or panfish in lakes or ponds and on smallmouth bass in streams.

Gammarus is widely distributed across the whole North American continent and in the British Isles. It thrives in cold, alkaline waters. *Hyalella* is more tolerant of its surroundings and is found in both cold and warm waters

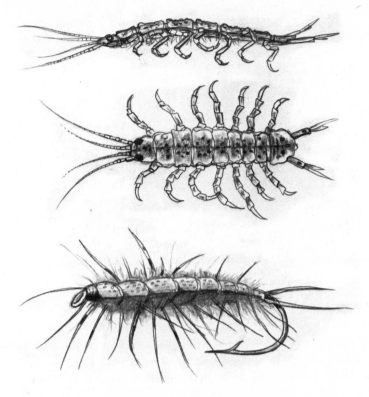

Sow bug (Asellus). *From top: side view, top view, imitation.*

that may be alkaline, neutral, or even slightly acidic; thus it is even more common than *Gammarus. Eucrangonyx* is at home in bogs or waters with very little lime content; its distribution is therefore limited and it need not be considered by fly-fishermen.

Gammarus and *Hyalella* also differ from one another in size and range of coloration, but in shape and silhouette the two are very similar; for purposes of imitation they may be considered identical in form and structure. Each has a compressed body, arch-shaped when at rest and elongated when swimming. Each has sessile eyes (flush with the body surface) and seven pairs of legs for climbing, grasping, and swimming, and each breathes through gills under the thorax. Each lacks the prominent carapace present in the opossum shrimp (mysid). Their heads are joined broadly to the thorax so that a definitive neck is lacking, and their bodies are covered by relatively hard, segmented exoskeletons (meaning, literally skeletons on the outside) that are manufactured from calcium absorbed from the water. As with many other crustaceans, they must periodically shed their exoskeletons in order to grow, forming a new and larger one in its place.

Both *Gammarus* and *Hyalella* are omnivorous scavengers, feeding on decaying animal and vegetable matter. They are enormously fertile little animals, mating frequently from early spring through late fall. In fact, it has been estimated that a single pair of gammarids could produce as many as 20,000 off-

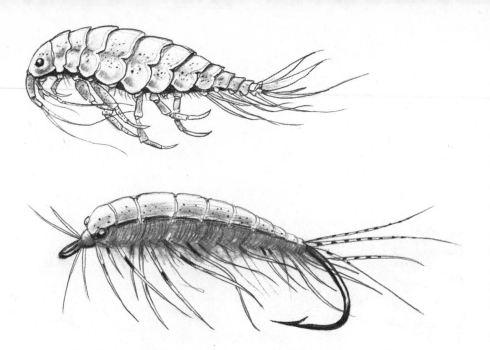

spring a year, although obviously this would be under ideal conditions with the longest possible breeding season. But even under less than ideal circumstances, scud populations grow very rapidly—especially in waters where predators are few.

Where trout and scuds coexist, scuds form the basic staple of the trout diet. Typically, a scud-fed trout is well-conditioned, fat and thick, with a small head in proportion to its body, its flesh firm and crimson-colored. Waters where scuds are present usually are famous for producing large trout. Such waters include streams like the Letort, Silver Creek, Upper Madison, Firehole, and many limestone spring creeks, and lakes such as Henrys Lake or the famous Kamloops trout waters of British Columbia.

Gammarus is more important to the fly-fisher than *Hyalella*. It is a free-ranging animal that may be found anywhere from the wave-washed shores of lakes or streams to depths of 50 feet. This, plus its size—up to 25 millimeters—makes it available and attractive to larger trout. Its size also makes it easier for the flytier to imitate.

Gammarus wears a coat of many colors, ranging from brown through turquoise, but various shades of olive are most common. Most imitations are tied with olive dubbing, floss or wool, although some patterns call for brown. *Gammarus* is light-sensitive and on bright days will take shelter in shallow water under rocks or other debris or in the tangled stalks of aquatic weeds. To check for their presence in unfamiliar waters, turn over rocks along the shoreline or pull up weeds from the bottom; if gammarids are present you will soon see them darting away from your intruding hand or find them writhing on the uprooted plants.

Hyalella seldom exceeds 8 millimeters in length. It prefers shallow waters and may be found in great numbers under rocks or plants along shorelines. In color it may range from a light blue to a bright red, although pastel shades of green, brown, and yellow are most common. It has a tendency to swim on its back or side. Its small size and preference for shallow water make it an important source of food for young trout.

Fly patterns designed to imitate gammarids are invariably called shrimp flies. But keep in mind that most of them really are intended to imitate scuds rather than shrimps. Of the many patterns found in fly-fishing literature, relatively few are really good imitations of the naturals. Those tied commercially and sold in stores are often much too large and are sometimes tied in bright colors never present in the naturals.

Many patterns are also tied on bait hooks to imitate the arched shape of the scud. But the scud holds itself in this shape only when at rest, and usually it rests only when it is under cover and safe from feeding trout. The best imitations are those tied on regular straight-shank hooks that imitate the elongated body of the free-swimming gammarid.

Of all the patterns I have seen, only three strike me as reasonably good imitations. I have a strong prejudice for one of them because it is my own, developed after nearly five years of experimentation in the scud-rich lakes of the British Columbia interior. It has been thoroughly tested by anglers for a good many seasons and has frequently taken trout that were feeding very selectively on the naturals (I have seen some trout caught on this pattern that proved to have as many as 300 scuds in their stomachs). But I am no less guilty than anyone else of misnaming the pattern; it is called the Golden Shrimp.

Golden Shrimp

Hook:	Sizes 8 to 12, sproat
Tail, hackle, and antennae:	Soft ginger hen or cock hackle feather, stripped on one side
Body:	Golden olive floss (rayon no. 163)
Rib:	Fine gold wire
Silk:	Olive monocord

The fly is tied as follows: Strip the fibers from one side of a soft ginger hackle feather, leaving the point of the feather intact plus a few long fibers at the butt. Tie in the feather at the bend of the hook so that its point extends backward and down as the tail of the fly.

Next tie in fine gold wire for ribbing. Then tie in four strands of floss and build up a cigar-shaped body, tying off the floss behind the eye (the floss will darken somewhat when immersed in water, giving a fine imitation of the most common coloration of *Gammarus*). Now lay the hackle feather along the underside or belly of the fly, stripped side up, so that the remaining fibers hang down as legs. Secure the butt end of the feather behind and under the eye of the hook.

Next wind on the gold wire, using a dubbing needle to separate the hackle fibers so they are not bound under the wire (this is the painstaking part). The wire serves the dual purpose of giving the body segmentation and holding the hackle feather in place. Tie off the wire when ribbing is complete and trim away excess.

Now take the butt end of the hackle feather and double it back on top of the fly so that the long butt hackle fibers extend forward over the eye of the hook to simulate the antennae. Whip finish and trim away excess, lacquer the fly, and you're done.

Shortly after this pattern first appeared in print, I received a letter from Bob Boyle, senior writer for *Sports Illustrated* and co-editor of *The Fly Tyer's Almanac*, detailing his own efforts to create a fly matching the grass shrimp (also known as the glass shrimp) that is abundant in the brackish lower reaches of the Hudson River. He enclosed one of his patterns, which looked so real I half expected it to crawl out of the envelope. It is most complicated, but I think it is the deadliest imitation I have yet seen. Here is the pattern, as given in *The Fly Tyer's Almanac:*

Glass Shrimp
(Pleopods are the small swimming legs between the main legs and the tail.)

Hook:	Mustad wide-gap bait hook, sizes 2 to 12 (since this pattern is meant to imitate a true shrimp, which has a "broken-back" appearance, the bait hook is in order here)
Thread:	Dyno transparent sewing thread
Tail:	Clear quill cut from end of goose or peacock primary or tail feather and cut to a fan shape (Bob says he also has used large shad scales for this purpose)
Body:	Strips cut from clear sheets of Clorpane or K-Clear, built up around shank and secured with transparent thread, then coated with clear fingernail polish
Segmentation:	Fine silver or gold Mylar
Small antenna:	Five polar-bear hairs, thin ends forward
Large antenna:	Two hog bristles, thin ends forward
Lips, plates, and rostrum (nose):	Clear quill, trimmed to shape
Eyes:	Two ends of a chicken or duck feather tipped with black enamel
Legs:	The butt ends of the small antenna.
Pleopods:	Polar-bear hair tied in and splayed (monofilament or white hackle wisps may be substituted)

Although intended to imitate a brackish-water shrimp, this fly has taken many different species of fish in both fresh and salt water. Boyle notes it is also sometimes effective as an imitation of small immature crayfish, which tend to lack coloration.

Both the foregoing patterns are difficult to tie. One that is much easier and also is a good imitation has been given a host of local names but is perhaps most commonly known as the "Baggie" Shrimp, because strips from clear polyethylene sandwich bags are used in its construction.

"Baggie" Shrimp
Hook: Sizes 8 to 14, sproat
Body: Olive or brown seal's fur dubbing or wool
Overlay: Clear polyethylene strip cut from sandwich bag or similar source
Rib: Tan or olive silk (gold or copper wire is sometimes used) to bind overlay in place and give appearance of segmentation
Legs: Wool fibers or guard hairs of dubbing teased out with dubbing needle

Some tiers prefer to weight their patterns by wrapping fuse wire around the hook shank before winding on the body material. Such patterns are a distinct advantage in fishing slow-moving, weedy streams where scuds are most often found. Using a floating line with a weighted fly, the angler can cast into pockets or channels among the beds of moss and the fly will sink quickly to the depth where trout are feeding.

Weighting the fly is usually unnecessary in lakes. The exception may be in very shallow, weed-choked waters, where again it is necessary to cast into pockets or holes in the weeds. Otherwise, a sink-tip or fast-sinking line will usually be sufficient to get the fly down over the submerged weed beds or rocky shoals where on bright days trout are likely to be foraging. In the shallows or in late evening, when the light-sensitive gammarids come out of hiding, a floating line with an unweighted fly may be used to good effect.

A dead-drift method is most effective if you are fishing upstream with a floating line. For best results, use a fluorescent indicator on the end of your line to help detect the very slight hesitation in the drift that usually indicates a trout has taken the fly. In lakes or in streams where the flow is not strong enough to permit the upstream method, gammarid imitations should be fished with a slow, gentle retrieve, occasionally interspersed with short quick strips to imitate the erratic, meandering movements of the naturals.

Asellus, the aquatic sow bug, has a reputation somewhat less glamorous than that of *Gammarus.* Perhaps that's because it is . . . well . . . a sow bug, very much like the ones you find when you turn over a board that has been lying on moist ground. It too is common throughout North America and the British Isles, where it is known more colorfully as the water louse, and it inhabits lakes and streams of both warm and cold water, thriving especially well in alkaline waters. *Asellus* has a body that is depressed in form, concave on the bottom and convex on top, and has sessile eyes, seven pairs of legs, and gills under the abdomen. It lacks a carapace but is strongly segmented.

Asellus ranges up to 20 millimeters in length and is usually dull brown or gray in color. Somewhat more common in static waters than in fast streams, it feeds primarily on decaying vegetation. As with *Gammarus, Asellus* is a mighty fertile fellow and produces numerous offspring throughout the warmer months of the year. Despite its awkward appearance, it is highly mobile and can move about with deceptive speed. Where present, it usually exists in large numbers and provides a major share of the trout's diet.

There are not many established patterns designed to imitate *Asellus*. One of the best known was developed by the British flytier C. F. Walker, as follows:

Sowbug

Hook:	Sizes 12 to 14, weighted with wire that is flattened with pliers to the concave-convex body shape of the natural
Body:	Mixed gray and brown hare's-ear dubbing wound over wire
Rib:	Silver tinsel
Legs:	Gray-brown partridge hackle

Because of its fondness for beds of watercress, *Asellus* sometimes is called the cress bug. Hence the name of the pattern given by Ed Koch in his book *Fishing the Midge:*

Cress Bug

Hook:	Sizes 16 to 22, sproat
Silk:	Gray
Body:	Gray foam-rubber strip wound on shank
Overlay:	Black ostrich herl
Collar:	Two turns of the black ostrich herl used for overlay

A third sow-bug pattern, ascribed to Dave Whitlock, is tied much the same way as the "Baggie" Shrimp:

American Sowbug

Hook:	Sizes 16 to 18, sproat
Silk:	Gray
Tail:	Two strips of gray goose quill, short and well forked
Body:	Muskrat and gray seal's fur dubbing
Shellback:	Clear plastic strip
Rib:	Gold wire to give segmentation and hold plastic strip in place
Legs:	Guard hairs from dubbing teased out with needle

Sow-bug imitations should be fished in much the same manner as the scud patterns.

These are the scuds and sow-bugs—less glamorous, perhaps, than the mayflies and their kin, but a major source of food for trout. Study them and imitate them, and you will surely find them a major source of angling pleasure.

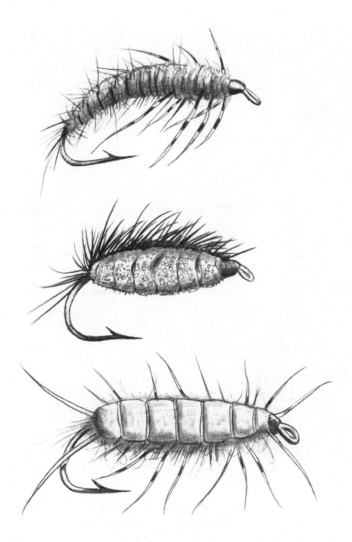

From top, C. F. Walker Sow Bug, Cress Bug, Whitlock Sow Bug.

Ed Zern, born in West Virginia of Pennsylvania Dutch parents, caught his first trout from a brook running into the then undammed Cheat River, using a cricket for bait, sixty-odd years ago, and has been an enthusiastic angler during most of the time since that splendid 2-ouncer. In 1965 he escaped from the advertising business and has since concentrated on fresh and saltwater fishing, upland bird and lowland waterfowl shooting, and occasional forays for big game, including several African safaris.

Ed began writing the "Exit Laughing" column in Field & Stream in 1958, having sold his first fishing article to that magizine in 1937, and became its Fishing Editor in 1976. He has traveled considerably on five continents and has fished for (and caught) trout on all of them. When indoors, he collects African and Oceanic sculpture, wildfowl decoys, bootjacks, sporting books, and sporting prints.

17
Bye-Bye, Wet Fly?

Ed Zern

I KEEP TELLING ANGLING NEOPHYTES that fly-fishing is simple, but sometimes I wonder. Sure, the theory and practice of dry-fly fishing is ABC stuff: flies come off the water, and trout eat them while they're floating along getting dry enough to fly away, and later trout eat them when they come back to lay eggs in or on or over the water or when they fall onto the water, exhausted and spent-winged after the mating flight. (Please note I said "onto the water" and not "into the water"; there's a difference, and it's important.) In any case they're floating on top of the water or in the surface film, and you can imitate them, and possibly fool a trout into trying to eat your imitation, by fishing a floater.

I was taught that procedure a long time ago, and I understood it. My mentors showed me artificial flies—Quill Gordons, Hendricksons, March Browns, Coffin Flies, and others—designed to represent specific mayflies and (in the case of the Grannom, Petrie's Egg Sac, and a few other artificials) specific caddis flies. Then, over the course of a season, they showed me the natural insects on the water, until I learned to identify the most important hatches on the rivers I frequented and to fish an artificial designed to imitate whichever fly was on the water. Fair enough; my brain isn't being willed to the Smithsonian Institution, but I was able to grasp the principles involved in dry-fly fishing and apply them successfully to the catching of trout.

So for several years I fished only dry flies—not out of snobbery but because my intelligence was unable to cope with the theory of *wet* flies. During long hours spent peering into pools and eddies I had never observed any *Iron fraudators* (Quill Gordon naturals) or *Ephemerella subvarias* (Hendrickson naturals) or, indeed, any other natural mayflies swimming about underwater—and yet that's what most of my wet flies were obviously meant to

255

imitate. They were tied not to represent any subaquatic stage of the insect, but to imitate the winged adult, the airborne fly, usually with the same hackle and wings as the dry-fly version, except that these were tied not to float the fly but to sink it.

Not all wet flies were tied to represent winged mayflies, of course, but a lot of them were, and it was this that bewildered and baffled me. It was true that a few caddises plunged beneath the surface to lay their eggs, and that at least one genus of mayfly, *Epeorus pluralis* (another Quill Gordon natural), sheds its nymphal skin underwater and swam from the bottom of the stream to the surface fully winged. But the great majority of emergent mayflies and caddises performed no such shenanigans; alive or spent, they floated on the surface, period. Nevertheless, many trout fishermen—most of them, when I started fly-fishing—persisted in using wet flies and somehow caught one hell of a lot of trout.

Finally I started using wet flies myself, mostly, I think, because the late Jim Leisenring was even then a legend for his ability to extract persnickety brown trout from hard-fished eastern-Pennsylvania streams, seldom with anything but wet flies, and I was fortunate enough to have fished with him a few times and even received some perfunctory coaching while we fished the lower Brodheads. I disliked the Leisenring flies—he gave me a dozen or so, of which I still have a few—because of their skimpiness, but I realize now that the reason for their effectiveness was not only the skill with which their tier presented them to the trout but also the fact that in their near-naked, wingless wispiness they came far closer to imitating the nymphal subaquatic stage of the insect than did the conventional wet fly of that day.

And that's the gist of this piece: that wet flies—those sinking versions of such dries as the Royal Coachman, Quill Gordon, March Brown, and Green Drake—are taken by trout either because to a slight degree they resemble the nymphal underwater stage of the insect (especially when fished with "the Leisenring lift," causing them to rise surfaceward like a nymph ascending to "hatch" on the surface) or because the trout mistook them, when they were fished with action, for tiny fry or shrimps (but *not* for mayflies swimming about underwater).

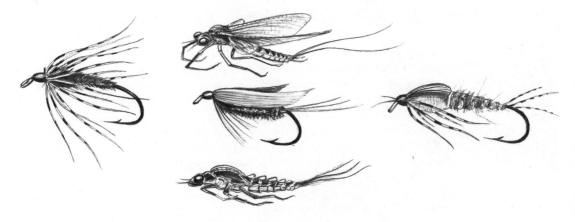

Does the wet fly suggest a drowned adult or live nymph? Flymph and nymph flies (right and left) suggest live swimming nymphs.

Those wingless, sparsely hackled wet flies with which Leisenring and his disciples wrought such havoc among the trout wherever they fished were in fact more nearly nymphs than wet flies, and Vernon Hidy, a close friend of Leisenring who helped him write *The Art of Tying the Wet Fly*, coined the word "flymph" when issuing a revised and expanded edition of that book (*The Art of Tying the Wet Fly & Fishing the Flymph*, Crown Publishers, 1971). Hidy defined the flymph as an imitation of the nymph struggling toward the surface, or in the surface film, on its way to becoming a winged insect—and Jim Leisenring's creations, wingless and with soft, straggly hackle suggesting clumsy legs or a half-shucked nymphal case, were indeed something between a wet fly and a nymph. Incidentally, the Breadcrust wet fly, which originated in the same part of Pennsylvania that produced Leisenring, is definitely the impressionistic representation of a nymph.

Let me recount one of those Leisenring lessons. I was sitting one morning beside the railroad bridge pool of the Brodheads, a quarter mile above the Hotel Rapids at Analomink, watching the water for any sign of activity, when Leisenring came wading down under the bridge, reeled in, walked up the bank, and sat down beside me. He was fishing a size 14 straw-colored wingless wet fly with a skinny raffia body and gave me two of them, saying he hadn't caught a trout all morning but assuring me that if they took anything it would be that fly. I thanked him and said I had been reading his newly published book, in which he urged wet-fly fishers to allow the fly to drift freely but to maintain contact, so that if a trout took it the angler could respond instantly and tighten to set the hook. "How can you let a fly drift freely in the current and still maintain contact?" I asked. "I should think any actual contact would cause some drag."

"I'll show you," Leisenring said, and walked down to the tail of the pool, where a fast run begins. Standing almost beside the run—much closer than I would have dared to stand until then—he flipped the wispish wet fly a few feet upstream and, holding the rod tip high, let the fly sweep down beside him and on downstream. Altogether the fly traveled not more than 15 feet, but it was obvious that (a) it drifted freely and (b) Jim would have felt—and probably seen—any trout that touched the fly. Then, having demonstrated, he fished his way on downstream, using the same technique.

When he had disappeared around the bend I thought I'd try his method, but didn't bother to change the fly I had on, a large, lumpishly tied Leadwing Coachman. I stood where Jim had stood, flipped the fly upstream as he had done, and held the rod tip high. When the fly came by me a 10-inch brown grabbed it, and I netted it and popped it into my creel. By the time I had worked downriver to the hotel, fishing each run the same way. I had seven browns in my creel and had seen a number of others flash at the fly and miss. I also had an acute case of embarassment at having caught trout with the wrong fly, and at having caught them when the Master hadn't, so I snuck around to the back door of the hotel, found Charley Rethoret in the kitchen, gave him the trout to put in the icebox, and urged him not to tell Leisenring under any circumstances, explaining my predicament. Charley, of course, told Leisenring at the bar while I was getting out of my waders, and Leisenring, of course, was amused.

This why-wet-flies? notion isn't a world-shaking heresy or even a new one. It has been hinted at for a hundred years or more by writers as troubled as I had been by the fact that moths and mayflies and most other flying insects don't go swimming about underwater, and that in fact most of them won't sink even when dead, except in turbulent water. A. Courtney Williams, in his *Trout Flies: A Dictionary and a Discussion,* published in 1932, ridicules Louis Rhead for his statement in *American Trout Stream Insects* that trout feed heavily on "drowned" flies underwater, and comments, "This is an astounding statement with which no observant angler will agree. Flies, as a rule, do not sink when drowned, but are carried along on the surface."

Why, then, didn't the angling world stop fooling around with wet flies, since the theory behind them was obviously wrong? For a simple reason: *Wet flies worked.* They worked in spite of the fact that they were tied to represent fully winged flies, which didn't make much sense. They worked because much of the time trout are *not* selective in their feeding and will seize anything that might conceivably be edible, including cigarette butts, beer-can tabs, and Parmachene Belles. They worked, and still work, because the average trout is even less intellectually ept than the average trout fisherman. They worked because sometimes, by design occasionally but more often by accident, the angler imparted to the fly a lifting movement that imitated a nymph swimming to the surface to shed its nymphal shuck and become a fly (and of course, it's difficult to cast a wet fly across current or quartering downstream and let it swing *without* achieving something akin to the "Leisenring lift"). They worked because under certain conditions they would be taken for tiny fry or shrimps, or for a nymph dislodged by the current or a nymph swimming.

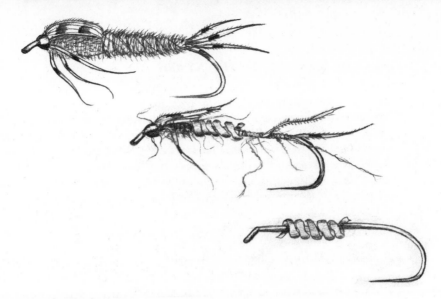

Raymond Baring's three phases of Pheasant-Tail Nymph: full nymph, fish-chewed reduced version, and leaded-hook, complete reduction.

But if that's the case, why shouldn't all wet flies tied to represent drowned or underwater-swimming mayflies and caddises be shipped off to the Museum of American Fly Fishing and be replaced with artificial nymphs and miniature streamers? I think the answer is that eventually they will be so replaced, as they're being (or already have been) replaced in the fly boxes of a great many trout fishermen.

This replacement process will gain speed as the lingering aura of mystery still surrounding nymph fishing is dispelled, and as anglers learn that upstream nymph fishing is even more productive, and not much more difficult, than dry-fly fishing. It will gain speed as the art of tying artificial nymphs—a relatively recent development in fly tying—advances to new and more effective patterns through the ingenuity and inventiveness of such innovators as Dave Whitlock, Len Wright, Carl Richards, and Polly Rosborough, and through the development of new synthetic materials.

A final note: I realized the possibilities implicit in the "new school" of imitation in 1961, when I first fished the Tichbourne in Hampshire, a spring-fed tributary of the Itchen, with the late Raymond Baring, then honorary secretary of the Test and Itchen Angling Association and a man of delightful wit and enormous angling skill. Raymond tied onto my 5X tippet a bare size 18 hook with three turns of fine copper wire around its short shank and nothing else—no fur, no feather, no silk, no tinsel. The turns of wire suggested a segmented body, but otherwise I was fishing a bare hook. When I cast it upstream on a slack line, a fine brown flashed out from under the weed bed, took it, and spat it out before I could tighten the line. Only after the fourth fish had taken and ejected the hook did I learn to keep slack line and leader to a manageable minimum and hook the trout.

Raymond told me that originally he had tied this creation as a Pheasant Tail Nymph, with the copper wire wound over several strands of pheasant tail and with a bit of dun hackle at the head; as trout chewed off the feathers the lure seemed to increase in attractiveness, until he began omitting the feathers altogether. The turns of wire, he felt, not only suggested a segmented body but also helped to sink the tiny hook faster. At any rate it was an eye-opening lesson, and of special interest because this was the first pattern I had ever seen that was "tied" even more skimpily than the ones Leisenring had given me twenty years previously. And, like Leisenring's flies, it worked.

THREE OF MY FAVORITE NYMPH PATTERNS

I consider the following three flies to be "all-purpose" or "utility" nymphs and fish them when I'm not sure what's on or in the water, while waiting for something to develop. My fourth favorite nymph would be whatever I can find in my fly boxes that best matches the nymph of whatever natural fly is emerging or should be emerging, or is in my opinion about to emerge.

The Dickey Fly

I tie this monstrosity (which I take to be an impressionistic representation of the dragonfly nymph and which was invented thirty years ago by the late Richard Jarmel) with a clump of peacock herl wrapped around a shaped cotton-batting foundation on a 3X-long size 6 light-wire Model Perfect hook, ribbed with flat gold tinsel, and with a tail and hackle made of the all-web butt ends of dun-colored hen hackle (it doesn't matter what color the feather is, as long as the web is some shade of blue or gray). The Dickey produces well, sometimes when dragonflies are skimming the water, and sometimes when they aren't. Sometimes, of course, it doesn't produce at all, but I've taken some fine trout on it, as well as a few smallmouth bass, Atlantic salmon, Arctic char, and grayling. I tie it weighted and unweighted, fish it as close to the bottom as possible, and consider it an ancestor of today's soft-hackle flies.

The Breadcrust

I believe this fly originated in eastern Pennsylvania; at any rate it was common in the fly books of many Brodheads Creek anglers when I first fished there in the late 1930s. There's something appetizingly grublike in its segmented, wingless body, which is shaped and tapered with orange wool wrapped in ostrich or some other fairly wide quill; the long, soft hackle should be light gray or grizzly. It's usually listed as a wet fly when it's listed at all (Mary Orvis Marbury doesn't, and you will not find it in A. Courtney Williams's *Trout Flies* or even in Wetzel's *Practical Fly Fishing*, although Wetzel was a Pennsylvanian), but I consider it a true nymph and fish it as such.

The Pheasantless Pheasant Tail

As I said, I first met this tiny but effective nymph in Hampshire, when my gillie and mentor, the late Raymond Baring, then living precisely midway between the Test and Itchen and fishing both frequently with exquisite skill, tied it on my leader. The Pheasant Tail had been invented by the Englishman Frank Sawyer; at any rate, it's of fairly recent origin. I have a deep faith in the magical fish-getting qualities of peacock herl, but all the herl and hackle had been chewed off the one Raymond gave me, and it still fooled the fish. As a result, I tie it without herl or hackle. Fished upstream in small waters (I've never really tried it in big, heavy, Madison River–type water), it sometimes gets splendid results, although to be fished properly it demands more concentration than I can usually muster.

J. Michael Migel was born in New York, but his early years were spent in Arizona—at school, at college, working on a ranch, and in mining. During this time his hunting and fresh-water fishing ranged from Alaska to Mexico, and his saltwater experiences were in the Sea of Cortez.

When he returned to the East, he joined the business world and today is a partner in the firm of Hamilton Associates & Co., Financial Consultants. His fascination with both fresh and saltwater fishing continues unabated.

He is a founding director of the American League of Anglers and was a member of the group that started the Bass Research Foundation. He belongs to the Angler's Club of New York, the Theodore Gordon Flyfishers, the Federation of Fly Fishermen, and Trout Unlimited.

His articles and short stories have appeared in numerous sports magazines, and he edited The Stream Conservation Handbook *and* The Masters on the Dry Fly. *Currently, he is the editor of the American League of Anglers' new quarterly,* Newscasts.

18

A Day's Nymphing

J. Michael Migel

MY SIZE 16 ADAMS settled comfortably on the quiet surface of Beaver Pool, its drift so gentle I imagined I could follow it from the corner of my eye, for I was completely beguiled by the sudden appearance of a flotilla. Introducing herself by soft chatter, *sotto voce*, a veritable Sarah Bernhardt entering from the wings, a smallish mallard hen, pride in every line of her body, glided from behind a nearby boulder. She did not use any visible means of locomotion, but ripples formed ahead of her breast and spread across the pool. Following this star were her progeny—downy ducklings—five, all in a row. Four sailed along dutifully; the fifth was Peck's Bad Boy. Time and again he left his station to dart with incredible speed after a bug or some such enticement, reluctantly returning to his place in line only after his mother first calmly voiced her disapproval and then practically shrieked. The same genes, so why this one adventurous soul among the five?

Suddenly, the entire family fled. The hen realized she was close to a dread human being when I jerked my rod. I'd felt a tug on my line and belatedly realized a small trout had hooked itself on my fly.

A quarter mile upstream from Beaver Pool I watched my Gray Fox Variant curtsy down a deep run while I stripped in line to keep the fly on a reasonably tight leash. While my lure was still wigwagging a little way upstream, it passed a miniature landslide. An earlier spate had undermined a sod bank and a large chunk had collapsed—half still hinged to shore and half being slowly chewed by the flowing race. A large clump of forget-me-nots had once decorated this slab; now a few blossoms lay submerged—turquoise spots tethered by dark-brown strings swaying back and forth in the current—while others jutted out over the water, their daintiness profaned by drunken angles. A monarch butterfly—bright orange dotted with ebony—flittered along the shore, touched down on the blue flowers, and fluttered for long seconds over the drowning forget-me-nots. Was it attracted to the underwater sprays by their movement or color? There couldn't have been any perfume.

Downstream, where my fly had drifted, there was a sudden shower of drops, and a curved, shiny back made me instinctively raise my rod tip; it arched against the sudden strain. In milliseconds a large trout became a memory-etched Winslow Homer watercolor, the fish's straining iridescence outlined against the color of the river and the mottle growths along the bank. There was a heavy splash and a hard, determined run. The slack portion of the line slipped through my half-closed fingers and then ran against the reel's buzzing drag. Suddenly, for no apparent reason, all motion stopped. Unbelieving, I reeled in. The fly's hackles were slightly matted but the fly itself looked all right. Then I found the answer. The lower portion of the hook with its barb was gone.

Seated on a comfortable slate overhang, feet dangling above the stream, I started to tie on a new variant. Sinuous, shadowy movements deep in the water gradually gained definition, becoming the broad, waving tail of a good trout nosing for nymphs.

Helene, my wife, had asked me to bring home two fish, big enough for a dinner she was planning for two special guests. I had enjoyed "pounding 'em up" with a dry for three hours, but this had produced only two small released browns, several chub, and a good strike lost because of a broken hook. Large trout weren't rising; they were feeding on nymphs. If I wanted to fulfill my wife's request, I had to change to a nymph.

I knotted a longer and heavier leader on my fly line and, having moved downstream, began casting a large, lead-underwrapped imitation of a stone-fly nymph. The weight was a bit awkward at first, but soon my timing was sufficiently good that I felt I wouldn't spook the trout near the rock. On my third cast, as the line drifted back toward me, there was a slight unnatural movement of the nail knot. Remembering Lefty Kreh's teaching on how to set a hook quickly while nymphing, my rod snapped downward. I felt heavy resistance. The line became a C string on a singing cello; I felt the fisherman's joy in knowing a good fish was fighting any restraint.

Fifteen minutes later, a cleaned, fat, beautifully marked 15½-inch brown lay in state on cut wet ferns in my creel, carefully measured by permanent marks on the butt section of my rod.

Then for almost an hour I nymphed conscientiously and with care, work-

ing spots where trout had formerly risen to dries or where there were good
lies. I even invented a new gadget—a pair of imaginary blinders, like those on
the headstall of a driving horse—so nothing would interfere with my gaze on
the nail knot. Only three small browns showed interest, and finally my attention wandered: the metallic clatter of a kingfisher's voice as it flew by with a
small minnow in its bill; how the dark-green needles of a pine, dipping in the
breeze, partially hid a small, white puffy cloud and constantly changed its
form. During the hours of fishing a dry fly there had only been three rises,
but in the shorter time I'd been nymphing there had been four rings—on the
opposite side of the river, of course.

Sitting on the bank, I reviewed what I'd been taught. Unless trout are actively rising, a man working a nymph upstream will outfish any dry-fly angler,
and the single most basic principle in this type of fishing is that trout understand a real nymph floating downstream and take this snack naturally and
casually. Their prey can't escape, so there is no slash, no rush. Therefore,
when a trout takes an artificial, correctly drifting downstream, it engulfs the
fly gently. Unlike dry-flying, intense concentration is necessary while nymphing, to detect the slightest odd leader movement. I needed one more good
trout and knew I would have to attend to this rule.

In July, some years earlier, an unprecedented searing, continuous heat
wave cooked the lower part of New Brunswick. Thermometers dangled in the
Maramichi River around noon read an unbelievable 82 degrees Fahrenheit.
Salmon either congregated and then aestivated near cold water, or they died.
Fishing, of course, became impossible.

At a breakfast-table conference, when one of our group mentioned
swimming as a possible diversion, someone suggested we buy a mask and
snorkel tube and float down our stretch of the river—to see if there were any
demented salmon in the pools or gaspers near possibly undiscovered small
underwater springs.

We were lucky. In Doaktown, the manager of the general store dug into
a bin in his storeroom reserved for mistakes, odd sizes, and specials and with
a triumphant smile sold me a child's mask and tube.

In our underwear shorts, three of us investigated our three quarters of a
mile of river. The underwater search made it obvious why salmon fighting
their way upriver rested in certain places and disdained others. The proven
favored stations were downstream from surprisingly small or big obstacles that
shunted away any current, or where deflectors created complete shelters. We
also explored several ledges and unsuspected drop-offs and plotted a run with
unexpected depths that was a natural roadway. Most of these could have been
discovered by careful study from the surface, but fishermen and guides are
creatures of habit; in the future, these might be new "drops."

In two of the finest pools on the Miramichi there were no salmon, nor
did anyone discover any cold water. But what also fascinated me were the
shad, trout, smolt, and parr that, seemingly undisturbed by the hot water,
watched me as I watched them. Shad—restless, driven by their burgeoning

reproductive urges—only flashed in and out of my vision. Trout were relatively stationary, finning behind boulders; smolt, being smaller, hid behind rocks. The pecking order was rigid; larger fish occupied the better holds.

With my face underwater, once I located a fish in residence I carefully overturned stones, and whenever there were nymphs clinging to the undersides I dislodged them. Currents carried these unlucky ones downstream, and from behind a boulder or rock sometimes a trout or smolt would appear and gulp. The almost absolute criterion of whether a nymph survived or became a meal was how far away from a hold the waters tumbled it.

If the fish only had to poke its nose out, the fate of the nymph was certain. If that same boarder had to navigate three or four times its own length out into the current, the nymph's chances were fifty-fifty. But if the householder had to make a long foray, the larva had at least a 95-percent chance of being carried to another downstream stone under which it could hide. Even more interesting was the fact that the trout or smolt almost always saw this distant food; several times I watched them dart out, perhaps halfway, hesitate, and then return to home base.

The many small young parr didn't have homes. With the exuberance and recklessness of youth, they lived around trailing water weeds or in any depth of water. Danger or its threat bothered them only momentarily. They'd flash away, returning quickly to their perpetual hunting in and about the fronds, pecking at the moss on the rocks, examining the bottom sand and cobble, or snatching at surface offerings. Filling their bellies in the plenty of summer was their only concern.

Then, on Pennsylvania's Brodheads Creek, I got another lesson. Al Caucci and Bob Nastasi were there doing fieldwork, and Dr. Fred Thompson, Paul Fitzgerald, and I watched the two men from a distance. They waded into different sections of the water, sampling riffles, runs, the deeper centers of pools, and back eddies. Their technique was identical at every area. Two sides of a 3-by-3-foot piece of fine-mesh hardware cloth had been lashed to wooden broom handles. One of the biologists pushed and shoved this net as close to the bottom of the river, upstream from himself, as the stones allowed. He then angled this trap back toward himself so the water flowed over the obstruction while the fine mesh could catch even the smallest particle of detritus—and nymphs. His partner moved from 6 to 8 feet directly above him and, like a horse pawing the ground, for several minutes kicked and with his feet tore at the bottom.

When the net holder raised his equipment clear of the water, the kicker joined him. With heads bowed, they made notes in their book and occasionally examined part of their catch with magnifying glasses. Several times they pulled from their pockets small mason jars filled with water and, aided by a fine-bladed knife, pushed what was probably a nymph into them.

I can get a lot out of reading, but my learning curve goes up drastically when I can see, touch, or feel any object I'm studying. When I read Al and Bob's *Hatches*, I understood their general classification of nymphs, grouping general families—the crawlers, the clingers, the swimmers, and the burrowers—and I was impressed by how their nomenclature accurately described specific types of nymphs and how each type inhabited a certain area in a stream, depending on the speed of the water and the kind of bottom. But it was entirely different to be *with* these men, to wade with them several times back to stretches they'd already covered, to find and examine with them the specimens that proved their groupings.

Bob and Al also had medicine vials with white plastic snap-on lids in their pockets, and they'd fill an inverted lid with drops of water. With the tip of a knife blade, they'd gently urge a nymph trapped in the hardware cloth into one of the lids before easing the rest of the insects in the seine back into the stream. There, brilliantly outlined against the stark-white background, the captive frantically wriggled about, searching for cover. Almost invisible to the naked eye, the gills would become pulsating opening and closing shutters under a 5- or 6-power glass.

In their chapter "Nymphs: The Primary Converters," these two scientists convince me that growing nymphs are almost inaccessible to trout. The brooks, browns, and rainbows don't have fingers with which to overturn rocks. It is only when the larvae are ready to metamorphose that their stomachs fill with air. Then they migrate, searching for an easy path to the surface, and often momentarily lose their grip on the bottom. Only at this time in their life cycle are they vulnerable to trout in sufficient numbers so as to make fish selective.

On the Brodheads, Al and Bob found a March Brown nymph (*Stenonema vicarium*) whose size, outline, and dark wing cases made the two men sense that perhaps this captive was ready to alter its life-style. Carefully all of us carried this possible changeling to a gentle side pocket of the pool. Fencing it in with a driftwood board, we let it go. Instantly it sought sanctuary under a stone. In an hour or so we returned and, to our amazement (Al and Bob were no longer with us), we watched our captive wandering about on the top of stones; on two occasions it floated an inch or two above the bottom and wriggled desperately to sink back to more solid footing. I thought perhaps it had been injured during its capture or release, but while we were staring it launched itself into upward flight and broke the surface film. There it struggled and struggled to rid itself of its chitin and finally flew away—a gossamer creature.

Having earlier borrowed one of Bob's mason jars, I pushed many nymphs into its branch water and carried them home to preserve and study. Only a short time later I'd assembled my own seine, bought a small magnifying glass, and transferred several medicine vials from our bathroom shelf to pockets in my vest. Often during the rest of that summer I spent hours learning about river life, but gradually its fascination waned. Two enthusiasts were needed to

net. Mostly, however, I quit because of my own love afair with dry-fly fishing
and my interest in stream conservation.

Toward the end of that summer I did make a change in my school books.
Art Flick had written a letter, published in *The Conservationist*, urging fishermen interested in collecting nymphs to examine them at streamside only, not
take them home, and, whenever possible, to return the specimens to their
habitat unharmed. He also cautioned about checking the legality of collecting
nymphs. New York's statutes, for example, do not allow this except by special
permit. Further, unless a collector is a professional and owns specialized ap-
paratus to keep aquarium water cool and moving, captured specimens seldom
survive. It was also recommended (by Al and Bob) that the average fisherman
use a mini-seine, such as a fruit strainer, in order to avoid disturbing the bottoms of streams. The nymph population was already in delicate balance in
many streams and declining in many others, so if too many anglers netted too
many larvae, the ecology of streams could be harmed. I gave up toting a
seine.

There was a splash in the river. I didn't see whether it was a kingfisher or
a trout. Picking up my rod, I waded in and made my first cast, determined to
concentrate on that nail knot. Then I stopped.

An hour earlier, the sight of several empty shucks clinging to rock forma-
tions had been behind my choice of a pattern tied to resemble a stone-fly
nymph, and a good brown had approved this selection. But since that victory,
that same fly had explored several different stretches of water and I hadn't
bothered to change.

I had nymphed seriously so few times in the past several years that cardi-
nal principles had slipped my mind: different types of nymphs live in fast or
lazy water, hard or soft bottoms, and nymphs wear unmistakable signals when
they are preparing to emerge.

The bottom of a stone lifted from a fast, rocky run had several Gray Fox
nymphs racing about in the green slime. I'd left my loupe at home, so I
couldn't see whether these insects were getting ready for their journey to the
surface, but by the calendar Gray Fox mayflies were scheduled to hatch, so I
tied on a size 10 nymph and continued my fishing.

The stretch above the one I'd finished Gray-Foxing was my favorite on
this entire river. A broad riffle, too wide to cast across, graduated into a deep
run that was identified as Buxom Pool—6 or 8 feet deep in times of normal
flow. Its middle was narrowed by two ledges, one on either side, pinched in
like the wasp waist of an 1890s lady of fashion laced into her corset. This
illusion was heightened by two huge chunks, pieces of the ledges, jutting up
out of the water above the pinch. Giant trout, well educated, fed in the slicks
behind these boulders and lived at their bases or in the deep drop-offs, crevices, valleys, and crests that corrugated the rest of the bottom.

The upper part of my shirt sleeve, where I'd reached too deeply trying to lift a bottom stone looking for nymphs, was wringing wet, so I sat on the grass to let it dry and contemplated that stretch of water.

I thought of an imaginary globe—an ever-spinning huge globe on a stand. Sculpted into it would be a contoured, moving, winding river, whose every rock rose in bas-relief below and above the currents. This moving water I was watching was the chisel and mallet that had shaped the track. The water, crags, ledges, rocks, stones, sunken logs, and pebbles really existed. They weren't figments of my imagination. Everything was there. It was up to me, from my 6-foot vantage point wading that river, without mask or snorkel but with my senses alive, to model that track in imaginary clay.

The next thing would be to people it with mosses, insects, and fish— starting with the premise that all living things in these waters are beset by the same problems: how to keep from being swept away, or how to stay still or make headway against ever-present currents. I would make these living creatures flesh out and grow through lore gained from word-of-mouth, books, and my own investigations. I would ask the whys about happenings to them.

No! Blinders weren't necessary. I wouldn't be enchanted by ducks or flowers; there would be no pane of glass to break refractions. Today, while nymphing, I could watch my line because at the same time I would start my bas-relief—not for this stretch only but for the river itself and all rivers I fished. Then whenever or wherever I nymphed, it would only be necessary to spin the globe.

While this modeling was being done, my carefully chosen artificials, cast with imagination to selected spots, would swim close enough to the living rooms of big trout that the fish would have to nose out and sample my offerings.

Learning to fish nymphs upstream had required that I try to understand the inner architecture of rivers, not merely the surface. It had been a revelation.

When I got into my car better than an hour later, I hadn't caught my second keeper, but for the first time I'd enjoyed nymphing. I hope, having finished this book, you will too.

FOUR OF MY FAVORITE NYMPH PATTERNS

Unless there is a strong specific hatch, I fish a nymph one or two sizes larger than the naturals.

For big rivers like the Delaware in the East, I like Charlie Brooks's *Montana Stone* (see chapter 13). Despite the fact that this fly is Western in origin, I've found it does well on Eastern rivers.

For small and medium streams, Poul Jorgensen's *Telleco Nymph* is good at almost any time. If there are a number of caddis on the water, I fish *The Breadcrust* as a caddis pupa. (See chapter 4 for these dressings.) And Art Flick's dressing of the Hendrickson produces for me all season long,

Hendrickson (Art Flick's dressing)
Hook: Art Flick size 12 (I use size 10)
Silk: Olive
Tail: Mandarin flank feathers
Body: Blend of gray fox belly fur, beaver, and claret seal worked together until the material is of a grayish-brown shade
Rib: Tying silk or fine gold wire
Legs: Partridge hackle

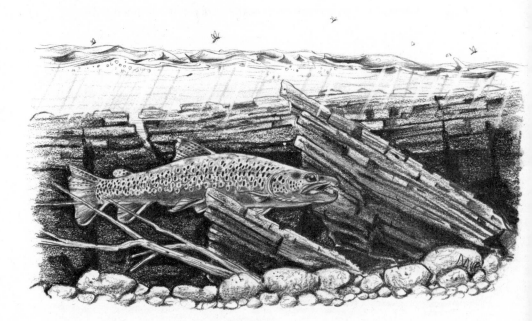

Conservation

Leonard M. Wright, Jr.

THE TROUBLE WITH our fishing is that we treat it like the weather: everybody talks about it but nobody does anything about it. Well, almost nobody. Only a small fraction of today's anglers are involved in preserving or improving our fishing.

Hardly a day goes by without a news item about a river being dammed, a stream, lake, or bay becoming polluted, or a fish-kill perfuming our shores. Our supply of fish seems to decrease as rapidly as the number of fishermen increases. If this trend continues we'll soon have our quarry both outnumbered and surrounded. Good military tactics, perhaps, but rotten conservation.

As a fisherman, you have four choices: You can grumble about the situation. You can dream about the good old days. You can spend a lot of money on a trip to the rapidly vanishing wilderness. Or you can spend very little and join a fisherman's organization, adding your voice, your vote, and your dues to those of other anglers.

Following is a list of groups dedicated to the betterment of our fishing. They can help only if you help. Joining one or more of them requires only a small investment of time or money. But the dividends may be enormous.

AMERICAN FISHERIES SOCIETY
1319 19th Street, N.W.
Washington, D.C. 20036

AMERICAN LEAGUE OF ANGLERS (ALA)
810 18th Street, N.W.
Washington, D.C. 20006

AMERICAN RIVERS CONSERVATIVE COUNCIL
324 C Street, S.E.
Washington, D.C. 20003

BASS
P.O. Box 3044
Montgomery, Alabama 36109

BROTHERHOOD OF THE JUNGLE COCK
10 East Fayette Street
Baltimore, Maryland 21202

BUREAU OF OUTDOOR RECREATION
United States Department of the Interior
Washington, D.C. 20240

BUREAU OF SPORT FISHERIES AND WILDLIFE
United States Department of the Interior
Washington, D.C. 20240

ENVIRONMENTAL DEFENSE FUND, INC.
162 Old Town Road
East Setauket, New York 11733

ENVIRONMENTAL PROTECTION AGENCY
United States Waterside Mall
Washington, D.C. 20460

FEDERATION OF FLY FISHERMEN (FFF)
15513 Haas Avenue
Gardena, California 90249

NATIONAL MARINE FISHERIES SERVICE
3300 Whitehaven Parkway
Washington, D.C. 20240

NATIONAL PARK SERVICE
U.S. Department of the Interior
Washington, D.C. 20250

NATURAL RESOURCES DEFENSE COUNCIL
1710 N Street, N.W.
Washington, D.C. 20036

RESTORATION OF ATLANTIC SALMON IN AMERICA, INC. (RASA)
Box 164
Hancock, New Hampshire 03449

SPORT FISHING INSTITUTE
Suite 801
608 13th Street, N.W.
Washington, D.C. 20005

STRIPED BASS FUND, INC.
45-21 Glenwood Street
Little Neck, New York 11362

THEODORE GORDON FLYFISHERS, INC. (TGF)
24 East 39th Street
New York, New York 10016

TROUT UNLIMITED (TU)
4260 East Evans Avenue
Denver, Colorado 80222

WATER POLLUTION CONTROL FEDERATION
3900 Wisconsin Avenue, N.W.
Washington, D.C. 20016

Note: A conservation directory, with a complete listing of prominent organizations and individuals engaged in conservation work, is available from THE NATIONAL WILDLIFE FEDERATION 1412 16th Street, N.W., Washington, D.C. 20036.